P9-DWK-777

THE PESTICIDES TRUST

The Pesticide Hazard

PESTICIDES are responsible for some 20,000 deaths and 3 million cases of acute poisoning annually – a burden borne, in particular, by agricultural workers and rural communities worldwide. The industry has felt compelled to respond to the international concern on both health and environmental grounds which has been expressed, notably by NGOs lobbying for higher safety standards and export controls. This policy-relevant, global survey, based on up-to-date research and data gathered by scientists and local organisations in Latin America, Africa and Asia, as well as information provided by the companies themselves to the EC's Product Stewardship Survey, assesses what progress has been made in both safety and environmental terms since the introduction of the FAO's voluntary Code of Conduct on the Distribution and Use of Pesticides in 1985 and the Prior Informed Consent procedure of 1989.

While there have undoubtedly been improvements, the picture is still a deeply disturbing one. It is not yet clear, this book argues, whether tighter information disclosure requirements and trade controls on the export of banned or severely restricted pesticides can effectively reduce the hazards posed by powerful agro-chemicals in the South. Instead, research effort and financial resources ought to be switched from 'risk reduction' and 'safe use' procedures, towards developing more environmentally-friendly techniques of sustainable agricultural production. This is essential if the health and environment of producers and consumers alike are to be protected.

THE PESTICIDES TRUST is an environmental charity and includes in its membership a wide range of interests – environment, food and consumer, farming and growing, conservation, wildlife, medical, health and safety and development organisations, all of which have long-standing concerns about pesticide issues. The Trust aims to create awareness among those who make decisions over the use and regulation of pesticides and among workers and consumers of the problems associated with pesticides; to provide a forum for discussion of the issues and to help coordinate action to tackle problems; to stimulate and promote the implementation of ecologically-sound, less pesticide-dependent methods and products in agriculture, insect vector control and other areas of pest control. With the Pesticides Action Network (PAN), the Trust collated evidence of pesticide use and abuse in 17 Third World countries and submitted this to the relevant United Nations Organisations.

THE PESTICIDES ACTION NETWORK (PAN) is an international coalition of citizens' groups and individuals who oppose the misuse of pesticides and support reliance on safe, sustainable pest control methods. Established in 1982, PAN currently links over 300 organisations in some 60 countries, co-ordinated by six Regional Centres located in East and West Africa, Asia, Latin America, North America and Europe. Because PAN is a network, no individual can direct or represent the entire coalition. Participants are free to pursue their own projects to further PAN's objectives, and benefit from their access to the collective resources of the network.

BARBARA DINHAM has worked at The Pesticides Trust for two years collaborating with Pesticide Action Network (PAN) groups to gather the information presented in this book. She previously spent many years carrying out research on transnational corporations and set up the Transnationals Information Centre, London. This research group was established to examine the economic, employment and environmental impact of transnationals, working with trade unions and community organisations to develop educational material, workshops and organise exchange visits. She has been involved in the Permanent People's Tribunal on Industrial Hazards and Human Rights, and in 1989 arranged for a group of survivors of the Bhopal disaster to visit Britain and exchange information with communities and victims' organisations concerned with the dangers posed by the production of highly toxic materials in the modern chemicals industry. She has written papers, reports and educational material on agricultural economics, transnational corporations, pesticides and industrial hazards. Previous publications include *Agribusiness in Africa*, and *Trade Union Internationalism: Solidarity for Survival*; *Deception, Demonstration and Debate: Toward a critical environment and development education*; *Greenprint for Action: an environmental issues course*; and *The Directory of Social Change: Education and Play*. She has also edited *The Directory of Social Change: Women*.

THE PESTICIDES TRUST

The Pesticide Hazard
A Global Health and Environmental Audit

Compiled by

BARBARA DINHAM

WITH A PREFACE BY
MONICA MOORE
Pesticides Action Network, North America

DISCARD

ZED BOOKS

LONDON & NEW JERSEY

363.1792
P476

*The Pesticide Hazard: A Global Health and
Environmental Audit* was first published in association
with The Pesticides Trust, 23 Beehive Place, London
SW9 7QR, by Zed Books Ltd, 57 Caledonian Road,
London N1 9BU and 165 First Avenue, Atlantic
Highlands, New Jersey 07716, USA, in 1993.

Copyright © The Pesticides Trust, 1993

Cover design by Andrew Corbett
Laserset by The Pesticides Trust
Printed and bound in the United Kingdom by Biddles
Ltd, Guildford and King's Lynn.

All rights reserved.

A catalogue record for this book is available from the
British Library

US CIP is available from the Library of Congress

ISBN 1 85649 201 X Hb
ISBN 1 85649 202 8 Pb

12/02

Contents

TABLES

FIGURES

Acknowledgements

This work could not have been put together without the active involvement of groups and individuals participating in the Pesticides Action Network, and innumerable others who have sought over the years to keep the issue of pesticides on the international agenda. I would particularly like to thank Topsy Jewell, Monica Moore and Sarojini Rengam, for reading and providing extensive comments on the drafts, my colleagues at The Pesticides Trust, Peter Beaumont, David Buffin and Mark Davis for comments and much support, to Chris and Bene Whitehouse for meticulous translations from Spanish and Portuguese, to Dorothy Myers for her excellent groundwork, to Robert Molteno for his faith and enthusiasm. Valuable contributions were received from Carina Weber and Juergen Knirsch of PAN Germany and from Liliana Cori of Greenpeace Italy. Thanks also to Martin Abraham, David Bull, Dr. Alastair Hay, Melanie Miller, Sue Milner, Dr. Elsa Nivia, Dr. Andrew Watterson and many others who have discussed trade, sustainable agriculture and pesticides issues with me over the last two years. My special thanks to Greg, Kate and Tess for putting up with my late nights and competition for the computer.

In practical terms, this would not have been possible without grants and financial contributions from the Goldsmith Foundation, The New Moorgate Trust Fund, Oxfam, Trocaire, Worldwide Fund for Nature, Royal Norwegian Ministry of Environment, Netherlands Ministry of Foreign Affairs, Danish Ministry of Foreign Affairs, The Commission of the European Communities, Directorate General XI.

While extensive material has been provided for this book and every effort has been made to check details, information has been interpreted from many sources, in different forms, from different countries and in making the final compilation I remain responsible for any errors.

Material provided by:

Latin America
Brazil: Reinaldo Onofre Skalisz, member of the State Council for the Defence of the Environment, Gert Roland Fischer of PAN Brazil and Onaur Ruano, agronomist. Additional material provided by Antonio Freire and David Hathaway.

Colombia: Dr. Elsa Nivia, toxicologist and Regional Co-ordinator of the Pesticides Action Network Latin America.

Costa Rica: Luisa Castillo and Catherine Wesseling, Programa de Plaguicides: Desarrolo, Salud y Ambiente, School for Environmental Sciences, National University, Heredia, Costa Rica.

Ecuador: Ing. Agr. Mercedes Bollanos, MSc (MAG), toxicologist and others at Fundación Natura.

Nicaragua: Martin Lezama Lopez, Departamento de Ecologia-UCA, Managua.

Paraguay: Jorge Abbate, Alter Vida.

Venezuela: Porfiria Mendoza de Linares, CIDELO.

Africa
Benin: Paul Djogbenou, Association pour la Sauvegarde de l'Environnement & le Dévéloppement (ASED).

Egypt: Dr. El Sebae, Alexandra University.

Senegal: Abou Thiam, Environnement et Dévéloppement du Tiers Monde (ENDA).

South Africa: Kate Emanuel, Environment & Development Agency and Group for Environmental Monitoring.

Sudan: Dr. Zuheir El Abjar, Department of Biological Control, Environment and Natural Resources Research Institute, Khartoum.

Togo: Akogo Yao Dzidula, Global Reform and Development (GRAD).

Additional material on **Egypt** and studies on **Morocco** and **Tunisia** were supplied through work commissioned by Greenpeace.

Asia
India: Dr. Daisy Dharmaraj, PREPARE. Sanjoy Sengupta of the Voluntary Health Association India and Dr. A.T. Dudani.

Malaysia: Vasanthi Arumugam and Sarojini Rengam, Pesticides Action Network Regional Office for Asia and the Pacific.

To Bilkis Banu and others who should not be nameless who have died at Bhopal, and especially to the women of Bhopal who continue their struggle for justice.

Foreword

In spite of the many bleak situations it documents, *The Pesticide Hazard: A global health and environmental audit* is a hopeful book, powerful in its refusal to accept widespread environmental contamination and the poisoning of millions of people each year as an 'inevitable price of progress.' Appearing 30 years after Rachel Carson's *Silent Spring* first alerted the general public to widespread ecosystem destruction from pesticide use, it is designed to assist contemporary efforts to change how societies view and regulate pesticides.

One of the most hopeful aspects of *The Pesticide Hazard* is the international collaboration that made it possible. Much of the material it presents is made available through the inspiring co-operation among organisations and individuals linked through the Pesticide Action Network (PAN) International. Formed 10 years ago by activists from five continents seeking a global approach to global problems, PAN connects and strengthens peoples' organisations throughout the world that are working to end pesticide damage and hasten implementation of environmentally sustainable, socially just pest management. The PAN network currently encompasses more than 300 groups in 60 countries, representing a tremendous diversity of experiences, expertise and perspectives. Since PAN is an international network, rather than an organisation, participants work independently and no one group speaks on behalf of the entire network. Based on their knowledge of their own local and national realities, PAN groups around the world work together to phase out hazardous pesticides and require producers to assume responsibility for the effects of their pesticide products. Longer-term network goals are to create the political will, scientific and social information base and infrastructures needed to overcome pesticide dependency in agriculture, public health, homes and other settings.

As *The Pesticide Hazard* clearly underscores, the primary human victims of the global pesticide trade are poor people, whose suffering tends to be invisible to those in positions of economic and political power. PAN participants regularly identify and publicise the impacts of specific products, incidents, problems and alternatives in specific locations, documenting the disproportionate impacts of pesticides on people and the environment and making the high costs of global pesticide addiction visible to governments, companies, pesticide users and the general public. Their findings consistently suggest that the true scale of 'the global pesticide problem' has never been acknowledged.

As deeply embedded in the global economy as they are in the environment, pesticide issues weave together a wide range of topics. Barbara Dinham and her PAN colleagues face this challenge in *The Pesticide Hazard*, presenting a comprehensive and detailed look at global pesticide issues. A series of special reports from public interest activists and scientists in 16 Southern countries document actual conditions and real-world barriers to 'safe pesticide use'. Trade issues are explored in depth, including pesticide import/export controls, relocation of pesticide production capacity and agricultural subsidies encouraging high pesticide use levels. The safety and health sections highlight the plight of occupationally-exposed workers and rural residents whose air, water and food supplies are repeatedly contaminated. The example of cotton as a pesticide-dependent crop appears in several chapters, and chapters on environmental impacts and alternatives discuss the growing international consensus that sustainable agriculture techniques offer a way out of the multiple dilemmas of pesticide addiction. In a fascinating annex, the environmental policies of major pesticide manufacturers are described in the companies' own words, which PAN participants and others will no doubt read with interest.

The Pesticide Hazard also surveys recent attempts by governments to control pesticide damages. It describes to readers several new concepts important to pesticide regulation, such as the 'Precautionary Principle', and reviews recent regional and international policies and regulatory mechanisms to control pesticide hazards, including the Food and Agriculture Organisation's (FAO) International Code of Conduct on the Distribution and Use of Pesticides. (PAN groups were deeply involved in developing the FAO Code, challenging and working with FAO member countries to include in its provisions concepts of social and environmental responsibility in a world characterised by increasing concentration of economic resources.) The Code's recently implemented Prior Informed Consent (PIC) process is also explained. Following years of heated debates, PIC has emerged as a widely-accepted (and in the EC at least, legislatively-mandated) mechanism for providing notice of regulatory status in producing-countries when pesticides are exported. PIC also firmly establishes the right of importing countries to refuse pesticide imports for reasons of health and environmental safety.

As important and life-saving as these incremental improvements are, ultimately Dinham and her collaborators make a strong case that 'damage control' measures within a fundamentally unsustainable pest-management paradigm cannot protect people or the environment from continuing harm. Much as Rachel Carson before them, they conclude that genuine solutions to ecosystem destruction and the epidemic levels of pesticide poisonings will be found only when pest management is put on an ecologically rational footing. This, of course, requires that resources be redirected in support of pest management methods based on naturally-occurring processes and away from chemical control models. *The Pesticide Hazard* should convince the sceptical of the need for just such changes.

Monica Moore,
PAN North America

1. Introduction

Background to pesticide hazards

Thirty years ago Rachel Carson alerted the world to the environmental hazards of pesticides in her book, *Silent Spring*. Since then, new pesticides have been developed which are less persistent in the environment, but which bring health hazards to pesticide users, particularly in Third World countries, or which damage wildlife.

The last decade has been one of substantial activity over the health and environmental hazards associated with pesticide use, and particularly with hazards in Third World countries. Important policy advances have been made. In 1985, the United Nations Food and Agriculture Organisation (FAO) introduced an International Code of Conduct on the Distribution and Use of Pesticides (the FAO Code), and in 1989 it incorporated provisions for governments to refuse to consent to hazardous imports, known as Prior Informed Consent (PIC). The PIC provisions are welcomed, not least because they have institutional back-up, and will provide an important link in transferring information on pesticides to resource-starved pesticide registrars in Third World countries. But as a trade-based mechanism, there are limits to what it can achieve.

This book provides evidence, documented by non-governmental organisations and researchers around the world, of health and environmental problems of pesticide use, which continue in spite of the efforts of guidelines developed in the FAO Code. It suggests that, in the long run, pesticide hazards can only be reduced by directing resources to non-chemical, sustainable methods of pest control.

NGOs show evidence

Over the last 10 years, non-governmental organisations have consistently fought to reduce pesticide misuse and abuse in Third World countries, lobbying at an international level for higher standards and trade controls, and working on the ground to develop alternatives. Many have collaborated informally through the Pesticides Action Network (PAN), an international coalition of over 300 groups and individuals who oppose the misuse of pesticides and support reliance on safe, sustainable pest-control methods.

This book is a result of PAN's efforts to continue drawing attention to the hazards. The FAO Code provides no mechanism or resources for monitoring. The evidence presented here ranges from academic research to interviews, from government sources to rural experience. It is beyond the resources of most governments, and particularly those in the Third World, to consistently document health and environmental hazards, and in the absence of such data the efforts of non-governmental organisations are crucial.

The death toll and the health burden

An accurate assessment of the numbers of people affected by pesticide use and misuse is impossible. The World Health Organisation (WHO) estimates that there are a minimum of three million acute severe cases of pesticide poisonings and 20,000 unintentional deaths each year, mostly in Third World countries.[1] This excludes cases of chronic pesticide poisoning. A 1990 study estimated that 25 million Third World agricultural workers are acutely poisoned every year.[2]

Perhaps even more worrying are the latent periods which reveal many chronic problems. For example the respected International Agency for Research on Cancer (IARC), part of the WHO, recently found that, on the basis of limited evidence, 'spraying and application of non-arsenical insecticides entails exposures that are probably carcinogenic to humans.'[3] This has profound implications for agricultural workers, and particularly for plantation workers who apply pesticides on a regular basis.

Precaution is paramount

As environmental awareness grows, a 'cradle to grave', or 'life cycle' approach to pesticides is increasingly endorsed. Ideally, this would ensure not only that pesticides are produced without harm to people or the environment, but are also used and disposed of in a non-polluting manner. An alternative is to take a broad view of agricultural production and to ensure that food and fibre is produced in a manner that does not degrade the environment, taking into consideration all natural resources, inputs and outputs.

In 1972, the rich industrialised countries, as members of the Organisation for Economic Co-operation and Development (OECD) adopted the 'Polluter Pays Principle'. Endorsed by the European Community (EC) in 1975,[4] it states that:

> . . . the polluter should bear the expenses of carrying out . . . measures decided by public authorities to ensure that the environment is in an acceptable state. In other words the cost of these measures should be reflected in the cost of goods and services which cause pollution in production and/or consumption. Such measures should not be accompanied by subsidies that would create significant distortions in international trade and investment.[5]

At present, the environmental and health costs are borne by agricultural workers, rural communities, consumers and governments. In plantation agriculture, in particular, labourers whose health is affected by pesticides are amongst the poorest in the country, and thus least able to seek redress.

There is even less information on the environmental impact of pesticide use in the Third World than on the health impact. Yet in many countries, pesticides have been applied relentlessly over decades—for example in the vast cotton acreage of Egypt and Sudan. To date, the polluter pays principle has not been widely utilised in agriculture, although a recent study of six EC countries argues for greater application.[6]

However, there are limitations to the polluter pays principle. For example, there are few cases where pollution can be directly traced to the polluter; it may be cheaper for a multinational to pay for pollution than to prevent it; big companies can afford to challenge their responsibilities in the courts; and it is difficult with pesticides to say which manufacturer is responsible for any particular poisoning or contamination case.

Environment and development groups believe that a precautionary or preventative approach, based on clean production, should be adopted. This has become known as the 'Precautionary Principle', which says that if further environmental degradation and health impacts are to be minimised, precaution must be the overriding principle guiding action. Past experience demonstrates that waiting for scientific proof or sufficient documentation of the impact of poisons may in the meantime result in irreversible damage to the environment and people's health. Adoption of the precautionary principle implies a shift in approach from proof of environmental harm, to proof of environmental safety.

The precautionary principle has been endorsed in a number of international fora. The Governing Council of the UN Environment Programme (UNEP) passed a declaration in May 1989 which recommends that all governments adopt Principles of Precautionary Action as the basis of their policies to prevent and eliminate pollution. In June 1990, the heads of EC member states announced that efforts to protect and enhance the natural environment would be developed 'on the principles of sustainable development and preventative and precautionary action.'[7]

International regulation for pesticides

Prior Informed Consent (PIC)

The FAO Code was adopted in 1985, to reduce the health and environmental hazards caused by pesticides, and to establish sound principles for the export and sale of pesticides. In 1987 the FAO accepted the principle of PIC and this was incorporated in the FAO Code in 1989. The PIC scheme was also adopted by the United Nations Environment Programme under the London Guidelines on the Exchange of Information on Chemicals in International Trade and is operated jointly by the FAO and UNEP through its International Register of Potentially Toxic Chemicals (IRPTC).

Pesticides will be placed in the PIC process if they meet one of three criteria: a chemical which is banned for health or environmental reasons in five or more countries; a chemical which is newly banned or severely restricted for health or environmental reasons in a single country after 1

January 1992; chemicals causing health or environmental problems under the conditions of use in developing countries. The FAO Code states that 'No pesticide in these categories should be exported to an importing country participating in the PIC procedure contrary to that country's decision.' [8]

While compliance is voluntary, a system is now in place to help make PIC work. Governments have been asked to nominate a 'Designated National Authority' (DNA) to receive and convey information. A data document, known as a 'Decision Guidance Document', is prepared on PIC pesticides and circulated to all governments through the DNA. Once governments have taken a decision on whether a pesticide can be imported, the DNA notifies the secretariat which in turn communicates this decision to all participating governments. The IRPTC is developing a database of importing countries' decisions which will be accessible by governments and exporters.

The pesticide industry has accepted the FAO Code and co-operated in its implementation. Their role in operating the scheme is crucial as PIC does not require exporting countries to introduce any export controls or to monitor exports (although some ask for notification). The PIC scheme therefore depends on the good will of the pesticide industry. Industries' approach is one of 'product stewardship', whereby all major corporations have now put in place policies to take their responsibility beyond the factory gate. Their policies include checks on labelling, advertising, marketing practices and other aspects set out in the FAO Code. The pesticide manufacturers' industry association, GIFAP, has made compliance with the FAO Code a condition of membership.

The EC member states will become the first to back the voluntary code with legislation. A Regulation passed in July 1992, which will come into effect in November 1992, amends a previous Regulation on export controls and makes compliance with the PIC provisions of the FAO Code mandatory.[9]

Implementation of PIC has been disappointingly slow, although this has to be set against the considerable work involved on limited resources. The process is now officially underway, with the first round of notifications having been sent out in September 1991. The first pesticides on the PIC list, and those under consideration for early inclusion, are set out in Chapter 2. As more pesticides enter the process, there is a danger that the potential for Third World governments to prevent hazardous imports will be limited by the lack of non-hazardous alternatives. It is therefore essential that greater priority is placed on resources for, and policies to encourage, sustainable, non-chemical methods of pest control.

PAN and other non-governmental organisations played a substantial role in achieving the PIC provisions, and have participated as observers in the Joint FAO/UNEP Experts Working Group (the Joint Group) developing guidelines for the operation of the PIC provisions. This study is a measure of their commitment to ensuring that the Code can become a workable standard, rather than empty words.

Controls on pesticide trade

Pesticides are big business, with sales of the top 25 companies amounting to around \$23.5 billion in 1990 and \$24 billion in 1991.[10] The top 10 companies account for around 73% of this. The overall pesticide market is larger, with production increasing in newly-industrialising countries. Because pesticides are traded which are widely banned, including at times in the exporting country, the case for tightening trade controls on these and other hazardous pesticides has grown. Many consumers have fought to have pesticides banned or severely restricted in their own countries, only to find residues returning in imported food. This is known as the 'Circle of Poison', and has led to consumer support for campaigns to ban the export of pesticides banned for use in the exporting country.

The PIC process, which introduces a mechanism for governments to stop imports of a number of named pesticides, is a control on trade. Under the terms of the General Agreement on Tariffs and Trade (GATT), PIC could be seen as a non-tariff barrier to trade, something which the GATT Uruguay round has sought to eliminate, although current negotiations have indicated that the PIC process would conform. However the PIC provisions require that decisions to ban or severely restrict a pesticide are 'not used inconsistently with the provisions of the GATT'.[11] This would mean a government could not ban the import of a pesticide which it produces and uses domestically, in order to protect its domestic industry. It does not prevent the production and export of pesticides banned domestically.

At the time of writing, the Treaty emerging from the GATT Uruguay Round has not been signed and many areas remain in dispute. If successful, it will introduce agriculture into GATT rules for the first time. It should also allow more access to Third World countries to the markets of industrialised countries for their processed products but, in turn, will further open the markets of Third World economies to multinationals.

One aspect which causes particular concern is the official GATT view that the environment will be protected through free trade. Environment and development non-governmental organisations are highly sceptical of this theory, which does not address the hidden costs of hazardous industrial or agricultural production and trade in hazardous products, which are borne by communities and the environment.

PIC is only one means of reducing or eliminating the hazards of trade in pesticides. Nevertheless, it is an important precedent, not only allowing governments to reject hazardous imports, but also as a means of transferring information and providing a structure for the work of advocacy groups in the Third World.

However, controls on pesticide trade are not sufficient to reduce hazards and the everyday use of pesticides exacts its toll on people's health, the environment and sustainable food and fibre production (see Chapters 3 and 4, and country reports). Without a redirection of resources into safer, particularly non-chemical, alternatives there will be no genuine choice. A fundamental change in approach to production is needed to protect people's health, the environment and sustainable food production in the long term.

Related international measures

The UN Conference on Environment and Development (UNCED) in June 1992, known as the Earth Summit, called for implementation of the FAO Code by the year 2000. UNEP favours a Convention to make the provisions contained in the Code internationally binding. However the FAO, at its biennial conference in November 1991, voted to keep the Code voluntary. While a Convention could strengthen aspects of the Code, Conventions are only as strong as the number of governments which ratify them, and the record of most governments is not strong in this respect. As a Convention binds governments, rather than industry, it does not eliminate the need for a Code which industry agrees to adopt. In addition, provisions in a Code, or a Convention, need to be implemented in national legislation in order to become legally binding in any one country.

In preparation for UNCED, governments met to draw up proposals for better risk assessment and management of chemicals. The meeting stressed the need for more control in managing chemicals in international trade, and its proposals were put to UNCED with the recommendation that an inter-governmental mechanism, under the auspices of the WHO International Programme on Chemical Safety (IPCS), should be set up to increase co-ordination among UN agencies.

A number of other Conventions have been agreed in recent years, with far-reaching potential. The Barcelona Convention is an agreement among 17 Mediterranean countries which, in 1991, agreed to phase out organophosphate pesticides by the year 2005, and to promote integrated pest management in agriculture. In Africa, frustration over the waste trade and pesticide dumping has led to the Bamako Convention on the Ban of the Import into Africa and the Control of Transboundary Movement and Management of Hazardous Wastes within Africa, which will include a ban on the import of hazardous substances which have been banned, cancelled, refused registration or voluntarily withdrawn in the country of manufacture for human health or environmental reasons.[12]

A sustainable way

UNCED placed both sustainable agriculture and trade in hazardous products on its Agenda 21, the action plan agreed at the conference. It endorsed the FAO Code, and called for more resources for sustainable agriculture. However, much of the planning for the Earth Summit focused only on risk reduction, safe management of chemical trade, and education and training for safe use.

The FAO defines sustainable agriculture as a practice which 'conserves land, water, plant and animal genetic resources, is environmentally non-degrading, technically appropriate, economically viable and socially acceptable.'[13] PAN groups believe sustainable agriculture should be promoted to bring a reduction in pesticide use and dependence, ultimately to eliminate the use of chemical pesticides, and to place food security, health and environment above increases in production.

A greater focus on non-chemical pest control is essential if the health and environmental hazards of pesticide use are to be reduced. A range of practices are advocated, including integrated pest management, better management policies to reduce use and investment in research to make sustainable agriculture a reality. Non-governmental organisations working on environment and development have advocated an approach embracing agro-ecology, or 'low external inputs for sustainable agriculture (LEISA).' Advocates of LEISA want a holistic approach to agriculture, which is 'economically feasible, ecologically sound, culturally adapted and socially just.' No technology is accepted or rejected, but rather it makes an attempt to draw lessons from past experiences in agriculture in both industrialised and developing countries.[14]

UNCED pledged a commitment to sustainable agriculture, and the FAO, as the relevant UN agency, adopted this approach in 1991. But at this stage little practical work has been undertaken in the UN system. In some of the countries reporting in this book, alternatives have been developed, in others there is little between peasant and industrial agriculture. In either case, it is important to allocate more resources in this direction. Methods which focus on tighter management of pesticides in international trade, and on risk reduction, are essential, but given the continuing hazards of pesticide use, these can only be considered a partial approach.

About *The Pesticide Hazard*

The Pesticides Trust is part of PAN, and published a previous report on behalf of the Network, *The FAO Code: Missing Ingredients*, which looked at hazardous pesticides unlikely to be included in the PIC process. This report was welcomed by the joint experts working group on PIC, and it was partly responsible for a broader definition of pesticides which would qualify for PIC. The groups and individuals who submitted this evidence have all been involved in PAN for many years.

This book is divided into two parts. Part I looks at the issues at stake, covering trade, health and safety, and the environment. The trade chapter focuses in particular on European exports, and asks whether trade controls can be effective in reducing pesticide problems in the Third World. Monitoring and assessment of the success of trade control measures to reduce hazards will assume a new importance. The section on trade focuses particularly on pesticide exports from the EC, the home of six of the 10 top agrochemical manufacturers. It highlights the lack of information about the nature and extent of exports, particularly those exported in bulk for formulation elsewhere. It looks at the extent to which trade controls, exercised through the EC, can be expected to reduce pesticide hazards.

Chapters 3 and 4 provide an overview of the health and environmental hazards identified by the PAN groups supplying information. Chapter 4 also looks at background to the Earth Summit, and the quest for sustainable agriculture. It documents initiatives undertaken in some of the countries surveyed in this report. Policies to promote pesticide reduction, and more sustainable alternatives would not be starting from scratch, but would require greater political and economic commitment than has been seen to date. It is clear from these reports that while awareness of hazards has increased, the marketing machines continue to sell pesticides, now with messages promoting safe use. But as the country reports (Chapters 5 to 13) in Part II indicate, safe use is not possible in many of the conditions under which these chemicals are used. Chapter 14 makes recommendations.

The nine country reports provide detailed information on the scale of pesticide use, health, safety, environment, and legislative issues in Brazil, Costa Rica, Ecuador, Paraguay, Venezuela, Egypt, South Africa, India and Malaysia. Material has also been supplied from PAN groups in Nicaragua, Benin, Senegal, Sudan and Togo. Some additional recent studies were available from Morocco and Tunisia. We have carried out a survey of the product stewardship practices of the 13 major agrochemical corporations, where they indicate steps taken to comply with the FAO Code. This is included in Annex 1.

Each chapter sets out some of the problems of pesticides, in trade, production, scale of use, and risks to health and the environment. The total picture which emerges indicates that pesticides remain a major problem, whose solution must remain central to the national and international agenda.

References:
1. WHO/UNEP, *The Public Health Impact of Pesticides Used in Agriculture*, Geneva, 1990.
2. Jeyaratnam, J., 'Acute pesticide poisoning: A major problem', *World Health Statistics Quarterly*, 1990, Vol. 43, pp. 139-144.
3. IARC Monographs on the evaluation of carcinogenic risks to humans, Vol. 53, 'Occupational exposure in insecticides application and some pesticides', IARC, 1991, pp. 612.
4. OECD, *The State of the Environment*, Paris, 1991.
5. OECD, *The Polluter Pays Principle: Definition, Analysis and Implementation*, OECD, Paris, 1975.
6. Baldock, D. and Bennett, G., *Agriculture and the Polluter Pays Principle: A study of six EC countries*, Institute for European Environmental Policy, London, December 1991.
7. Announced by heads of EC Member States at summit meeting, Dublin, June 1990.
8. *International Code of Conduct on the Distribution and Use of Pesticides (Amended version)*, FAO, Rome, 1990, p. 24.
9. Council Regulation (EEC) No 2455/92 of 23 July 1992 concerning the export and import of certain dangerous chemicals, *Official Journal of the European Communities*, No. L251/13, 29/8/92.
10. Agrow, *World Crop Protection News*, No. 165, 7/8/92.
11. The FAO Code, *op. cit.*, p. 25.
12. Organisation of African Unity press release, 29/1/91.
13. FAO, *Sustainable Development and the Environment*, FAO Policies and Actions, Rome, Italy, 1992, p. 7.
14. Reijntjes, C., Haverkort, B. and Waters-Bayer, A., *Farming for the Future: An introduction to low external input and sustainable agriculture*, Macmillan/ILEIA, Leusden, Netherlands, 1992.

Part I
The Issues at Stake

2.   Trading in Hazard

Pesticide problems in Third World countries have led to a focus on trade controls to reduce the transfer of hazardous products from the North to the South. It is increasingly accepted that products which are banned or severely restricted in the North should not be exported to the South, yet no country prohibits the export of pesticides banned in their own country. There are limits to how much can be achieved through trade controls: many products are used only in tropical regions, and will not be banned or restricted elsewhere; others may be used with minimal risk in the North, but are hazardous under the conditions of use in Third World countries.

In spite of the health and environmental risks, pesticide sales to Third World markets are expanding. Most companies are looking to parts of the South, particularly the richer countries in Latin America and South East Asia, for growth. Trade liberalisation, and monetary policies which encourage cash crops for exports, will tend to increase pesticide sales in agricultural-exporting countries.[1] This chapter looks at whether controls targeted at trade can adequately address health and environmental concerns.

In particular, exports from Europe are examined to see what impact might be gained through trade controls on hazardous pesticides, and the unintended impact of trade controls in transferring production. We look at whether the considerable international effort directed to tighter measures on the trade and marketing of pesticides adequately covers problem pesticides, in order to eliminate pesticide problems.

The global pesticide market

From the 1950s to the end of the 1970s was a period of pronounced growth in pesticide sales. Sales dropped in the early 1980s, but then stabilised and began to increase. In 1990, the world pesticide market was valued at $26.8 billion and, in spite of the last two years where the recession brought a small drop in sales in real terms, industry commentators predict the market will remain stable.[2]

The pesticide market is dominated by a small number of transnational corporations: the top 10 companies, all of which are European or US-based, control 73% of the world market, and 20 companies control 93%.[3] The top 15 are all based in Western Europe or the United States, led by Ciba-Geigy (Swiss), ICI (UK), Bayer (German) and Rhône Poulenc

(French). In 1991 pesticide sales of the top 25 companies were estimated at $23.9 billion.[4] Japanese companies command a small but significant share, and are growing (see Table 2.1).

Western Europe and North America are the largest users of pesticides, with 31% and 26% of sales respectively in 1991. Japan is the next largest single market, with 9% of sales in 1991 (10% in 1990). The rest of Asia and Australia accounted for 15% in 1991, Latin America 11% (8% in 1990), Eastern Europe 4% (6% in 1990) and Africa 4%.[5] In the North, herbicides account for the majority of sales, and in the South insecticides.[6] The international monetary policies influencing Third World development, led by the World Bank and the International Monetary Fund, encourage investments in cash crops for export, and this will tend to increase pesticide sales in developing countries unless other methods of production are promoted.[7]

Introducing new products onto the market is becoming more difficult. Until the end of the 1970s, research and development uncovered 20-30 new products each year. However, the more accessible chemistry has been exhausted, and increasing awareness of the health and environmental impact of pesticides has brought tighter controls on testing before introducing new products in Northern markets. Bayer now examines around 23,000 potential pesticidal compounds each year, of which only about 100 progress beyond even the initial screening stage and only a handful reach the marketplace.[8] Each new pesticide product takes on average 10 years research to develop, test, and deliver to the market. The major companies see the future in genetic engineering, use of viruses and biotechnology, as well as control of the seed market, in order to breed seeds which are resistant to particular pesticides. The newer pesticides are more selective, have much lower application rates at grams per hectare rather than kilos per hectare, and are more biologically active, as well as more expensive.

The costly process of finding new pesticides, and the stable nature of Northern markets, means many companies look to the South for expansion, and some industry observers expect Third World pesticide use to double over the next 10 years.[9]

Pesticide use in the South

Pesticide use in developing countries climbed 23% between 1971 and 1973. A Worldwatch paper published in 1987 showed that between 1972 and 1985, imports of pesticides increased by 261% in Asia, 95% in Africa, and 48% in Latin America.[10] The 1991 figures indicate that Latin America and Asia together accounted for 21% of the market, with Africa just under 6%,[11] whereas in 1985 developing countries consumed 21.6% of the world's pesticides (see Table 2.2).

Many companies see Latin America and South East Asia as target areas for their products. For example Ciba-Geigy says 'Agriculture in developing countries will rely more and more on the use of pesticides.'[12] Rhône Poulenc predicts its Asian sales will accelerate until the year 2000 and its

Table 2.1 Major pesticide corporations and their countries of origin, 1990 and 1991 sales.

Company and home base	World Rank (1990)		1990 sales (US$m)	1991 sales (US$m)
Swiss (17%)				
Ciba-Geigy	1	(1)	2,704	2,920
Sandoz	12	(11)	858	806
Total Swiss			$3,886	$3,726
German (24%)				
Bayer	4	(3)	1,989	1,927
Hoechst	8	(8)	1,346	1,356
BASF	9	(9)	1,224	1,294
Schering	10	(10)	897	918
Total German			$5,389	$5,495
UK (14%)				
(+ UK/Netherlands)				
ICI	2	(2)	2,522	2,412
Shell (Anglo/Dutch)	13	(12)	804	780
Total UK			$3,208	$3,192
French (9%)				
Rhône Poulenc	3	(4)	$1,917	$1,958
US (30%)				
Du Pont	5	(5)	1,755	1,768
DowElanco	6	(7)	1,500	1,593
Monsanto	7	(6)	1,508	1,551
Am Cyanamid	11	(13)	825	890
FMC	14	(14)	435	475
Rohm and Haas	17	(17)	363	361
Uniroyal Chem	25	(—)	240	244
Total US			$6,645	$6,882
Japanese (5%)				
Sumitomo	15	(15)	416	430
Kumiai	16	(16)	381	405
Sankyo	18	(18)	330	358
Ishihara	19	(19)	114	346
Nihon Nohyaku	20	(19)	306	328
Sostra	21	(—)	294	n.a.
Hokko	22	(—)	257	258
Takeda	24	(—)	246	246
Total Japanese			$2,344	$2,371
Israeli				
Makhteshim-Agan	23	(—)	$247	$250
Sales of top 10			$17,362 (74%)	$17,697 (73%)
Sales of top 25			$22,819	$23,874

Source: *Agrow World Crop Protection News*, 7/8/92.

priority areas for growth are Eastern Europe, Asia, China and Iran.[13] Important markets for Cyanamid are Brazil, Eastern Europe, China, Thailand and Malaysia.[14] BASF is targeting Eastern Europe and is developing products for the Latin American markets.[15] ICI is continuing to expand in the Asia-Pacific region.[16] Bayer sees the main agrochemical markets remaining in Western Europe, the US and Japan, but it still targets the bigger Third World agricultural markets, such as Brazil, Mexico, South Africa and South East Asia.[17]

Table 2.2   Increasing pesticide sales in Latin America, Africa and Asia (US$ millions).

Latin America	1980	1985	1990
Argentina	102	164	241
Bolivia	9	13	18
Brazil	695	1,225	1,993
Chile	8	12	17
Colombia	96	155	259
Ecuador	41	60	86
Paraguay	-	-	23
Peru	14	21	30
Uruguay	7	11	18
Venezuela	22	38	61
Mexico	199	351	565
Total LA	$1,193	$2,050	$3,288
Africa			
South Africa	-	-	(1991) $160
Egypt	$77.97	$84.89	(1989) $105
Asia			
Malaysia	Average increase 6% a year between 1984-1989		$300
India	Average increase of 12% a year over 20 years		

Sources: For Latin America, Burton & Philogene, 1988, in *Preliminary diagnosis of the use of pesticides in Brazil and their impact on human health and the environment*. Henao H. Samuel, and others, Brazil, April 1991. Various other sources, including country reports.

However, the markets targeted for growth are likely to be selective, and among the richer Third World countries which are already significant users, such as Brazil, Mexico, Argentina, some South East Asian countries such as Malaysia and Thailand, and China. Few companies expect any increases in the African market, apart from South Africa, although in many African countries pesticides form a significant part of expenditure on imports.

In the poorer markets, companies frequently market older pesticides which are more broad spectrum and cheaper, but which remain profitable:[18]

for example two of Bayer's leading products, carbofuran and methamidophos are widely used in the Third World. ICI's paraquat, one of its biggest selling lines, is widely used on Third World plantations. Hoechst's products endosulfan and deltamethrin command large Third World sales.[19] Many of these older products have been named by Third World non-governmental organisations as causing concern under the conditions in their country.

Do pesticides address hunger?

The push for pesticide sales in the South depends on three assumptions: that increased agricultural production will increase access to food and thus reduce hunger; that increased production will mean more exports and more foreign exchange and thus make the exporter richer; and that pesticides are the only way to increase agricultural production. The simple equation between increasing agricultural production and reducing hunger is widely subscribed to by agrochemical corporations. As Bayer says:

> Given the abundance of food in the industrial countries, it is easily forgotten that people in other parts of the world are in dire need . . . There can therefore be no doubt that crop protection is of crucial importance in the fight against hunger. It is more necessary than ever before.[20]

The industry association, GIFAP (Groupement International des Associations Nationales de Fabricants de Produits Agrochemiques), states in the objectives of its Asia Working Group:

> The rising population and its demand for adequate food will increasingly put governments and its agriculture under pressure. In many Asian countries it will not be possible to expand the arable land beyond its level today. In order to feed an increasing population higher yields per given acreage have to be obtained. Together with new varieties, advanced crop production techniques and the use of Crop Protection Products this goal can be achieved.[21]

In spite of poverty and food shortages affecting many Third World communities, the export agricultural sector consumes the most pesticides. Cotton crops accounted for 11% of all pesticide use in 1991,[22] and in Third World cotton-growing countries, it can consume up to 90% of annual pesticide expenditure. This is mainly for export, and not as part of a strategy to increase access to food, fibre and fuel for the poorest communities. Pesticide inputs in Third World countries rose dramatically following the Green Revolution, which increased yields from wheat and rice harvests. But, while production increased, many small farmers lost their land, unable to afford the expensive inputs. One consequence was that access to food decreased for many.[23] There is no simple equation between increasing agricultural production, and access to food. There is, however, a more direct connection between increased pesticide use and the export agricultural sector. This has not proved a satisfactory motor of development. Low commodity prices have meant agricultural exporting countries accumulate more debts than profits, as well as a distorted economic base. The assumption that pesticides are the route to increased agricultural production is discussed more widely in Chapter 4.

Pesticide trade and the FAO Code of Conduct

With increasing pesticide use in the South, and in recognition of associated hazards, the FAO adopted the International Code of Conduct on the Distribution and Use of Pesticides (FAO Code) in 1985 to raise industry marketing and distributing practices. Pesticides have proved hazardous in all countries, but more so where there are high rates of illiteracy, a lack of protective equipment, hot and humid climates making the wearing of protective clothing virtually impossible, lack of washing water, absence of medical facilities, difficulty of keeping antidotes and lack of training. The Code also addressed standards of advertising, which frequently promised high yields for less costs from using pesticides.

Pesticide trade is most directly addressed through the Prior Informed Consent (PIC) provisions in the FAO Code. The concept of PIC was

Table 2.3 Pesticides included in the PIC procedure, and those identified as candidates for inclusion.

Initial pesticides for PIC	In process/under consideration*	To be included if still in use
aldrin	methamidophos	chlordecone
captafol**	methomyl	DBCP
chlordane	methyl bromide	endrin
chlordimeform	monocrotophos	kelevan
cyhexatin	paraquat	lead compounds
dieldrin	parathion methyl	leptophos
dinoseb	phosphamidon	mirex
DDT		nitrofen
EDB		schradan
fluoroacetamide		strobane
HCH (mixed isomers)		telodrin
heptachlor		thallium sulphate
hexachlorobenzene		
mercury compounds**		
parathion ethyl		
phosphides:		
aluminium and		
magnesium**		
toxaphene**		
2,4,5-T		

* Some formulations of these pesticides are likely to be included in the process, on the grounds that they may cause health problems under conditions of use in developing countries.
** Decision Guidance Documents are still in preparation for these pesticides
Source: Minutes of the UNEP/FAO Experts Meeting on PIC, Geneva, February 1992.

introduced early in the negotiations for the FAO Code, but was deleted from early drafts, only accepted in principle in 1987, and finally added in 1989. Under PIC, governments may register a refusal to allow the import of pesticides banned or severely restricted for health and environmental reasons, which meet an agreed criteria (see Chapter 1). At present the PIC procedure covers only a small number of pesticides (see Table 2.3). The scheme is in its early stages, and few governments have indicated their decisions on imports. None of these lists can be regarded as exhaustive, and more pesticides will be added. Any pesticide now banned for health or environmental reasons is automatically included in the PIC process, but before it can be fully entered, the secretariat must have a Decision Guidance Document prepared, reviewed and checked.

The General Agreement on Tariffs and Trade (GATT), under the Uruguay Round, has been working to eliminate non-tariff barriers to trade, and one area of concern is whether PIC would run counter to GATT rules. As things stand at present, international agreements such as PIC should be exempt. Under its own working group, established in 1989, on export of domestically prohibited goods and other hazardous substances, GATT has been developing guidelines for products domestically-banned or severely restricted on the grounds of being harmful to human, animal or plant life, or health, or harmful to the environment. Although the working group has suggested that prior informed consent be required for the export of domestically-banned chemicals and pesticides, this has not won general agreement, with the United States in particular arguing for only prior notification.

The FAO Code addresses only a limited aspect of pesticide trade. Bearing in mind that as much as 40% of foreign trade is made up of transnationals trading within the same company, there is scope for a much broader code of conduct. A Code of Conduct for transnational corporations, covering responsibilities and accountability, has been on the UN agenda for over 20 years, but is virtually moribund. A more far-reaching code would address issues such as commercial secrecy, accounting methods which allow transfer pricing to move profits without full disclosure, and thus avoid tax responsibilities, corporate responsibility for hazards and pollution in Third World subsidiaries.

As the FAO Code is voluntary, industry's commitment is essential for it to be effective. The major pesticide corporations have all indicated their support for the Code and GIFAP has made compliance a condition of membership. All the major companies have established policies of 'responsible care and product stewardship'.

Product stewardship—an approach to safety?
A survey of the product stewardship policies set out in Annex 1 indicates the approach taken by the major agrochemical corporations, particularly those which are members of GIFAP, to implement the Code of Conduct. While no company was prepared to indicate its budget allocation for product stewardship, it appears that all companies have reorganised their

management structure to promote safe use, and to take on board the provisions of the Code covering labelling, packaging, storage and disposal, advertising and training. Companies do not see compliance with the FAO Code as incompatible with efficient and profitable use of pesticides.

In fact, the companies have little to lose from safe-use initiatives. Pesticide use is increasing, and education and training initiatives based on safe use still promote agrochemicals. In addition, in markets where over-use has increased insect resistance and resurgence, education to promote safe and effective use, in the context of Integrated Pest Management, will help create a long-term, stable market for pesticides.

Companies emphasise the approach of 'training the trainers', such as agricultural extension officers and agricultural colleges. While this is an efficient way to emphasise safe use, it does not promote alternative, non-chemical methods of agricultural production. Several corporate projects have produced popular information, such as posters, videos and cartoon books, and some work in rural schools to raise awareness of pesticide hazards. For example, a pilot programme in Costa Rica sponsored by the major companies, and run in co-operation with the government, introduces safe use in rural elementary schools as a regular part of the curriculum.

The continuing hazards of pesticides clearly indicate a need to stress safety, which it would be misplaced to criticise. However education and training cannot only work in the context of safe use of pesticides, and must address safe agricultural production in the context of non-chemical alternatives. The largest group of users in Third World agriculture, agricultural labourers on plantations, cannot exercise the option of safety in their working conditions, and millions of other small farmers cannot afford to wear even simple protective clothing (cotton shirt and trousers covering arms and legs, washed after use), regardless of the level of training.

The PIC process could serve to focus particular attention on pesticides which fall into the category of causing concern 'under conditions of use in developing countries', and thus raise hazard awareness in countries where these are used. There are many pesticides shown in the country reports which consistently cause health problems, for example paraquat (whose status in PIC has not yet been confirmed), endosulfan, deltamethrin, profenofos, and organophosphates and carbamates which cannot be specifically identified. To date, the manufacturers of pesticides falling into this category have all challenged their inclusion in the PIC process. They may not be included until they are banned in one country for health or environmental reasons. But companies also dispute the government's right to ban a product. For example, the Philippines government recently banned endosulfan, and the producer, Hoechst, challenged this in the courts, winning a temporary order allowing it to continue importing and selling.[24]

The companies' replies to the survey on product stewardship policies indicate they accept the scale of the problem. However their resources to promote pesticides in the context of safe use is far greater than the resources to promote non-chemical agricultural practices.

Safe use or product promotion

The scale of health hazards in Third World countries has prompted GIFAP to launch pilot projects on safe use in three Third World countries—Kenya, Guatemala and Thailand—to train farmers through distributors and government extension services, supported by radio, poster and protective-clothing campaigns. In addition to improving standards of formulation, packing, labelling, storage and transport, medical personnel will be trained to diagnose and treat pesticide poisoning.[25] However, these programmes are intended to run for several years before being introduced elsewhere. One danger of campaigns run by industry is that exposure to information about good practice, will also focus on pesticides, and will tend to increase use. Safe-use campaigns need to run with a programme proposing non-chemical alternatives.

Integrated pest management (IPM) involves a broad ecological approach to pest control, using a variety of methods to control pests. Methods can involve protecting and preserving natural enemies to pests, intercropping, crop rotation, a knowledge of when pest infestation is likely to cause economic damage greater than the cost of treatment, improving the quality of the soil, introducing biological controls. IPM also involves the judicious use of pesticides. In many Third World countries, the use of insecticides has brought problems of insect resistance and resurgence, which mean farmers cannot grow crops, or switch to other pesticidal products. This has prompted many of the big agrochemical corporations to embrace IPM as it would provide a long-term, stable market for pesticides. Ciba-Geigy, for example, has set up a team to train smallholders in Latin America, Africa and Asia in IPM techniques, as well as safe handling of pesticides. Environmentalists have suggested that companies are in fact developing 'integrated pesticide management', and do not subscribe to the theory that managing pesticides is the same as managing pests. The original IPM concept aimed to reduce and, if possible, eliminate pesticide use.

The pilot projects on safe use address a very limited audience. In Third World countries, the education, training, marketing, and other strategies which promote pesticides have not been matched by resources for alternatives. In Sudan, where a successful IPM project has run for many years, there is still no general application of the lessons, and large-scale aerial spraying is the norm. A method of spraying which encourages pesticide over-use was pioneered by Ciba-Geigy in 1970, and still applies today, with different contractors (see Chapter 4).

Exporters' responsibilities

There is no provision through UN agencies or governments for monitoring or enforcing the FAO Code. For pesticides not in the PIC process, but banned or severely restricted for any reason in an exporting country, the exporting country is required to notify the importing country that a shipment should be expected. Few governments have set up schemes to notify of such exports, and many banned or severely restricted products are exported without notification.

Once a pesticide is part of the PIC process, its export should not take place unless the importing country has indicated it still allows its imports. The governments of pesticide exporting countries are obliged to keep their pesticide exporters and industry informed of the decisions of importing countries, and to take appropriate measures to ensure that exports do not occur contrary to the decision of participating importing countries.

To date, only the European Community has made this mandatory, through Council Regulation (EEC) No. 2455/92, concerning the export and import of certain dangerous chemicals, dated 23 July 1992, which is effective from the end of November 1992. However there are no sanctions against exporting contrary to the regulation. The regulation states that 'Member States shall take appropriate legal or administrative action'. As many importing countries do not have the means to stop unwanted imports, the success of the scheme is yet to be tested.

More far-reaching responsibilities for the export of hazardous products have still to be addressed. For example, could a manufacturer be sued for the effects of its products? In February 1991, the US Texas Supreme Court ruled that Costa Rican farmworkers who claim to have been made sterile through exposure to the pesticide DBCP can sue the former manufacturers, Dow Chemical (now DowElanco) and Shell, through this court. This is part of a long-running struggle for compensation, but earlier suits filed in 1983 and 1987 were dismissed by the courts.[26] If these cases succeed, they will establish important precedents for health and safety responsibilities of exporters. Other workers believed to be affected by DBCP worked on banana plantations in Honduras, where DBCP was used between 1968 and 1980, and caused the deaths of 14 workers, and cancer and sterility in hundreds. The two US companies using the pesticide, Standard Fruit and Tela Railroad, have denied these charges.[27] In a case in South Africa, farmers affected by spray drift from 2,4,5-T used on sugar plantations lost a court action against the manufacturer.

European exports

The European agrochemical corporations command the major share of the world market, with 47% of sales generated by companies whose home base is in the EC, or 54% including Swiss companies. As all these companies are transnationals, their operations are worldwide. While companies tend to locate their major production facilities, particularly of the active ingredient, in their home country, they also locate production in other important markets. This means that most US companies have production facilities in Europe, and European companies in the USA. Japanese companies still have weak outlets in Europe and the United States, but are seeking ways of strengthening these. In addition to the major producers, many smaller companies formulate and export, or specialise in a narrow range of active ingredients—for example the UK company AH Marks, which is one of the world's major manufacturers of phenoxy herbicides.

Production in, and exports from, Europe are immense, however statistics record the export of formulated products only, and tracing the extent of bulk exports of active ingredients for formulation and sale in other markets is virtually impossible. Most European trade in formulated products takes place within the European Community, or with other OECD countries, as shown in Figures 2.1 and 2.2, but the UK, Spain, France and Denmark export the same or slightly more outside the EC as within it. EC countries exporting most formulated products to Third World countries are Germany, France, UK, the Netherlands and Italy. Eastern Europe is a growing market, particularly for Germany. Table 2.4 shows the destination of formulated pesticide exports from the major EC-exporting countries.

Table 2.4 Destination of exports of formulated pesticides in 1989 and 1990 from the eight main EC-exporting countries: Belgium/ Luxembourg, Denmark, France, Germany, Italy, the Netherlands, Spain, UK.

Importing country group	1989 (ECU million)	1990 (ECU million)	% Change
East Europe	211.9	234.9	11%
NW Africa	36.7	39.5	8%
Africa	233.5	160.5	-31%
North America	168.8	150.3	-11%
Central America	80.6	71.5	-11%
South America	59.3	66.5	12%
Middle East	163.7	216.6	32%
Asia	88.8	93.7	6%
Far East (incl. Japan)	141.8	129.9	-8%
Pacific	32.2	23.5	-27%
Total all exports	**3,247.3**	**3,426.2**	**6%**

Source: Eurostat COMEXT, compiled by The Pesticides Trust.

In 1990 exports to Africa made up 6% of the total exports of formulated pesticides from the EC; the Middle East took 6%; Central and South America 4%; Asia (excluding Japan and China) and the Pacific 3.5%; and Eastern Europe 7% (see Figures 2.3 and 2.4). While the proportions are small, the quantities and value are significant, particularly in relation to imports in those regions. As an example, the UK is a major supplier of pesticides to Egypt, with annual sales averaging nearly £12 million (1987 £16.7 million; 1988 £12 million; 1989 £20 million; 1990 £4.67 million; and 1991 £4.77 million).[28] This amounts to between 20% and 30% of Egypt's imports,[29] while constituting a tiny proportion of UK exports of

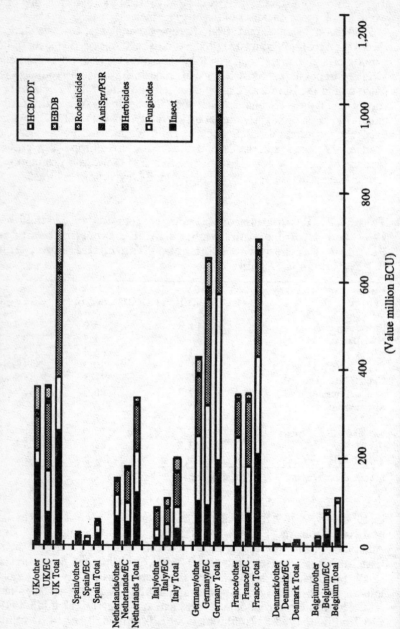

Figure 2.1   Major EC Pesticide Exporters 1989

(Value million ECU)

Figure 2.2

Comparison of Formulated Pesticide Exports from Main EC Producers to OECD and non-OECD Markets, 1990

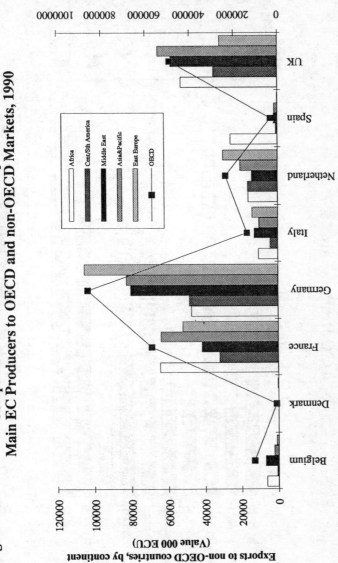

Source: Eurostat COMEXT, Compiled by The Pesticides Trust

Figure 2.3   Total EC-Formulated Pesticide Exports
to Non-EC Destinations, 1990

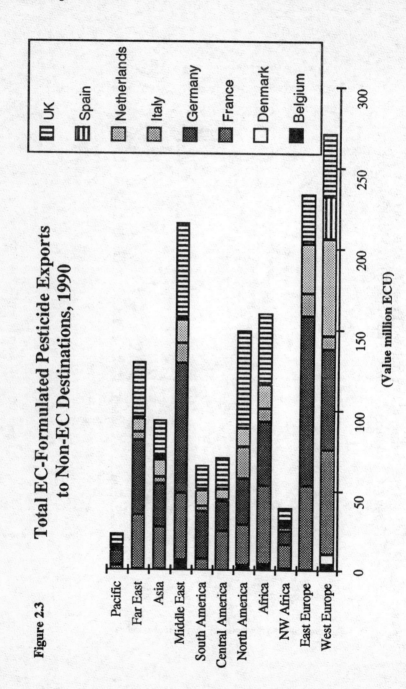

(Value million ECU)

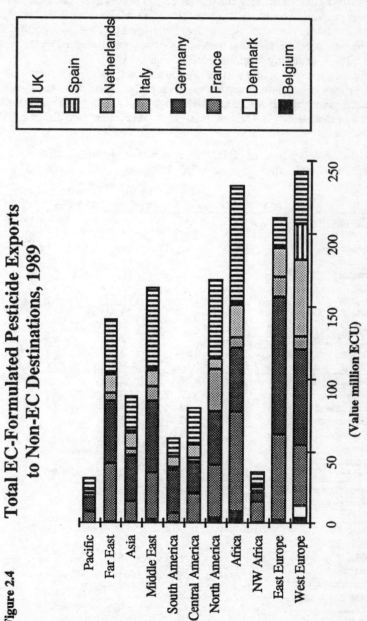

Figure 2.4   Total EC-Formulated Pesticide Exports to Non-EC Destinations, 1989

(Value million ECU)

Legend:
- UK
- Spain
- Netherlands
- Italy
- Germany
- France
- Denmark
- Belgium

formulated pesticides. The UK supplies nearly half of Sudan's pesticide imports, which are mainly for use on cotton.[30] It is also likely that a much higher proportion of active ingredients for formulation would be exported to Asia and South America, which have significant production capacity. This is supported by the fact that these regions account for approximately 15% and 11% respectively of global pesticide imports.

Tracing exports of any particular product is difficult. The export statistics are broken down into insecticides, fungicides, herbicides, anti-sprouting agents, plant-growth regulators and rodenticides. Only two categories are given in more detail, DDT and benzene hexachloride (see Table 2.5); and

Table 2.5 Exports of DDT and benzene hexachloride from the EC, showing non-EC importers.

	1989 000 ECU	1989 000 kg	1990 000 ECU	1990 000 kg
Belgium to				
Other EC	135		78	
Switzerland	19		15	
Poland	31		32	
Hungary	14		17	
USA	3		9	
Brazil	3			
India	5		23	
Japan	14			
South Korea			2	
Taiwan	2		2	
World	227	N/A	187	N/A
Germany to				
Other EC	52	30	24	6
Switzerland	12	25	4	3
Czechoslovakia	3	0	3	0
Honduras	4	0		
Syria	2	0		
Australia	1	1		
World	75	82	32	17
Netherlands to				
Secret (sic)	4	0		
World	4	0		
UK to				
Other EC			12	2
Norway	4	1	4	1
Malta	1			
Gambia			3	1
Namibia			1	
Canada			3	
Thailand	13	10	31	27
World	19	11	55	51

Source: Eurostat COMEXT, Compiled by The Pesticides Trust.

the triazine group, which includes atrazine, propazine and simazine. There is a strong case for better accountability of exporters, and better access to this information. With information available only on exports of formulated pesticides, it is impossible to have a true picture of both the scale of pesticide exports, and of particular products. Corporations say that commercial secrecy is essential to protect their markets.

Exports of technical grade products

The lack of data on exports of technical grade products is even more significant than the difficulty tracing particular products. Companies may export bulk active ingredients without publicly revealing the designation. For example Brazil, traditionally thought to be the preserve of United States exporters, in fact imports more from Europe, with the inclusion of Switzerland, than from the United States (see Figure 2.5).[31] This is not clear from looking only at exports of formulated pesticides. Looking at Brazilian imports, a number of pesticides on the PIC list could be traced: in 1989, Shell exported aldrin from the Netherlands (though its imports had dropped steadily through the 1980s); Hoechst, Germany, exported endosulfan; Enschem, Italy, exported carbofuran. From Switzerland, Ciba-Geigy exported two pesticides which are candidates for the PIC list, dichlorvos and phosphamidon.

Figure 2.5

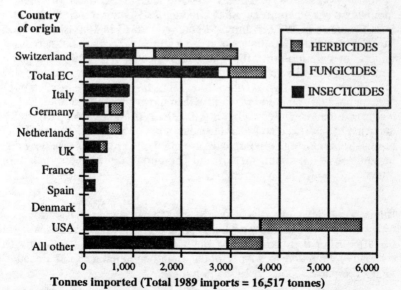

Brazilian pesticide imports, 1989

Source: Compiled by The Pesticides Trust from data of the Associadad National de Defensivos Agricoles (ANDEF), Brazil.

Exports of hazardous pesticides from the EC

No major companies are based in Belgium, Italy or Spain. However, Belgium and Italy are important exporters. Annexes 2 and 3 show details of producers of pesticides on the PIC list and candidate PIC list. Some European exporters of pesticides and potential pesticides for the PIC process could be traced.

Belgium

Ameco Belgium is not a pesticide manufacturer, but formulates and exports a wide range of pesticides, including chemicals in, or potentially in, the PIC process: aluminium phosphide, captafol, carbofuran, chlordane, DDT, dicofol, dieldrin, heptachlor, methamidophos, methomyl, monocrotophos, parathion ethyl and parathion methyl. Ameco also appears to export thallium sulphate, previously thought to be no longer produced.[32] Belgium exported DDT or benzene hexachloride to the value of ECU 227,000 in 1989, and ECU 187,000 in 1990. These went predominantly to other EC markets, Poland and Hungary. Small quantities were exported to Brazil, India, South Korea and Taiwan. Another Belgian company, Chimic-Agriphar, a subsidiary of Protex NV/SA, exports chlordane, DDT, aldrin and dieldrin, according to Greenpeace Belgium.[33]

Denmark

The Danish company, Cheminova, produces and exports parathion ethyl and parathion methyl, and is one of the major producers of parathion in the world. However, Danish statistics do not show any insecticide exports, indicating parathion is largely exported as a technical product for formulation elsewhere. Venezuela imported 280 tonnes of parathion methyl from Denmark in 1989.[34] Import figures for Brazil in 1989 show imports from Cheminova of 30 tonnes of insecticides.[35] These are not necessarily imports of parathion, but illustrate the difficulty of tracking source and destination. Cheminova has focused on organophosphate manufacture since the 1960s, claiming to now have the largest and most modern organophosphate plant in the world. Cheminova now sells intermediates or manufactures organophosphates on behalf of other companies. The company has invested considerable sums, some $15 million, supporting the re-registration of organophosphates around the world.[36] Its product range, in addition to parathion methyl and parathion ethyl, covers malathion, dimethoate, fenitrothion and ethion.

France

Rhône Poulenc is one of the fastest growing pesticide transnationals. It took over Union Carbide's pesticide products division when this was sold off after Bhopal, making it the main global supplier of aldicarb. The company is reputed to supply lindane, and supplied 15% of Ecuador's monocrotophos imports in 1990 (14 tonnes).

Germany

Hoechst Germany is a major manufacturer and supplier of endosulfan globally. For instance 1990 exports to Ecuador were 48 tonnes. Endosulfan is not on the PIC list, but has caused widespread concern and has been responsible for many accidental deaths. For example 31 died in Sudan in 1991 as a result of poor storage of grain baited with endosulfan.[37] It was banned in the Philippines in 1992, but Hoechst challenged the ban in the courts and won a temporary reprieve.[38] The Germany company Bayer is the major producer of carbofuran and methamidophos, both potential PIC pesticides. The German company, Hentschke & Sawatzki, supplies thallium sulphate. Venezuela imported methamidophos from Germany in 1989.

Italy

Italy is a major supplier of triazines, with total exports amounting to ECU 27.5 million in 1989, and ECU 17.7 million in 1990, although this includes exports of all triazine-based chemicals. The triazine pesticides, such as atrazine and simazine, have been banned in a number of EC countries because of their presence in water supplies, although these are not yet potential PIC pesticides. In Italy itself, there is a temporary ban on the use of atrazine (in place for three years), and it has been banned in Germany and Belgium and severely restricted in the UK. Italy's exports of triazine go primarily to the United States, which accounted for 82% of exports in 1989, and 95% in 1990.[39] Italy exported 42 tonnes of technical grade carbofuran to Brazil in 1989[40] and has supplied methamidophos to Paraguay.[41]

Netherlands

The Netherlands was a major exporter of aldrin, but the Shell plant synthesising this pesticide has now closed. The Netherlands does not have a major pesticide industry, but is the base of a number of companies which re-export. A quantity of either DDT or benzene hexachloride shipped from the Netherlands in 1989 went to a 'secret' destination.

UK

The UK company ICI is the major producer and exporter of paraquat, although the company also has production facilities in the USA, Japan and Brazil, and formulates in India and Malaysia. Several importing countries identified the UK as their major source of paraquat, including 65% of Ecuador's supplies in 1990 (264 tonnes). AH Marks in the UK is the world's main supplier of dinoseb, banned in the UK and on the PIC list. Other UK exports of PIC pesticides include: methamidophos to Paraguay in 1990;[42] demeton-S-methyl to Venezuela in 1989.[43] A UK company, MTM, exports demeton-S-methyl.[44] The UK is a major supplier of pesticides to Egypt, with annual sales averaging nearly £12 million (1987 £16.7 million; 1988 £12 million; 1989 £20 million; 1990 £4.67 million; and 1991 £4.77 million)[45] and amounting to between 20% and 30% of all imports.[46] Pesticides imported and in major use in Egypt which may come from the UK, and are potential PIC pesticides, include paraquat and methamidophos. The UK supplies nearly half of Sudan's pesticide imports, which are mainly for use on cotton.[47]

Other European—Switzerland

Outside the EC, Switzerland is the major European exporter. As home to the largest pesticide corporation, Ciba-Geigy, as well as Sandoz, the twelfth largest, Swiss exports are high. In 1991 formulated pesticide exports alone amounted to Sw.Fr. 824.3 million. Europe is its largest market, with 7% going to Africa, 14% to Asia (including Japan), and 9% to South America (see Table 2.6). Exports from Switzerland of PIC candidates includes monocrotophos where, for example, Ecuador identified Switzerland as its major supplier, with 1990 imports of 76 tonnes.

Table 2.6   Total Swiss pesticide exports in 1991, by value.

Destination	Total (million Sw. Francs)	%
Europe	538.67	65
Africa	56.10	7
Asia	116.92	14
North America	13.08	2
South America	76.27	9
Australia & Oceania	18.01	2
Diverse	5.28	1
Total	824.33	100

Source: Swiss Chemical Industry export figures.

Production moving to Third World

An unintended impact of controls on trade in hazardous pesticides, particularly controls aimed at closing the 'circle of poison' which prevent industrial markets from exporting pesticides banned or severely restricted in their own countries, will almost certainly be the transfer of production facilities of these pesticides to Third World countries, particularly if the market in those countries is sufficiently large. In some cases this will happen unilaterally, when newly-industrialising countries will establish their own production facilities for products which are out of patent. Where major markets are developing in the Third World, such as in Brazil, Mexico and China, pesticide corporations will license or establish production facilities in or near these markets and this trend could accelerate if they are prevented from exporting hazardous pesticides from industrialised countries. In fact, much production has already shifted.

Since the 1970s, about one-fifth of the new production and formulation plants have marketed products to the Third World.[48]   According to the 1991 World Investment Report, the most attractive areas for investment are the East, South and South-East Asia, while Africa is becoming increasingly marginalised as an area for investment, apart from the oil-rich nations. The top foreign investors are transnational corporations—500 of which control 70% of world trade, and are also responsible for most foreign investment, leading to intra-firm trade. As much as 40% of foreign trade takes place within transnational corporations, making identification of pesticide exports even more difficult.[49]

Domestic pesticide industries have grown in Latin America, India and other newly-industrialising countries.[50]   According to United Nations Industrial Development Organisation (UNIDO) figures in 1985,[51] pesticide production is already significant in parts of Asia, Latin America and Africa—together, these continents now export slightly more pesticides than they import. Thirty-three tropical and subtropical countries have facilities for formulating pesticides and at least 11 produce technical grade active ingredients. Third World factories not owned by the major transnationals may manufacture pesticides with expired patents, early inventions which tend to be highly toxic or persistent, and among the most widely banned in the North. They include, for example, DDT, toxaphene and parathion.

The major Third World producing countries are in Asia with China accounting for 7.3% and South Korea 5.7% of global production. India, Taiwan and Indonesia are also major producers. In Latin America, where the major producers are Brazil and Mexico, the share of global production was 3.7% in 1985. Eastern Europe and the then-USSR produced 21% of the world's pesticides in 1985.[52] The largest industrialising nations in Asia and Latin America have significant under-utilised capacity for pesticide manufacture, and are anxious to expand.

In Asia foreign corporations have co-operated with local companies to establish joint ventures. But the initial rush into South America has slowed, and some corporations are pulling out.[53] Some plants manufacture the active ingredients, others formulate active ingredients imported from the North. Many of the production facilities are exported from Europe and the United States. US researcher Angus Wright points out that

> Richer countries also frequently support investment in pesticide production plants and encourage pesticide use through development policies, foreign aid, multilateral development banks, and influence on agricultural research. Many Third World governments enthusiastically promote such programmes.[54]

This foreign direct investment in technology-intensive manufacturing in developing countries, and the growth of pesticide manufacturing in newly-industrialising countries, which has increased during the second half of the eighties, may undermine the potential of trade controls, and shows the importance of all countries participating in PIC as both importers and exporters.

Large Third World markets attract investment

Brazil is one of the largest pesticide markets in the world, with annual sales of around $1,200 million, larger than Germany before unification. With a market this size, Brazil has also become the major Latin American producer, and pesticide manufacture has been expanding for over 15 years. In 1990 nearly 30 companies were producing about 50 different pesticides. In 1988, Brazil synthesised 65.3 million metric tons of active ingredients, imported 13.4 million tons and exported 18.8 million tons. Exports from Brazil to other Latin American states have expanded enormously, from 1.5 million tons in 1975, to 18.8 million tons in 1988.[55]

However, the majority of Brazil's industry is in the hands of transnationals, six of which control over half the value of production; eight Brazilian-owned synthesisers take 15%. The others synthesise low-tech products and commodities such as dichlorvos, phosphine, trichlorfon, copper-based fungicides, alachlor, diuron, glyphosate, propanil and trifluralin. Investment in pesticide production continues; for example in 1989 Bayer doubled its insecticide production in one plant, and Ciba-Geigy planned to increase its herbicide production by 8,000 tonnes a year.[56] Shell Quimica formulates a range of pyrethroids and organophosphates, including monocrotophos. Others are fenbutatin oxide, fenvalerate, cypermethrin and cyanazine.

Markets the size of Brazil attract not only investment in production facilities, but also serve as a magnet for pesticide promotion. Shell, for example, planned over 1991-92 to target sugar cane in the country with a herbicide, isoxyl, it had acquired from a Japanese company.[57]

Without a sufficient market, production plants in Third World countries cannot be guaranteed to run profitably. In the early 1980s, Egypt attempted to cut its foreign exchange cost for pesticide imports, and established a plant to manufacture about 10% of its annual consumption of dimethoate and malathion. The plant was established with help from the United Nations Industrial and Development Organisation, using second-hand equipment bought from an Italian company for $US10 million. However, at current international prices, the cost of the locally formulated product is higher than the cost of importing it formulated from abroad. The country must import most solvents, surfactants, and other adjuvants used in formulation, as well as drums, packaging materials and vials (see Egypt country report).

Lack of safety in Third World factories

The Bhopal gas leak, which has killed over 3,000 to date, from a Union Carbide pesticide plant manufacturing carbaryl and aldicarb for use on India's cotton crop, raised the question of standards of production. At the time of the gas escape, all safety systems designed to contain leaks were out of action. In addition, the highly volatile methyl isocyanate was stored in large quantities in a tank whose refrigeration system had broken. In a similar Union Carbide plant in Beziers, France, the active ingredients were synthesised without storing methyl isocyanate, but only making quantities as required.

There have been attempts to interpret the General Agreement on Tariffs and Trade (GATT) in such a way that the transfer of environmentally harmful industrial production processes to countries with poor environmental standards could be defined as 'environmental dumping', under the definition referring to:

> products where goods containing materials which have toxic or dangerous properties, and to production processes, where a method of production is transferred internationally to somewhere with lower environmental input and emission charges so that the financial benefits of this can be reaped.[58]

However it is not at all clear that the present GATT Uruguay Round— should it be completed—would include a strong definition. If production continues to move to the Third World, controls need to be introduced to ensure health and safety standards are as high as elsewhere.

Trade liberalisation and the free market

The UN Conference on Environment and Development attempted to include the responsibilities of transnationals in Agenda 21, but all references were deleted after lobbying by the Business Council for Sustainable Development, through the International Chamber of Commerce.[59] The governments of the rich industrial countries want discussion of the linkage between trade and environmental sustainability transferred to the Uruguay Round world trade talks, where free trade will take precedence over environmental policy. Transnationals argue that there is no incompatibility between free trade and the environment, and this is the official GATT position. If the goals of Agenda 21 are to succeed, they would need to be taken seriously by transnational corporations, however transnationals' objectives remain the further opening of markets. Transnational corporations argue that free trade is the only way to defend environmental interests and on development they adopt the conventional economic wisdom that economic growth, measured by the gross national product, is essential and that the wealth created by a few will benefit the many.

World Bank and International Monetary Fund structural adjustment policies have been influential in promoting pesticide sales, by encouraging developing countries to export crops to earn foreign exchange as a fuel for development. The same policies have encouraged deregulation of pesticides to promote sales on the open market.

When pesticides were deregulated in Ghana in the early 1980s, the effect was to take use out of the hands of the Cocoa Board, whose extension officers were responsible for spraying. It seems likely that small farmers, who now buy and apply their own pesticides, will have less access to training, protective clothing and washing facilities than did the extension workers.

In many countries, pesticides have always been available on the free market. In Egypt, where subsidised pesticides are easily accessible, insecticides intended for use on cotton appear to have been sprayed on fresh fruits such as grapes, prunes and watermelon. Ill health has been attributed to eating contaminated fruit and vegetables for over 20 years.[60]

Venezuelan non-governmental organisations have voiced fears that pesticide deregulation now being discussed by the government will increase trade in pesticides illegally smuggled into the country.[61] The government is also concerned about the practice of smuggling, and believes many of the smuggled products are banned elsewhere. It has indicated it will undertake a joint programme, with the National Guard, to control and monitor this trade.[62]

Third World governments maintain that access to finance, and particularly aid funding, to buy agricultural chemicals is easier than for other products.[63] In Sudan, which spends $30-$40 million annually on pesticides, financing comes from donations and loans by some EC countries, the World Bank and some Gulf countries. Sometimes donors stipulate that their funds be used to purchase pesticides from a specific origin. Others go further, and specify both the type of pesticides and the exporter. A researcher with the US Environmental Protection Agency has pointed out that many excessive pesticide shipments are linked with other commodities in an aid package. A country may be able to receive highly desired commodities, such as Toyota vehicles, only if an equally valued portion of the aid package consists of pesticides regardless of whether a legitimate need for them exists. Benin and Guinea-Bissau have both received pesticides with Toyotas as part of Japanese aid packages.[64]

This concentration on the export sector has an impact on domestic food production. Food imports have risen, partly as a consequence of focusing on the export agricultural sector, and partly as a consequence of cheap food policies in the United States and Europe. Cheap foreign imports depressed local prices, and undermined smallholders producing for this market. Food imports into sub-Saharan African, which were insignificant in the early 1960s, now account for around a fifth of local consumption, and absorb some 20 per cent of total foreign exchange earnings.[65] Yet food self-sufficiency needs to be given a greater priority, as one economist pointed out:

> Production of food is the most effective form of import-saving investment. For a country with a deficit on its balance of payments to import food means that it is borrowing to eat. The debt remains to be paid after the food is eaten. This is the rake's progress that has led many Third World countries into the present impasse.[66]

Should the GATT Uruguay Round be completed, agriculture will be included for the first time, and it is thought this may increase export agriculture in Third World Countries, with the effect of increasing trade in pesticides. GATT has proposed that food security be ensured through international trade. One GATT economist, Kym Anderson, suggests that a free market in agriculture would lead to the international relocation of cropping production from high-priced to low-priced countries, which in turn would substantially reduce the use of chemicals in world food production, and thus reduce agricultural pollution. It is difficult to follow this reasoning, as it is likely this would encourage pesticide trade, with no guarantee of access to food for the poor, or food security for the country. Indeed, Anderson points out that:

> Food consumers in densely populated Western Europe and Japan, where price and trade policies and high land prices currently encourage the heaviest use of farm chemicals, would have the most to gain from the effect of such reforms.[67]

Arguments for increased pesticide trade are based on the premise that pesticides are essential to sustain agricultural yields, and particularly to feed the increasing world population. Instances of starvation and increasing population in Third World countries are frequently cited to justify the approach. However the connection between agricultural inputs and food security, in particular food for the poor, is tenuous. Distribution is a greater problem than production, as access to food is limited by poverty, not the quantity of food produced annually.

Conclusion

The PIC provisions are an important advance as a mechanism for reducing trade in hazardous chemicals. The process is in its initial phase, and it is as yet too early to tell whether the political will exists to ensure it operates as intended. However there are drawbacks. In particular, the success of PIC will depend on decisions taken by importers and a lack of non-hazardous alternatives, or inability to regulate the pesticide industry in the importing country, could lead to inaction. Many environment and development groups favour a halt to the export of products banned in the exporting country, as controls on trade are in themselves not sufficient to reduce hazards.

However, there are limitations to both import and export controls. Pesticide trade to Third World countries is increasing and is likely to continue to do so. Should trade controls become too constricting, they will encourage production to move, a trend already observed where the market is sufficiently large. While it may be in the interests of richer Third World countries to develop their own pesticide industries, this is unlikely to promote health and environmental interests. Policies to reduce pesticide hazards in the Third World based on trade controls, and legislation to prevent export of pesticides banned in industrial countries, will not address the fundamental problems, many of which are caused by the scale of pesticide use, the difficulty of using pesticides safely under certain conditions of use and particularly in hot tropical climates, occupational health and safety standards, and poverty.

There is a need for a broad approach to the problems of pesticide hazard, not only based on controlling and managing chemical trade, but also looking at trends in investment. This will place pesticides in the wider context, focusing on safer methods of agricultural production, based on principles of sustainability and prioritising the health and safety of pesticide users, their communities and the environment.

References:
1. *British Agrochemicals Association Annual Report*, 1992, for example, sites trade liberalisation as the reason for increased sales to Argentina.
2. *Agrow World Crop Protection News*, No. 163, 10/7/92, pp. 18-19.
3. Agrow, *Future Trends in the Agribusiness Industry*, PJB Publications Ltd, December 1990.
4. *Agrow*, No. 140, 2/7/91, and 10/7/92.
5. *Ibid.*
6. *Ibid.*
7. See, for example, interview with Bayer, in *Agrow*, No. 129, 15/2/91.
8. 'Bayer emphasis growth from within', *Agrow*, No. 129, 15/2/91.
9. Industrieverband Agrar, the German agrochemical trade group, 1989 figures, quoted in Knirsch, J., translated from *Gefahrliche Exporte* (Dangerous Exports), a study of German pesticide exports, PAN Germany. Quoted in *Global Pesticide Campaigner*, PAN North America, Vol. 1, No. 3, June 1991.
10. Postel, S., *Defusing the Toxics Threat: Controlling pesticides and industrial waste*, Worldwatch Paper 79, September 1987.
11. *Agrow*, No. 163, 10/7/92, pp. 19-20.
12. Ciba-Geigy, 'Safety depends on you', Agricultural Division, p. 3.
13. *Agrow*, No. 158, 1/5/92.
14. *Agrow*, No. 146, 1/11/91.
15. *Agrow*, No. 155, 13/3/92.
16. *Agrow*, No. 157, 10/4/92.
17. *Agrow*, 15/2/91.
18. Knirsch, J, 'Pesticides in the global marketplace' (translated from *Dangerous Exports*); and Wright, A., 'Third World pesticide production', in *Global Pesticide Campaigner*, PAN North America, June 1991, Vol. 1, No. 3.
19. *Agrow*, No. 157, 10/4/92.
20. Bayer brochure, 'All Climates under one roof: World's largest crop protection research centre completed at Monheim', undated.
21. GIFAP (Groupement International des Associations Nationales de Fabricants de Produits Agrochemiques), Asia Working Group Objectives and Structure, undated.
22. *Agrow*, 10/7/92.
23. This is well documented but see, for example FAO, *Sustainable Development and the Environment*, FAO Policies and Actions, Rome, Italy, 1992, pp. 33 and 38.
24. 'Hoechst blocks Philippines Government attempt to ban endosulfan', *Pesticides News*, No. 16, June 1992, p. 3.
25. *GIFAP Bulletin*, Vol. 17, No. 3, 1991.
26. *Agrow*, No. 128, 1/2/91, p. 18.
27. *Agrow*, No. 156, 27/3/92, p. 25.
28. UK Export Statistics.
29. Calculated against Egyptian imports, converted at 1991 exchange rates (£1=$1.75).
30. Eurostat, COMEXT, 1990.
31. ANDEF (Associadad National de Defensivos Agricoles, the pesticide manufacturers' industry association), export figures, Brazil.
32. *International Pesticide Directory*, MacDonald Publications, UK, October 1991.
33. Wattiez, C., *L'exportation de pesticides interdits a l'origine du cercle du poison, une etude de cases: La Société Chimic-Agriphar exportatrice de Chlordane, mais aussi de DDT, d'Aldrine, de Dieldrine et de Toxaphene*, Greenpeace Belgium, August 1991.
34. See Venezuela country report.
35. ANDEF, *op. cit.*, pesticide imports to Brazil, 1989.

monocrotophos (Azodrin 250 R) . . . everything points to the fact that the affected children have been the victims of a 'micro-poisoning': that is to say they have been continuously exposed to low levels of the toxic substance. Two or three weeks of frequent exposure has caused paralysis. The adults show symptoms of acute poisoning.

Press reports have revealed eight cases of monocrotophos-related paralysis in children in 1990 and 1991. Recovery took five to six months. Parents of the affected children suffered from nausea, vomiting, abdominal pains, severe headaches, profuse sweating and other discomforts. Farmers do not use personal protective equipment, though many say they know they should. Other press reports point to more than a dozen monocrotophos-related paralysis cases in two other towns.

There have been numerous cases of poisoning in the Second Public Health Region of Paraguay. The Pollution Control Department of the Environmental Health Services is conducting research into the most widely used pesticides, with the co-operation of the Agriculture and Livestock Service. These have now been identified as carbofuran, cypermethrin, DDT, deltamethrin, endosulfan, fenvalerate, monocrotophos, parathion methyl, phosphamidon, profenofos and cypermethrin and trichlorfon. This has identified potential pesticides causing the problems, but not yet found solutions.

Brazil[10]

While the country as a whole does not monitor the health impact of pesticides, regional poison control centres keep records. Brazil is among the world's major pesticide users. In 1988, 2.21 kilos of pesticides active ingredients were used for each of the 23 million rural workers.

Between 1986 and 1989, registered pesticide-related poisonings numbered 2,164. Most are not registered as they do not receive medical attention, and doctors are not trained to recognise pesticide-poisoning symptoms, commonly mistaking symptoms for food poisoning or other illnesses.[11] A toxicologist from the Poison Control Centre in São Paulo State assessed that 280,000 Brazilians, 2% of the population, are contaminated by pesticides each year. The Agriculture Secretariat in the state of Santa Catarina surveyed 7,498 farmers between May 1986 and March 1990, to investigate the number of times they had been poisoned by agrochemicals, and found over 28% had been poisoned at least once, and 2% more than seven times.[12]

During the visit of a delegation to a cocoa plantation in 1989, pesticide sprayers spoke of headaches and throat and skin irritation arising from use of BHC, officially banned in Brazil in 1981, but still available under-the-counter from many shops selling agrochemicals. Chronic health problems are common: Nestor Bispo da Silva, aged 55, has heart, chest and eyesight problems which he said are common among older workers who have been spraying BHC without protection for nearly 20 years.[13]

In Parana State, between 1982 and 1991, a reported drop in pesticide poisonings from 1,356 to 328 was believed to be a result of lax methods of reporting during the mid-eighties. What does appear from the statistics is a trend away from incidents related to organochlorines, and the 'dirty dozen' pesticides aldrin, BHC and endrin, as well as demeton-S-methyl. Pesticides responsible for more than five incidents in this state alone in 1990 or 1991 were: 2,4-D+picloram, carbofuran, chlorpyrifos, cypermethrin+profenofos, deltamethrin, endosulfan, glyphosate, malathion, methomyl, monocrotophos, organophosphates generally, paraquat, parathion methyl, profenofos, tridimenol+disulfoton, trifluralin (see Table 5.1). There is no breakdown of the seriousness of incidents, however it is noted that the greatest number of pesticide poisonings, up to 70%, occur on cotton plantations.

In the Brazilian State of Bahia, cocoa is grown on plantations, making the state virtually a monocrop economy. Among the agricultural labourers employed to spray pesticides, illiteracy is 60%, 73% of applicators did not use gloves, 85% did not use masks, over 43% smoked during the application of pesticide products. Other workers return to their jobs immediately after pesticide application, and over 86% ate meals at the workplace, mainly fruits found on the same land as the treated crops. All workers wore the same clothes for days or sometimes weeks.[14]

Venezuela[15]

In Venezuela during the period 1980-1988, 10,309 cases of pesticide poisoning were reported to the Ministry of Health. Of these, 5.6% resulted in deaths. The deaths increased throughout the 1980s, from 975 in 1980, to 1,553 in 1988 (see Table 9.3) although this could be a result of improved reporting.[16] The true picture is unclear because medical attention is not always available, many people do not seek medical help, and cases treated in the private sector are not always reported. More than 40% of poisonings are caused by organophosphates (mainly by parathion) or carbamates. Gramoxone (paraquat) was responsible for nearly 60% of deaths, and parathion for 30%.

An analysis of monthly bulletins on poisoning between 1985 and 1990 produced by the Centre West Region Toxicology Centre, which includes the States of Lara, Portuguesa, Yaracuy and Falcon, showed that 1,235, or 21% of all poisonings, could be attributed to pesticides. Pesticides caused 74 deaths, 63% of all those who died as a result of some kind of poisoning. The Ministry of Health's epidemiology statistics show 130 cases of poisoning and 52 deaths in 1989 and 92 deaths in 1990. The highest number of deaths occur in the Zulia and Mérida regions, where the trade in contraband pesticides is highest.[17] The cause of poisoning is rarely noted, and only occasional press reports cover details. From these, it seems that while suicide by pesticide ingestion is common in the rural areas, accidental death is also common.

hospital, of whom two died. The cases included 25 who ate pesticide-contaminated wheat or vegetables; 12 cases treated for contamination of skin or inhalation during spraying; two cases from drinking water from the canal; six cases of children below seven years who unwittingly ingested pesticides.[31] None of the pesticides were identified.

Organophosphates have also caused concern in Tunisia, which reports that these can easily be bought in small quantities from retailers. It is thought that organophosphates cause scores of accidents and deaths. As there are few physicians in the countryside, and hospitals and medical workers are out of the reach of most peasant farmers, poisonings and deaths go unreported. The majority of peasant farmers are illiterate, and prosperous farmers hire labour to spray—a cheap 'commodity' in Tunisia. Pesticides are badly stored, and come in close contact with food, water and beverages. Pesticide containers are used to store water, olive oil, milk, etc. It is hoped in future to present a better view of problems in the countryside as two new medical faculties have been launched, one in Sfax (south) and one in Sousse (centre): both have emergency help and are building a team of toxicologists and personnel trained to deal with chemical hazards and poisoning.[32]

In South Africa, apartheid laws have created a special situation for the country's 1.4 million farmworkers. Illiteracy is high, workers have few basic rights, and racial prejudice has allowed farmers to dictate unsafe practices. As farms are isolated, farmworkers have little possibility of organising to improve their conditions. In addition, lack of proper training means there is a general lack of awareness about pesticide problems by farm owners. This problem has been acknowledged, but no formal study has been undertaken to determine the national rate of poisonings among farmworkers. One case which reached the press in 1991 indicates the problems facing farmworkers. It reported that:

> Mr. Andries Sefoor, 46, collapsed on the farm Helpmekaar outside Montague on January 4 1991 after spraying pesticides for three days. An artery burst after he had inhaled poisonous substances. His wife, Mrs Marta Sefoor, said he came home two days earlier complaining of blurred vision and a blinding headache. 'He had been working for years with poisons and had never been given protective clothing or a mask,' she said. 'He told me he had complained about his headaches to the farmer, Mr. Hermie Kriel, who insisted that he return to work.'[33]

Farmers are required to provide all employees with safety equipment for spraying, including protective helmets, goggles, gloves, overalls, chemical-resistant clothing and boots. However, a survey of pesticide sprayers conducted in 1989/90 by the Farmworkers Research and Resource Project revealed that of 39 workers interviewed, only four were supplied with sufficient protective gear. The rest were either given nothing or overalls. The farmworkers were mainly from maize farms in the Transvaal, Northern Cape, and Northern Orange Free State.[34] Only one of the workers knew the name of the chemical he was using. One farmworker said:

No, they have never given us masks . . . If I hadn't spoken about gloves, they wouldn't have even given us that . . . We scoop the poisons like that, without gloves . . . you put your hand into the container and when you pull it out, the poison is there on your hand . . . they don't tell us that we have to use masks.[35]

West Africa—some controls, but no monitoring

Surveys of pesticide use in cotton in Benin, Senegal and Togo confirmed that none of these countries monitor health effects, keep statistics or records of pesticide poisonings or incidents, and information is particularly difficult to come by. In all three countries, cotton is grown exclusively by smallholders. The region has strong links with the French institute for research on cotton and exotic textiles (IRCT), which offers support to francophone countries in the shape of improved seed varieties, assessment of fertiliser requirements and advice on pesticide application.[36] The main pesticides used are pyrethroids and organophosphates, and farmers are advised to 'calendar spray'. This means application whether or not pesticides are needed: however IRCT advice seems to have prevented the overall escalation of spraying on cotton observed elsewhere, including in anglophone Africa.

In Senegal, a semi-private company, Société de Développement des Fibres Textiles advises farmers on cotton cultivation. It has helped reduce pesticide treatment on cotton, eliminated some toxic pesticides and promoted pyrethroids, although paraquat is still used. Nevertheless no protective clothing is used by cotton farmers and, as most housing is in or near the cotton fields, families are constantly exposed. No surveys of the health effects are known to have been carried out.

In Benin cotton, grown throughout the country, is the main source of foreign exchange and the main consumer of insecticides. Since 1981, pyrethroids and organophosphates have replaced organochlorines. However imports of pesticides have increased dramatically from 1984-85 onwards, doubling between 1984-85 and 1987, though subsequently dropping slightly. The area sprayed is increasing, particularly since 1990 when it reached 122,767 hectares. In Benin, 70% of agricultural workers are illiterate, there is no training in pesticide use, and protective clothing is unknown.

In Togo, cotton is the main export crop, and while the exact percentage of pesticides used on cotton is unknown, it is thought to be the main use for pesticides. Cotton production increased from 20,000 tonnes in 1980 to 100,000 tonnes in 1990, and over the same period pesticide imports for use on cotton increased from 436,226 litres (CFA francs 588 million) to 1.2 million litres (CFA francs 1,189.5 million). There is no pesticide legislation, and few controls, and the government welcomes the PIC process. Monitoring is a remote possibility, and little is known about the impact of pesticides in rural villages. Pesticides are sold through technical distributors, who are ill-equipped to advise on appropriate use, and whose information is often inaccurate. The company responsible for cotton in

Togo, Société Togolaise du Coton, said there had been significant cases of poisoning during previous seasons. Known cases of poisonings are registered at the Central University Hospital in Lomé, however the nature of the incident and the product involved are rarely cited.

Chronic exposure—a chronic problem

Cases of chronic pesticide poisoning amongst users are more difficult to trace. In the Venezuelan state of Guarico, at Calabozo, Dr. Moratino of the local hospital claims there is evidence to suggest that pesticide poisoning has caused birth defects and other health problems to local people. In the Andes zone, a study of agricultural workers found high levels of organochlorine pesticides in the workers. Some of the group also had very low cholinesterase levels, an indication of exposure to organophosphate and carbamate pesticides.[37]

Indian research by King George Medical College of the Industrial Toxicology Research Centre, Lucknow, carried out a series of tests on workers spraying DDT and malathion regularly. At least half of the workers developed psychological symptoms such as anxiety, sleep disturbance, depression and severe headaches. One out of five had impaired memory and performed simple drawing tests clumsily. Some suffered retinal damage, blurred vision and saw flashes of light and black dots.[38]

Cancer

Few Third World countries have attempted to analyse incidents of cancer and pesticides. In Egypt, one researcher pointed out that cancer deaths were recorded for the first time in 1964, almost eight years after the commencement of large-scale use of pesticides. The cancer death rate has increased steadily, and is greater in governorates where pesticides are widely used. The death rate from cancer is also higher among villagers than town dwellers in the same governorate, which could indicate greater occupational exposure. It is also higher among males than females, however male villagers are more exposed to bilharzia, which is linked to bladder cancer.[39]

In India, there is concern among doctors that cancer is increasing among communities exposed to pesticides. Dr. KT Shenoy of the Thiruvananthapuram Medical College has pointed to frequent cases of cancer of the lip, stomach, skin and brain, leukaemia, lymphoma and multiple myeloma, among farmers in Kuttanad. The area has 52,000 hectares of paddy fields, and pesticide consumption has shown a steady increase from 1,200 tonnes in 1972 to a peak of 13,400 tonnes in 1980, in recent years stabilising at 4,000 to 5,000 tonnes a year.[40]

An environmental toxicologist working in Tamil Nadu, increasingly concerned about the chronic impact of extensive pesticide spraying on agricultural labourers, conducted a small survey in three villages.[41] Dr. Muthu studied 20 labourers, 15 men and five women who had been spraying between five and 20 years at Thiruvarur Taluk in Tanjore District. Many Indian farmers spray pesticides for 8-10 hours a day without protective clothing and this area, the granary of Tamil Nadu, is one where pesticide spraying is high. Dr. Muthu carried out a preliminary survey, which showed that 90% of farmers are ignorant about the environmental and health hazards of pesticides; 80% work without taking any protective measures; 92% have direct skin contact while spraying; 30% of women are involved in pesticide spraying.

The variety of pesticides used makes it impossible to differentiate the impact of particular pesticides responsible—active ingredients include DDT, monocrotophos, BHC, mitacid, endosulfan and parathion. The study, as yet unpublished, is still underway, however the results of cancer assessment tests indicate cause for concern. Dr. Muthu used established methods to test for chromosomal aberrations and sister chromatid exchanges as indicators of increased carcinogenic risk. These measured significantly higher in the study group, compared to the control group, indicating that pesticide sprayers in agricultural fields are at risk of acquiring chromosomal anomalies, which increase significantly with duration of service. Smoking also significantly increases the risk.

Women and reproduction

There is little information on the impact of pesticides on women and reproduction. However, women work with pesticides and/or live near sprayed fields. These reports indicate one case which linked pesticide exposure to birth defects, where a woman spraying carbofuran during the early stages of pregnancy, collapsed. She later suffered a threatened miscarriage, and when her son was born, one arm had not developed beyond the elbow (see Ecuador). There are reports from Brazil, as yet not substantiated by research, that two different birth defects have been observed, and it has been suggested that these could relate to seasonal variations in spraying pesticides. The incidence of miscarriages and birth defects in areas subject to high pesticide spraying appears a neglected area of study.

A number of studies exist on breast milk, and there is considerable data showing the presence of organochlorine pesticide and polychlorinated biphenyl residues in human milk from Third World and industrial countries. Organochlorine compounds in human milk are highest in developing countries.[42] In South Africa, samples of breast milk of Kwa-Zulu mothers exposed to DDT sprayed for malaria control showed total DDT consumed by babies was 0.1 mg/kg per day, and in one case 0.375 kg/mg per day. These exceed the Acceptable Daily Intake for DDT, 0.02 mg/kg per day, by an average of five times, and for the extreme case of exposure, by 18.8 times.[43]

Records over-emphasise suicides

Where figures on pesticide poisonings exist, they frequently come from hospital poisons units, which tend to receive very acute cases of poisoning—predominantly, though not exclusively, cases of suicide or attempted suicide. These figures thus skew the overall statistics relating to pesticide poisoning, and may give the impression that suicides are the most significant problem.

In Brazil, researchers pointed out that deaths are commonly noted as suicides, without due investigation into whether these are accidental or possibly murders. In Brazil, the main pesticides used for suicide are parathion, monocrotophos and paraquat.

In 1989, in Negri Sembilan, Malaysia, there were 171 pesticide-related suicides, and 84 attempted suicides—this state has the second highest incidence of pesticide-related suicides.[44] The easy availability of pesticides leads to suicides which might not otherwise occur. In January 1990, in Tanah Rata, three school girls who had been threatened with bodily harm by a villager, apparently saw no way to resolve their dilemma and drank paraquat in school. One of the girls, Vanaja Gopal, had died when the incident was reported, the other two were in a critical condition. One of the girls had brought the bottle from her home.[45]

Paraquat has caused widespread concern because of its use as a suicide agent. It is acutely toxic, and there is no antidote. To discourage both suicidal use, and accidental poisoning, ICI began adding 'alerting agents' to some formulations in 1975, with the addition of a foul smell. In 1977 it included an emetic to induce vomiting and a blue dye to reduce the likelihood of mistaking paraquat for a cola drink or coffee. These are now added to the majority of, but not all, formulations (on importers' request). No studies appear to have been carried out to analyse the impact of these additives. In Malaysia, paraquat is still commonly used to commit suicide.

Malaysia has been one of the countries most concerned about paraquat use for suicide purposes, and approximately three-quarters of hospitalised cases of paraquat poisoning there have been due to suicides. However this pattern is not the same in all developing countries. In Costa Rica, a study of the occupational accident and disease register between 1980 and 1986 indicated that 75% of severe hospitalised paraquat cases were non-suicidal. Pesticide use has not basically changed in Costa Rica since that date. In Costa Rica, the change of colour from brown to blue, and the addition of an emetic substance, do not appear to have reduced paraquat-related accidents.[46]

Several NGOs point out the inadequacy of hospital data. In Egypt, for example, one-third of 1,154 patients admitted to hospital with acute poisoning during 1988 were pesticide-related, and a high proportion of these were attempted suicides. Chronic cases of pesticide exposure were not picked up through these hospital sources.

In Tunisia, a study over the period 1975-79 also showed that nearly 80% of hospitalised pesticide poisonings were suicides. This still left 155 cases of accidental poisoning. A further study of pesticide-related deaths in hospitals, through the records of the Forensic Medicine laboratory of the Faculty of Medicine of Tunis between 1976-1986, again pointed to a majority of suicides, 93%. Parathion was largely responsible (83%).[47]

Pesticides are freely available in South Africa, and are widely used to commit suicide. Pesticide poisonings are notifiable, under the Health Act 63 of 1977, to the Department of National Health and Population Development. These statistics largely reflect suicide cases, which are far more likely to be reported to the Department of Health than occupational cases. In all areas, the official notifications were lower than the numbers of pesticide-related deaths registered in hospitals or health districts. In 1989, 42% of reported cases were suicide attempts and in 1990, 31%.[48] Details are set out in the Table 11.1. Organophosphates are the main pesticide-linked suicide cause. Between 1986 and 1987 organophosphates were responsible for 51% of known agricultural poisonings.

In industrialised countries, the favoured form of suicide is an overdose of sleeping pills. In poor countries the easy accessibility to toxic pesticides makes them the most common method. Unfortunately, the prospects for survival when the attempted suicide is a gesture or cry for help is far lower when the agent is a pesticide. A teaspoon of paraquat provides a slow painful death. The suicide issue is a reflection of the easy availability of pesticides, not an indication of the level of pesticide poisoning.

Aerial spraying—a blanket hazard

Aerial spraying is frequently carried out carelessly, without due regard to the population, to non-target crops and to non-target areas such as rivers, dams and other water sources. Even carried out within guidelines, aerial spraying is more likely to cause contamination than ground spraying. Aircraft travel faster, making over-runs more likely, and pilots are insulated from the weather and less able to judge wind conditions in the target area. To minimise weight, low water volumes are used in aerial spraying, so that more concentrated mixtures are applied. Pilots run less risk of poisoning than ground crews who mix and load the pesticide. Flaggers, who direct the aircraft from the ground, run the greatest risk because of over-spraying or exposure to drift.[49]

In Egypt, about 1.26 million workers are potentially exposed every year to pesticides during aerial application, as field workers carrying out spraying, or as field workers in the sprayed field. No data is available on exposure under field conditions, yet it is known that the application of hazardous organophosphorus pesticides is high. As recently as 1990, the government adopted a tactic of widespread aerial spraying of the River Nile and its irrigation branches to kill an outbreak of water hyacinth. The two pesticides used, acrolein (an aquatic herbicide, intended for injection below the water surface[50]) and ametryn, killed a large number of fish, polluted drinking water, and caused a number of people to be hospitalised. The incident was criticised in Parliament, and the Minister of Irrigation promised to rationalise the use of aquatic herbicides.

In Tunisia, drift from aerial spraying causes additional hazards on local foods such as couscous, pimento, spices, dry meat and fish, which women spread on their roofs to dry in the sunny hours of the day. Cotton has now been introduced as an industrial crop in central Tunisia, attracting increased aerial spraying, and a large proportion of the 55 million olive trees is aerially sprayed with parathion.[51]

In Paraguay, cattle ranchers, who are large landowners, employ aerial sprayers to apply herbicides on their pastures. In many regions, their land is bordered by smallholders . The disregard for smallholders rights, and lack of control on ranchers leaves them unaccountable for careless spraying, which destroys smallholders' crops, and has caused health effects on children in the affected areas. The Paraguay country report documents three cases where this has occurred, in November 1989 when 200 hectares of smallholders land was sprayed affecting 334 families, in Arroyo Moroto where 112 people were affected destroying 50-100% of cotton crops and causing illness to children and adults, and in Republicano, when 176 people were affected and 67.55 hectares of cotton lost. Compensation has proved to be elusive and derisory.

In Brazil, pesticides are commonly applied by aircraft. In Parana State, the second main agricultural region, aerial application has only been inspected since July 1991. Farmers have not been required to observe marker flags, wind direction or the dangers of pesticides falling outside the target area. A number of workers remain in the field holding marker flags.

Storage and disposal—limitations

Obsolete and out-of-date pesticides—on both a small and large scale—continue as a problem, intensifying health and safety hazards to communities. Disposal of used pesticide containers equally continues to encourage unsafe practices, such as use for food storage, or simply exposure through proximity to housing and farmworkers.

On a large scale, obsolete pesticides have accumulated to reach identified stocks of over 6,500 tonnes, including hazardous pesticides such as HCH, lindane, parathion, DDT and dieldrin. Quantities have accumulated through past policies which established a number of African countries as 'storage' centres for pesticides used in locust control. Other stocks have accumulated through unwanted aid donations and through inefficient storage and accounting measures which lead to over-ordering or overlooking pesticides in store. The FAO has begun to address this problem, as have some pesticide manufacturers. Shell, for example, shipped back obsolete dieldrin from Nigeria to the Netherlands for incineration. However cost is a barrier to safe and speedy disposal.[52]

In May 1985, the inhabitants of the city of Kalaa Seghira, 150 km south of Tunis in the Sahel, signed a motion asking the Ministry of Agriculture to deal with 600 tons of HCH and 70 barrels of malathion which are deteriorating, and whose fumes are intoxicating the neighbourhood making people sick.[53] In December 1990, the Ministry of Agriculture was still seeking ways of disposal. As of the end of 1991, there were still reported to be more than 500 tonnes of obsolete HCH in Tunisia. The malathion had not been removed.[54]

In Sudan, the government attempted to deal with surplus obsolete pesticides by bringing these to a central store. A Sudanese group, the Sudan Development Association (SDA), collected evidence on three sites: one area where 60,000 litres of Torbidan had been left since 1980; another dump on a Blue Nile Agricultural Corporation site which has existed for more than 20 years, where pesticides have 'corroded, spilled out and (been) washed down with heavy seasonal rain to pollute the surrounding water ponds which are used by domestic animals and in some other household utilities.'[55]   SDA is particularly concerned about a site at Hasahissa town which the government took over in 1987 as a central dump for obsolete and banned pesticides. Old and rusted containers are stored inside the barbed wire compound of a cotton gin. The ground is dry and dusty and the perimeter dirt road constantly stirs up more dust. The major worry stems from a large quantity of unidentified pesticides which were buried. Hasahissa is in the middle of a populated region and irrigation schemes, being only 1.5 kilometres from the Blue Nile and less than half a kilometre from the Gezira main canal. Health has deteriorated in the area, and residents believed that the pesticide containers stored outside sheds were the source of the hazard. However during the rainy season in 1988 the situation worsened and it appears that the buried pesticides are now leaching into water supplies. Ill-health is common and, according to SDA, the rate of animal deaths is high. Researchers interviewed nearby residents and found a high incidence of headaches, nausea and dizziness, skin hypersensitivity, loss of appetite, running nose and sinusitis, sore and stinging eyes. More than 60% of the families interviewed lost their domestic animals or poultry during the last few years.[56]

At a farm level, containers are thrown into water courses, or left on farms. This was identified as a common occurrence in Brazil, Paraguay, Sudan and South Africa. In South Africa, under the Hazardous Substances Act 1973, empty pesticide containers and the remaining contents are required to be disposed of in a responsible manner—either punctured and flattened or buried. But in fact drums are generally left in the fields or orchards and not properly destroyed. In April 1989, 50 migrants from the Transkei, employed on a potato farm in the Orange Free State, were poisoned after drinking water from a disused drum which had contained monocrotophos. A three-year-old girl died and eight people became critically ill.[57]

In a study of 27 farmers in the grape-producing Hex River valley of the Western Cape, 51% of the farmers claimed they had a problem with the disposal of empty containers and unwanted chemicals, 18% had unwanted chemicals which they could not dispose of, and 70% of the farms had empty containers lying around. Only 7% of the farmers knew of companies that dispose of chemical waste.[58]

Philip Masia of the South African Farmworker Education Project pointed out that there may only be one communal tap on a farm, or people may have to obtain their water supply from a nearby stream: 'You're talking about people who earn so little that they can't even afford a bucket, so they use whatever container will hold water.'[59]

Food contamination

Accidents will happen

Tragic reports still emerge of food treated with toxic pesticides which is consumed *en masse*. Accurate documentation is sometimes hard to come by. One well-documented case occurred in Sudan, in March 1991, when 31 people died after eating bread made from maize flour treated in 1983 with endosulfan as a poisonous bait for birds.[60]

The government committee investigating the deaths uncovered a trail of carelessness and greed, made possible by the difficulties of keeping toxic substances safely over many years under the prevailing conditions. Maize was treated with 50% endosulfan, and was distributed to farmers, all of whom were instructed in its use and its possible harm to human beings and animals. Over the years, these injunctions faded. About 16.5 pounds of the treated maize remained in the storeroom of the Shaykh of Obeydeya: he sold it to a restaurant proprietor, who washed the maize, left it to dry and gave an amount to a neighbour to feed poultry. When the poultry died, the maize was sold on to a village supplier. An inhabitant of the village bought part of the contaminated maize for a funeral party, had it ground and prepared bread. The funeral guests thus became its victims and 31 died, mainly younger people. Over 350 people were affected, and months afterwards the survivors were reporting continued loss of memory. Others, particularly female victims, experienced continuing weakness and a tendency to faint. The incident confirms the difficulties of guaranteeing safe storage and disposal over any period of time.

In another recent mass poisoning, 150 people were reported to have died in India, in the village of Rajpura in Uttar Pradesh after eating food contaminated with lindane served at a village wedding.[61]

Our daily bread . . .

On a more day-to-day level, there is concern about pesticide residues in foods treated as part of the normal production process. It is difficult to impossible in parts of the world to carry out regular testing to ensure Maximum Residue Levels (MRLs) and intervals between spray and harvest are complied with. A number of Third World countries now conduct residue testing on foods, and while this is sporadic and scanty, there are indications of problems. In fact, MRLs are only intended to check good agricultural practice. A comprehensive programme of monitoring MRLs is expensive, and requires trained staff with access to good equipment.

Some of the most damaging evidence came from Egypt (covered in more detail in the country report). Although there is little routine monitoring, and sample sizes are very small, it appears that subsidised cotton insecticides have been misused, and sprayed on fresh fruits such as grapes, prunes and watermelon. Instances of diarrhoea have been common for the last 20 years, associated with eating these fruits and others contaminated with toxic compounds not recommended for use on vegetables or fruits, such as ekatin, triazophos, phosfolan, methamidophos and monocrotophos.

Since 1986, Egypt has seen a very large increase in the production of vegetables grown under plastic houses and in tunnels. This has been accompanied by an increase in incidents of poisoning due to heavy residues from frequent applications of pesticides, without observing the safe interval between the final spray and harvesting. Some of the pesticides involved have been methomyl, methamidophos, dimethoate and monocrotophos. Although fatal cases are reported every season, the Ministry of Health has never carried out thorough investigations.[62]

A food monitoring survey was carried out by the Faculty of Agriculture of food samples in all governorates in Egypt, for residues of DDT, lindane, dieldrin, endrin, methoxychlor, malathion and pirimiphos methyl. The results indicated that most areas of Egypt have a high percentage of pesticide residues in their foods: over 50% of the samples in five of the 11 governorates.[63] In a random sample of the diet of Cairo residents, more than 23 pesticide residues and their degradation products were detected, mainly endrin, dieldrin, lindane and DDT. In endrin, dieldrin and lindane, the levels were above the acceptable daily intake.

In Tunisia, spray drift from aerial spraying contaminates many vegetables with organophosphates, including parathion. A study showed that in citrus fruits, malathion was detected in 57% of samples, parathion in 4% and methidathion in 30%; parathion was also detected in 17% of artichokes, 43% of carrots, and in pimento, apple and tomato. However, the sample size is not stated.[64]

Latin American countries all reported evidence of unacceptable residues. In the capital of Ecuador, Quito, random tests on milk, including breast milk, found that all samples had traces of some of the hazardous pesticides BHC, lindane, aldrin, endrin and chlordane. This was confirmed by a report written by the National Science and Technology Council, which concluded that all the country's foodstuffs are contaminated by pesticides. And in 1986, research found that a large proportion of food and drinking water consumed in urban areas contained pesticide residues.[65]

In Venezuela,[66] there have been reports of pesticide residues in vegetables, grains, flours, pastas and even in drinking water in certain regions of the country. Research carried out by the State Experimental Agricultural Production Research Centre (CIEPE) found that samples of wheat flour, pastas and celery were contaminated with malathion and dithiocarbamate pesticides residues. No studies have been carried out to show the extent of contamination of cereals like rice where highly toxic pesticides like parathion are indiscriminately used. CIEPE is currently investigating residues in the country's cereal-growing zone.

In Brazil,[67] a limited survey suggested that 2-5% of food contained residues in excess of recommended limits. A more thorough, but earlier, survey showed 41% of produce in São Paulo supermarkets contained residues surpassing legal limits. Residues of pesticides restricted to non-food crops, such as cotton, are regularly found on food.

Pesticide poisoning—can doctors diagnose?

In Britain, a report on pesticides and health by the British Medical Association (BMA) pinpointed a lack of training and awareness of pesticide-related illness in doctors, stating:

> Not all doctors need to be expert toxicologists, but all doctors need to be aware of the possibility of disease resulting from toxic substances and to have more training and practical experience in the differential diagnosis and treatment of chemically-induced diseases. [68]

This report goes on to point out that the General Medical Council recommendations on basic medical education do not mention toxicology, and a survey of all 24 medical schools in Britain revealed that two taught no toxicology at all. The maximum devoted to toxicology in any course was 12 hours: most were far less, including as little as one hour. The same was true of pharmacology courses (between one and 12 hours). No consultant physician is employed on a full-time National Health Service contract in clinical toxicology, and only about 12 are employed with part-time contracted commitments to this discipline.[69] If this situation exists in a country such as Britain, with more resources for health care, what is the situation in Third World countries?

A common complaint from groups investigating pesticide abuses in Third World countries is the lack of training for doctors, and their failure to anticipate, or recognise, symptoms brought on by exposure to pesticides, particularly chronic, work-related exposure. It seems there is little training geared to help doctors. In South Africa, for example, there is no course or registered specialised field in clinical toxicology at any of the country's universities. This problem has also been identified by the pesticide manufacturers' association, GIFAP, which is undertaking a project to improve pesticide safety in three Third World countries. The Guatemala project specifies the need to train doctors to recognise pesticide symptoms.

A greater problem in poor countries, and particularly in remote rural areas, is that medical care is frequently not available at all. Where pesticides are regularly applied on a large scale, such as on plantations and estates, there is sometimes a clinic. However this is often inadequate, with poorly trained staff, a shortage or lack of antidotes. The medical officer frequently puts the estate-owners interests above those of labourers. Should hospitalisation be necessary, it can be many hours travel away (see Malaysia country report).

Labelling—not an antidote

The major pesticide manufacturers have all tried to address labelling shortcomings, however pesticides are still used by workers speaking a different language to printed instructions and by illiterate agricultural labourers, or are too complex to be taken in quickly.

Many of the countries providing information point to the problem of illiteracy, in particular Benin, Togo, South Africa, Brazil, Ecuador and India. In countries speaking multiple languages, the label language is frequently incompatible with the users' language. For example, in Tamil Nadu, where the main language is Tamil, labels were almost always in English or Hindi. In Tunisia pesticides are commonly sold without labels in Arabic.[70]

In Brazil, inaccurate information was found on labels. For example the herbicide lactofen, formulated by Hoechst, was sold in Brazil with a label warning that no fatty materials should be taken in the event of poisoning, but the next line said 'a large quantity of milk should be drunk in the event of poisoning.' Some labels had correction stickers over these instructions.[71] A leaflet on the DowElanco product Esteron (2,4-D) said the product could not be absorbed in dangerous quantities through the skin, while health and safety guides indicate that skin contact is dangerous.

Health and safety requirements are often impractical under the prevailing conditions of use. One example, not unusual, is the product Lorsban (chlorpyrifos) in South Africa where the label states 'If you get it on your clothes, change and wash them'; 'Wear rubber gloves, if you get it on your skin, wash it off at once'; 'Notify all inhabitants of the immediate area to be sprayed and issue the necessary warnings.' But many workers in South Africa do not have gloves, or access to clean water, and are rarely able to simply leave the field and change clothes. The Malaysian survey[72] also pointed to the impracticality of following label instructions.

Accurate label instructions are essentially long and complex, and encouraging farmers to read and follow these—even literate farmers with access to protective clothing or equipment—is difficult. A rural advisor in Natal, South Africa, said: 'Farmers take one look (at the label) and you can see the doubt on their faces.'

In poor rural areas, pesticides are repacked into small, affordable size packages, and these are not fully labelled. A number of countries, notably Venezuela and Ecuador, mentioned that illegal pesticides are smuggled into parts of the county. These are sold without any control, and checks on adequate labelling is impossible.

Conclusion

In the countries providing information for this study, there appears to be a trend away from organochlorines and some other compounds now widely-banned for agricultural use, such as DDT, aldrin, dieldrin, chlordane, heptachlor, toxaphene, 2,4,5-T. Other organochlorines, particularly endosulfan, are still widely used. Numerous other pesticides which have not been banned, however, have been identified as causing health problems in the countries studied here. Trade controls limited to banned products therefore may not effect the cause of most present-day pesticide hazards. There is, therefore, an urgent need to include these pesticides in the PIC scheme.

Organophosphates, which are more acutely hazardous as a group to the health of pesticide applicators, are in common use, and many countries studied here identified health problems of rural workers with use of organophosphates as a general category. Their impact arises not through oral toxicity, but general exposure to these pesticides. Pesticides which have been identified as causing health or environmental problems by more than one group in the country reports are set out in Table 3.1, however in most cases identification of particular pesticides is not possible. Two pesticides, parathion and paraquat, widely regarded as hazardous under conditions of use in Third World countries, are in common use. They have been identified as causing severe poisoning, sometimes death, stemming from the conditions of use, and not only from their acute oral toxicity. Yet paraquat and parathion methyl have to date been successfully kept off the PIC list by the manufacturers, ICI and Bayer, undermining the effectiveness of the scheme.

The use of hazardous pesticides is partly determined by cost. Later generations of pesticides, often regarded as more 'safe', are targeted for a narrower range of insects, and are generally more expensive putting them out of the price range of many farmers. However some of these, for example the pyrethroids, have brought their own problems where they are widely used, because of their impact on non-target organisms, and natural enemies.

While there are still labelling shortcomings, improvements have been made. However, in many Third World countries the majority of applicators are illiterate, and find the increasingly comprehensive labelling information, which is essential to convey the conditions necessary for safe use, too complicated.

Agricultural labourers and pesticide applicators on large estates are most seriously at risk. The risk to communities in rural areas is also great. The lack of health monitoring or treatment, particularly to communities regularly exposed to spray—either through living in areas which are aerially sprayed, near intensively sprayed estates and plantations, or near pesticide disposal dumps—remains severe.

The pressure is likely to increase to reject the use of certain pesticides identified as hazardous, such as monocrotophos. However, as long as equally or only slightly less toxic chemicals are substituted as an alternative, health and safety issues are not advanced. In spite of increasing commitment to 'sustainable agriculture' which does not threaten the health and environment of pesticide users, this is a long way from the reality operating in the countries surveyed here.

Table 3.1 Pesticides identified as causing health concern in these studies.

Named pesticides	Brazil	Costa Rica	Ecuador	Egypt	India	Malaysia	Morocco	Paraguay	Sth Africa	Sudan	Tunisia	Venezuela
2,4-D						✗			✗			
acrolein				✗								
aldicarb		✗		✗								
aluminium phosphate						✗						
azinphos methyl				✗								
BHC	✗											
carbamates												✗
carbaryl						✗		✗				
carbofuran	✗		✗	✗				✗				
chlorpyrifos	✗											
deltamethrin	✗							✗				
demeton-S-methyl	✗											
dichlorvos			✗	✗								
dimethoate				✗		✗						
disulfoton	✗											
endosulfan	✗		✗					✗		✗		
endrin					✗							
malathion											✗	
methamidophos		✗	✗	✗								
methomyl		✗	✗	✗								
monocrotophos	✗		✗	✗	✗			✗				
organophosphates				✗			✗	✗	✗	✗	✗	✗
oxamyl				✗								
paraquat		✗				✗						✗
parathion ethyl/methyl												✗
parathion methyl	✗							✗				
phosphamidon			✗					✗				
profenofos	✗							✗				
terbufos		✗										
triazophos				✗								

Unfortunately, the trend appears to be towards education and training for safe use of pesticides, rather than an approach based on the precautionary principle, which would give greater priority to less hazardous production methods, whether this is integrated pest management, cultural techniques to reduce use, or non-chemical, sustainable alternatives. It is doubtful whether the safe use approach alone can begin to address the problem, and many more changes are essential to combat the health impact of pesticide use.

References:
1. WHO/UNEP, *Public Health Impact of Pesticides used in Agriculture*, WHO, Geneva, 1990.
2. Jeyaratnam, J., 'Acute pesticide poisoning: A major problem', *World Health Statistics Quarterly*, 1990, Vol. 43, pp. 139-144.
3. IARC Monographs on the evaluation of carcinogenic risks to humans, Vol. 53, 'Occupational exposure in insecticides application and some pesticides', IARC, Geneva, 1991.
4. Loevinsohn, M., 'Insecticide use and increased mortality in Central Luzon, Philippines', *Lancet*, 1 June 1987, Vol. 13, p. 5962.
5. Trade union organiser from the State of Bahia, Brazil, speaking at an international cocoa meeting organised by the Transnationals Information Exchange, 1989.
6. PREPARE, India Rural Reconstruction and Disaster Response Service, report for The Pesticide Trust, Madras, October 1991.
7. Dinham, B. 'Paraquat and occupational hazards', *Pesticides News* , No. 16, June 1992, p. 4. Interviews with Honduran workers provided by C. Brady.
8. Morocco and Tunisia studies were provided by Greenpeace from reports provided to them as evidence submitted to the Barcelona Convention.
9. See Paraguay country report, Chapter 8.
10. See Brazil country report, Chapter 5.
11. Hathaway, D., unpublished report produced for Greenpeace Brazil, *Production in Brazil*, 1991.
12. See Brazil country report.
13. Hurst, P., Hay, A., and Dudley, N., *The Pesticide Handbook*, Journeyman, London, 1991.
14. See Brazil country report.
15. See Venezuela country report.
16. Ramirez, M., *Toxicologia de los plaguicidas Epidemiological bulletins*, Ministry of Health, 1989.
17. 'Unregulated import of pesticides: a public health drama', *El Universal*, 18/3/91.
18. Dinham, *op. cit.*
19. *Ibid.*
20. *Ibid.*
21. See India country report.
22. Nowell, Dr. H.A., Professor de Medicina del Trabajo, Facultad de Medicina, Universidad de San Carlos de Guatemala, Conocimiento, 'Casuistica y hallazgos anatomopatologicos derivados de las intoxicaciones por plaguicides', unpublished report, 1991.
23. Dinham, *op. cit.*
24. This and the following information was extracted from the manuscript of *Victims Without Voice*, now published by Tenaganita in collaboration with PAN Asia and the Pacific, Malaysia, 1992.
25. Association pour la Sauvegarde de l'Environnement et le Developpement (ASED), report for The Pesticides Trust, 14 April 1992.
26. See Ecuador country report.
27. *Hoy*, 5/1/91

28. Gallego, Dr. H.A., toxicologist, compiled these figures which were supplied to Dr. E. Nivia by Dr. O.N. Zapata, Chief Environmental Health Officer, Antioquia, Colombia, 25 June 1992.

29. Pesticide National Committee, Khartoum North, covering the seasons 1986/87 to 1990/91, in report for The Pesticides Trust, Dr. Z. ElAbjar.

30. ElAbjar, Dr. Z., 'Cotton and pesticides: Sudan case', report to The Pesticides Trust, September 1991.

31. Occupational Health Department, Sudan, Annual Report, 1990/91, 13 pp.

32. Bouguerra, Prof. M.L., Faculty of Sciences, Tunis, 'Report on organophosphorus pesticides in Tunisia over the period 1987-1990', for Greenpeace International, 1990.

33. *South*, 12-23/1/91, South Africa.

34. Farmworker Research and Resource Project Farmbase Surveys: designed to identify some of the problem areas that face farmworkers and compare trends across the country. Conducted by rural advice employees and fieldworkers 1989-90.

35. Emanuel, Kate, report of interview with Botha, W., Rainbow's End farm, Banhoek, Western Cape, 5.9.91

36. Technical Centre for Agriculture and Rural Cooperation, 'Cotton's fluctuating fortunes in Africa,' *SPORE*, bi-monthly bulletin, No. 37, February 1992, France.

37. Contamination of Andes zone, organochlorinated pesticides and cholinesterase level in the blood [translation as in source]. In Acta Cientifica Venezolana, XL Annual Convention, ASOVAC. UDO, Vol. 41, 18-23 November 1990,

38. 'Pesticide Poisoning', *India Today*, June 1989, p. 74.

39. Abdel-Gawaad, Prof. A.A., Professor of Environmental Pollution, Secretary of the National Society of Environmental Protection, General Secretary of the Egyptian Society of Toxicology, 'Ecotoxicological impact of organophosphorus pesticides in Egypt', report prepared for Greenpeace International for submission as evidence to the Barcelona convention, 1990.

40. 'Concern over pesticide residues', *The Hindu*, 11/3/91.

41. Muthu, Dr. P, 'Assessment of the occupational hazard - carcinogenicity in farmers as a result of pesticide usage, and their education in the scrupulous use of pesticides (Thanjavur District, Tamil Nadu, India)', report submitted to Ashoka Innovators for the Public, July 90-June 91,

42. Jensen, A.A., 'Chemical contaminants in humans' milk', *Residue Review*, Vol. 89, pp. 2-128, 1983.

43. Bouwman, H., Cooppan R.M., *et al.*, 'Levels of DDT and metabolites in breast milk from Kwa-Zulu mothers after DDT application for malaria control', *Bulletin of the WHO*, 1990, Vol. 68, pp. 761-768.

44. *New Straits Times*, Malaysia, 14/1/90.

45. *The Star*, Malaysia, 18/1/90.

46. Wesseling, C., and Castillo, L., PPUNA, School for Environmental Sciences, National University, Heredia, Costa Rica, quoted in a report on 'Current status of paraquat use and impact in Costa Rica', Programa de Plaguicidas, Escuela de Ciencias Ambientales, Universidad Nacional, Heredia, Costa Rica, March 1992.

47. Bouguerra, *op. cit.*, quoting Dr. Zouhir Hammami.

48. Department of National Health and Population Development, Western Cape Region, 'Pesticide poisonings in the Western Cape 1989 and 1990', Belville, April 1991.

49. Described in more detail in , Hurst, P., Hay, A. and Dudley, N., *The Pesticide Handbook*, Journeyman, London, 1991.

50. Worthing and Hance, *The Pesticide Manual*, British Crop Protection Council, 1991.

51. Bouguerra, *op. cit.*

52. 'Dealing with obsolete pesticides,' pp. 3-4, 'Pesticide Donations and the Disposal Crisis in Africa', pp. 5-6, *Pesticides News*, No. 14, December 1991.

53. Ben Hamida, S., *Réalités*, 5/7/85, Tunisia.

54. Bouguerra, *op. cit.*

55. El Gadi, M.I., 'Hasahissa pesticides graveyard', Sudan Development Association, unpublished report sponsored by Oxfam, Oxford, 1991. See report in *Pesticides News*, No. 14, December 1991, pp. 3-4.

56. El Gadi, *op. cit.*

57. Koch, E., 'A mass poisoning highlights flaws in farm health codes', *The Weekly Mail*, 7-13/4/89.

58. Reed, Dr. A., 'A descriptive study of accidental agricultural chemical poisoning in the Western Cape', Child Health Unit, June 1991.

59. Personal interview with Philip Masia of the South Africa Farmworkers Education Project, 30.4.91, in report for The Pesticides Trust, 1992.
60. Report of fact-finding by the Sudanese Ministry of Agriculture, Natural Resources and Animal Health, 1991, translated for the Pesticides Trust.
61. Thomas, C., 'Misuse brings harvest of death to India', *The Times of India*, 19.4.90, and *Agrow* No. 110, p. 21.
62. See Egypt country report.
63. See Egypt country report.
64. Bouguerra, *op. cit.*
65. Press clipping, 2.6.91
66 See Venezuela country report.
67. See Brazil country report.
68. *The BMA Guide to Pesticides, Chemicals and Health*, published on behalf of the British Medical Association by Edward Arnold, London, 1992 (original report published by the BMA in 1990), pp. 149-151.
69. *The BMA Guide, op. cit.*
70. Bouguerra, *op. cit.*
71. Photocopy of label supplied.
72. Tenaganita and PAN Asia and the Pacific, *op. cit.*, pp. 30-31.

4. Dare We Spray?
Environment and Alternatives

Chemical pesticides cause widespread environmental problems and are the only toxic chemical deliberately introduced into the environment. They are responsible for water pollution, soil degradation, insect resistance and resurgence, the destruction of native flora and fauna, and some, as ozone depleters, contribute to the greenhouse effect. As part of an approach to agricultural production, they have helped bring about large-scale monocrop economies. The appropriateness of this is now being questioned, particularly in Third World countries and the demand to construct positive alternatives is growing.

The evidence presented here by PAN groups is not an attempt to provide a comprehensive environmental audit, as environmental information on the day-to-day impact of pesticides in Third World countries does not exist. For example, material from Paraguay stressed that while local environmentalists are concerned about the widespread effects of pesticides, including disappearance of beneficial insects, contaminated water, fish losses and animal deaths, the evidence is based on local observations and an environmental hazard audit is lacking. Most material here reflects this problem, and provides recent information drawn from local research and newspaper reports, collated by PAN groups.

The problems which are particularly apparent include insect resistance and resurgence; contaminated water sources at farm level, plantation level, and in major agricultural zones; inaccurate aerial spraying which affects non-target crops, canals and dams; and destruction of non-target species. It is difficult to separate the health and environmental aspects. For example pesticides from a dump/storage depot in Sudan have leached into surrounding water sources, killed animals and affected villagers' health. [1]

The second half of this chapter highlights some of the alternatives to pesticide use, which were surveyed by PAN groups for this report. Against the background of the UN Conference on Environment and Development, there has been increasing awareness of links between high-input/high-yield models of agricultural production, environmental degradation, health and poverty. Sustainable agriculture is now finally beginning to be seriously considered on the international political agenda.

Pesticides in the environment

At a 1992 conference on water and the environment, the Assistant Director of the FAO attributed the degradation of water quality to excessive use of fertilisers and pesticides in areas with highly intensive agriculture, which uses over 70% of available fresh water.[2]

Stable pesticides, such as organochlorines which do not degrade quickly, can bioaccumulate, by building up in the body fat of animals, and can also 'travel' over long distances. They have, for example, been found in the body fat of Antarctic penguins. Atrazine, a newer generation of pesticide, has also been found in the Arctic.[3]

Large-scale use of pesticides has contributed to soil degradation, and to damaging monoculture cropping. For example the development, by the ex-Soviet Union of the region which is now Uzbekistan, into a vast cotton-producing monoculture led to an overuse of pesticides, polluted rivers and exposed hundreds of thousands of cotton pickers to poisonous insecticides and defoliants, which in turn have caused severe health hazards. The diversion of rivers for irrigation has shrunk the Aral Sea, once the world's fourth-largest inland lake, to 60% of its former size, and the formerly diverse agricultural region became highly dependent on cotton production.[4]

Over-use also provokes insect resistance and resurgence of pest populations, a feature particularly associated with cotton production. In the Rio Grande Valley of Mexico, 700,000 acres of cotton production were abandoned in 1970, when the tobacco budworm, a once harmless pest on cotton, kept in check by natural enemies, had become resistant and rampant. In north-east Mexico alone it wiped out cotton crops worth £35 million a year. An entomologist, Prof. Ray F. Smith, said in 1974 'Their resistant strains cannot be controlled by any available insecticide at any dosage.'[5] The area still cannot grow cotton.

Organophosphate pesticides are less environmentally stable, and have less tendency to bioaccumulate, however they have contributed to pollution in the Mediterranean Sea. At a meeting of the Barcelona Convention in October 1991, all countries in the area, except Albania, agreed to phase out the use of hazardous organophosphates by the year 2005. The meeting called for greater monitoring of organophosphates in 'hot spot' areas. It also acknowledged the need for financial and technical support of extension and educational services to train farmers in integrated pest management for non-chemical methods of control.[6]

Concern over pesticide pollution led the North Sea Conference to call for a 'substantial reduction in quantities of pesticides reaching the North Sea and to this end, by 31 December 1992, to control strictly the application and use of pesticides to reduce, where necessary, emissions to the environment.'[7] The use of lindane, one of the pesticides targeted, doubled in the UK between 1988 and 1990. It is persistent and stable, and is transported by both rivers and in the atmosphere.[8]

Insect resistance

Over-use of pesticides creates insect resistance, destruction of natural enemies and resurgence of pest species leading in turn to increased spraying—a syndrome known as the 'pesticides treadmill'. In the Sudan the economy is highly dependent on cotton exports from the massive Gezira scheme, developed in the early 1900s to supply Lancashire's textile mills. Pesticides were introduced after the Second World War, and aerial spraying began in 1949.

Gezira now supports a population of 1.5 million, plus 400,000 seasonal labourers. Pesticide use increased steadily from the 1940s. By 1976, insecticide use had reached 2,500 tonnes a year. Cotton production costs quadrupled over 10 years, while yields fell from 420 kg per hectare in the early 1970s to 250 kg per hectare by 1980—about the same yields as obtained before World War Two and the widespread introduction of pesticides.[9]

As a consequence of the scale of pesticide use, two pests in particular, white fly and American bollworm, are now dominant. These were not known when chemicals were first used in the Gezira scheme. White fly remains resistant to some commonly used insecticides,[10] and the two pests impose a threat to cotton production. In the late 1970s the cotton aphid also became a pest. The pests thrive mainly because extensive use of chemicals over a long period has eliminated their natural enemies. In 1990, Professor Bashir warned that *Spodoptera littolaris* might become a major pest in the very near future—population counts have shown its tendency to build up. There has been almost no monitoring of the ecological impact of pesticides used in cotton in Sudan, but some scientists regard this resistance and resurgence as the most serious ecological effect.[11]

In India, widespread resistance to pesticides used, particularly in cotton production, has been reported. In 1990, farmers in Punjab and Haryana lost 20% of their cotton crop to the American bollworm, and three other states suffered high losses. Losses were estimated at $500 million a year, with uneven impact, meaning that some farmers will lose 90% of their crop, while others lose little. Over-use of pyrethroid insecticides has generated pest resistance, and an entomologist from the Indian Agricultural Research institute says the incidence of pyrethroid resistance has increased at least 100-fold over two years.[12]

Water pollution

The Medjerda is the largest river in Tunisia. Rising in Algeria, it stretches 500 km and crosses some of the most important agricultural areas of the country, where wheat, barley, corn, sugar beet, beans and chickpeas are grown—and large quantities of pesticides are used. One-third of the Tunisian population depends on the Medjerda for drinking water, and this is expected to reach nearly half by the year 2000. Although the Ministry of Health recently carried out a study of pollution of the river with Canadian consultants, it did not include pesticides, which must be present.[13]

A study is planned for Lake Ichkeul in the North of Tunisia: this is an important bird sanctuary and a unique ecosystem because it is connected to the sea by a narrow channel, and renewal of its waters is rather slow. It also collects the waters from many small rivers which cross a densely cultivated area, in which are used large quantities of pesticides. A preliminary study of the lake sediments and birds' eggs reveals organochlorine pesticide and PCB residues.[14]

In Brazil, tests of drinking water carried out by the Santa Catarina Agriculture Secretariat indicated high levels of polluted drinking water in the state. Of samples taken between June 1988 and December 1990 in 10 regions, the percentage of samples polluted ranged from 68% at Blumenau to 100% in Videira.[15]

In Egypt, a major environmental impact arises from the continuous aerial spraying on cotton, which covers up to 1.2 million feddan (2.8 million hectares) a year. Because of the special canal irrigation system in the country, all the water sources, which includes Nile River water, canals, ponds, and underground water, are polluted by pesticides from direct aerial spraying, leaching and washing pesticide containers. Organophosphorus pesticides detected have been found in underground and surface water at levels between three parts per billion (ppb) and 19 ppb, depending on the type of water source and the time of spraying. As a comparison, the UK total limit is five parts per 10 billion, which is rarely exceeded. Higher concentrations are found in canals and branch canals which are directly sprayed. Lower rates of four to nine ppb have been measured in Nile river water; and traces measuring one to three ppb in underground water.[16]

Another indication of high residues in water came from research in the Bhopal area of India during 1990 which reported high levels of organochlorine pollution, in this area also devastated by the impact of pesticide production. Sixty water samples were taken from wells and hand pumps, which showed that HCH levels varied from 1.6 to 8.7 parts per million (ppm) and DDT varied from 3.2 to 22.34 ppm,[17] again far in excess of EC permitted levels. The pesticides made at Union Carbide's Bhopal plant were carbaryl and aldicarb, and high levels of 1-naphthol, a breakdown product of carbaryl, was found in soil, surface and ground waters around Bhopal at levels ranging from 0.153 to 0.656 ppm.[18]

Destruction of non-target animals

In the Gezira scheme acute intoxication of fish, birds, cattle and wild animals is common during the spraying season, specially in areas where compounds like monocrotophos, parathion methyl and endosulfan are used. Shortly after the start of the spraying season the bird *Milvus migrans*, locally known as hadaya, suffers heavy mortality from dimethoate poisoning. Incidents involving domestic animals include the death of cattle.

Documentation is rare, but exists for cases in 1973 and 1978, and for 1990 when goats died after eating a bait of sorghum bran stored in an open area in Aldewim city, the capital of Blue Nile. The use of zinc phosphide as bait for rats claims a heavy toll on wild and domestic fauna. The use of endosulfan in baits for bird control in the Nile Province nearly wiped out that area's population of grain-eating birds, and of cats, dogs and other small carnivorous animals.[19] Some of this poisoned bait subsequently found its way into a food store and was responsible for 31 deaths (see Chapter 3).

In Sudan, scientists believe irreversible damage to native flora and fauna and vital ecological processes might have been done. Some scientists have pointed out that during the 30 years of chemical spraying in the Gezira, Blue Nile and White Nile schemes, scores of species of beneficial organisms might have been wiped out. Due to the absence of accurate data and the continuous changing in the cropping system, it is difficult to estimate the nature of the damage. In 1989 one scientist suggested that introduction of pesticides in newly-developed areas should be preceded by a study on the prevailing fauna and flora and studies on the existing ecological relations.

Studies in Brazil showed degenerated livers and kidneys of sheep which drank herbicide-contaminated water (see Brazil country report).

Shrinking fish supplies

Falling fish yields and losses of traditional fishing grounds were identified in a number of reports. The area of Gabes, 450 km south of Tunis on the Tunisian coast, and the nearby island of Djerba, suffer from growing pollution from industrialisation, including fertiliser and phosphoric acid plants which dump solid and liquid wastes into the sea, and from agriculture, although no scientific studies have been conducted to identify accurately the source. Yields of crustaceans, particularly shrimps, and of fishes and sponges, are dwindling. Sponge production was one of the most important activities on the island. No scientific studies have been performed to trace the source of pollution.[20]

In Egypt, fish production has declined, particularly in Lake Karoon, Lake Manzallah, Lake Mariut and Lake Burullus. First announced in 1986, this decline appears to be getting much worse, and has been attributed to water disposal of toxic pollutants, including pesticides.[21]

In Brazil, large numbers of dead fish appeared several days after Tordon— the herbicide picloram + 2,4-D, a DowElanco product—was sprayed for three days in one area. Studies of fish from River Miranda, Mato Grosso State, and also from Guaraquecaba Bay, Parana State, identified Tordon as being responsible; in River Miranda U-46 (BASF product containing mecoprop and MCPA) was identified.[22] The worker applying the product, who had no training and wore no protective clothing, was badly affected on his legs. He received no help in seeking medical assistance. Farmers apparently wash their tractors and other equipment in rivers, contributing to environmental pollution.[23,24]

Fish deaths have been recorded in the irrigation canals in Sudan, connected with the Gezira cotton scheme. A 1988 paper revealed that drivers from the plant protection department had washed barrels containing residues of endosulfan in the canals, causing high fish deaths. It was reported that three people subsequently died after drinking water from the canals.[25]

In Venezuela, many fish died in the Dos Cerritos reservoir, which supplies drinking water to three towns in Lara State, with a total of 1.5 million inhabitants. The reservoir is polluted with pesticides used on the surrounding vegetable and sugar cane crops, and the State Agricultural Development Department has appointed a Regional Pesticides Committee to look into the situation.[26]

In the Philippines, the traditional fish-rice culture which provided food and protein to farmers and their families, has been virtually wiped out by pesticides, whose use escalated after the introduction of a golden kuhol snail. Ironically, the snail, which has attained plague-like proportions in the country, and spread rapidly throughout water courses, was introduced to supplement farmers' diets as well as in a failed attempt to reach an export market.[27]

Rice farmers in Malaysia also believe that fish have been adversely affected by pesticides, and this has been confirmed in an academic study.[28] Scientists are concerned that rivers and lakes near rice fields are also affected.[29]

Localised pollution

Apart from large-scale pollution of water courses, disposal of unwanted containers threatens both the environment and health, as is highlighted in several of the country reports. Lack of hazard awareness, and of alternative disposal methods, means the agricultural areas are littered with empty containers. A survey of horticulturists in Paraguay revealed that 24% of farmers threw empty containers into streams, sewers, ditches or drainage channels.

In Brazil, an estimated 10 million containers are thrown into rivers, by roadsides, burnt without adequate controls, inappropriately buried, or used as containers for food and water. A regional conference, held in Toledo, Parana State in 1991, on the disposal of toxic waste, which was organised by the municipal authorities, agronomists and the state departments of agriculture and the environment made several recommendations (see Chapter 5).

* Disposal should be regulated by government authorities
* Industry should collect for recycling or destroying
* Community dumps for containers should be established

The conference linked the problem of disposal to the use of agrochemicals, and also recommended that promotional material on pesticides should only be directed at agronomists and forestry technicians, and all advertisement of products in the mass media should be prohibited.

Aerial spraying

The blanket approach of aerial spraying runs counter to sustainable agriculture and integrated pest management. Spray drift, accidental spray onto non-target areas, destruction of non-target crops, and effects on human habitation are unavoidable consequences of this application method.

Aerial spraying of the herbicide 2,4-D in Sudan against water hyacinth in the White Nile between 1959 and 1983 caused regular defoliation of cotton cultivated around the area. Under the Water Hyacinth Control Act of 1960, farmers are not entitled to any compensation for damages to their crop resulting from control measures of this aquatic weed.[30]

In South Africa, hormonal herbicides including 2,4-D, 2,4,5-T and MCPA were aerially applied to kill broad-leaved weeds in the Natal sugar cane fields. The spray drifted over five km, killing many vegetables and crops, causing million of rands in damage to local farmers. A temporary ban on these herbicides has been in place since 1989 in the province. However, farmers received no compensation, having lost the legal action they instituted against the manufacturers of the products involved.[31]

In Paraguay, smallholders experience crop losses quite regularly, when ranchers, who are large landowners, use aerial applications of herbicides to control weeds in pasture. In one case in November 1989, 334 families lost parts of their vegetable and cotton crops (see Paraguay country report).[32]

Aerial spraying in Sudan[33]

The average area of cotton treated annually in Sudan by aerial application ranges between 220,000 and 300,000 hectares, about 85% of the total cotton cultivation. In the irrigated schemes, chemical spraying uses one of two methods: firstly the 'concerned scheme' in Gezira, where the project unit of crop protection provides the chemical, hires aircraft and directs and supervises operations. Secondly, the 'package deal method (PDM)' where an agrochemical company is contracted to spray the crop. The PDM system focuses on yield, without giving due weight to environmental considerations. Spraying is carried out on an insurance basis until a certain yield is achieved, but regardless of the level of pest infestation. When that yield is reached, the contractual obligation has been fulfilled and spraying stops, even when additional pickings would be possible with extended pest control.

Some Sudanese scientists are highly critical of PDM, whose history goes back to 1970,[34] when severe insect attacks in the late 1960s, a direct result of previous over-spraying, prompted the Gezira Board to seek a solution. In 1970/71 season, Ciba Geigy proposed a research project to develop a strategy for boll worm control. The company recruited scientists from research centres, and proposed using the most advanced equipment, including light traps, suction traps and special aeroplanes to attack the pest. The plan was to carry out 24-hour monitoring, using infra-red devices, to track insect activity. In the first year, 800 feddan were allotted for a pilot project, but the next season the company asked for 15,000 feddan. In the third year, the company wanted to expand PDM to 30,000 feddan, and wanted the Gezira Board to share the cost. Professor El Bashir describes what happened next:

> In fact that was the beginning of the end of the research component of the package deal, and the start of the commercial side of the project. The success of Ciba-Geigy in dragging the Gezira authorities and dominating the pesticide market encouraged other companies to ask for similar opportunities. Thus in 1976/77 Montedison presented a research project to control *Heliothis armigera*. The project started on 11,151 feddan and then jumped to 33, 657 feddan in the second season. Other companies followed on condition that they will provide acceptable yield on similar contracts so as to stay in business.[35]

According to Professor Abdelrahman,[36] this continued until the area put under PDM ranged between 250,000 and 300,000 feddan annually. Many Sudanese environmentalists called upon the Gezira authority to review or halt PDM (now carried out by a range of contracted companies). The Gezira Board exercises no restrictions on the type and nature of the chemicals used; it is more expensive than the tender system, as companies frequently add items which would not otherwise be incurred, such as salaries of non-Sudanese staff paid in foreign exchange, consultation, 'experts' visits; it is incompatible with integrated pest management. In addition, when the contracting company reaches the contracted yield, they stop pest control, even though two or three additional pickings may be possible. The Gezira Board has then found that additional sprayings are needed, adding to the overall cost.

Sudan spends $30-$40 million annually on pesticides, of which 90% is for cotton. There is concern about the extent and effectiveness of certain imports. In April 1991, the pesticide national committee decided to stop future imports of mixed active ingredients, and in particular to review those containing endosulfan and dimethoate, which have been in use for more than 30 years. However this will not reduce use, rather Sudan will import single active ingredients, and the research corporation will supervise to ensure precision in achieving the required formulation.[37]

The European Community exports to Sudan amounted to ECU 18 million in 1989, and ECU 17 million in 1990, and of this nearly half came from the UK in 1990, 18% from Germany, 16% from France, 10% from Italy and 8% from the Netherlands.[38]

***   ***   ***

Alternatives

Small farmers in Africa, Asia and Latin America have successfully farmed and nurtured the land for centuries without recourse to chemical agriculture. The pressure to adopt industrialised agricultural methods came initially with the demand for land in these countries to supply crops in the North, and was later reinforced with economic strategies, promoted by the World Bank, the International Monetary Fund and other major lending institutions, for development based on the export of cash crops. Internal food security too has been seen in terms of a shrinking number of large farms supplying food needs.

These ideas have increasingly been resisted (although always resisted by peasant agriculturalists), and the last 10 years in particular have given greater voice to alternatives through the development of farmer networks and the work of non-governmental organisations.

In a recent study of several hundred organic farms spread over 14 countries and four continents, published by the United Nations Development Programme, it was concluded that 'organic agriculture is a feasible option for environmentally and economically sustainable production strategies in developing countries.' [39]

The study found that in most of the cases reviewed the total output value of the farm was higher than in conventional farming. This was due to a wider mix of crops and livestock and sometimes because of higher yields. In some countries yields were more stable on organic than conventional farms over a number of years, an important factor affecting food and income security. Organic farmers link to each other through the International Federation of Organic Agricultural Movements. Grassroots conservation efforts in Latin America are expanding, promoting traditional agro-ecosystems which respect the accumulated experience of interaction with farmers who use locally available resources to manage farming systems giving sustained yields. [40]

The concept of a low external input and sustainable agriculture (LEISA), is now taken seriously by UN agencies. A recent book setting out the principles behind this approach, as well as practical examples, defined LEISA as:

> agriculture which makes optimal use of locally available natural and human resources (such as soil, water, vegetation, local plants and animals, and human labour, knowledge and skills) and which is economically feasible, ecologically sound, culturally adapted and socially just. The use of external inputs is not excluded but is seen as complementary to the use of local resources and has to meet the above mentioned criteria. Neither the conventional Western agricultural technology nor any alternative technology is completely embraced or condemned. The attempt is made, rather, to draw lessons from past experiences in agriculture in industrialised and developing countries and to merge them into a process of technology development which leads to LEISA. [41]

In preparation for the Earth Summit, the FAO and the Netherlands government held a joint conference on Sustainable Agriculture and Rural Development (SARD). The resulting declaration and programme for action included a commitment:

to carry out inventories and study diverse forms of agriculture systems, including low external input sustainable agriculture and organic agriculture farming systems, and determine the scope of their agronomic, environmental and socio-economic viability in different farming and population density conditions, as well as evaluating their environmental and social performance. . . . This should be an integral part of the review process for sustainable agricultural policies and plans.[42]

This commitment to sustainable agriculture was subsequently adopted by the FAO at its biennial conference in November 1991 as an approach to future agricultural projects. At the Earth Summit in June 1992, these plans were endorsed with emphasis on the need for farmer participation, and to build local institutional capacity through national and local agricultural planning bodies.

The planning and organisation relating to the Earth Summit highlighted the contribution to agriculture of small farmers in creating and maintaining genetic diversity. The agro-ecology movement which has grown in Latin America over the past 10 years has established a practical basis for developing alternatives. Proponents of this movement maintain that the use of pesticides and hybrid seeds in agriculture may threaten the genetic base of agriculture. Field experience shows that, in terms of increasing access to food and fibre for the poor, autonomous seed production and conservation of local crops are critical factors.[43]

The SARD recommendation to establish inventories of alternatives has already been undertaken in Costa Rica, where Dr. Jaime Garcia has documented the known plant control methods in the country from 1913 to 1991, which do not use synthetic pesticides. The inventory links the method to the target pest, and covers most crops.[44]

An inventory of alternatives—Costa Rica

Through an environmental education programme, the diversity of experiments and approaches has been documented in a database, with the aim of building an inventory of institutional and non-institutional resources on alternatives to pesticides, and of recording agricultural methods used by farmers either now or in the past. The database shows the range of agricultural alternatives in Costa Rica, which includes the use of sexual pheromones, natural enemies, native parasites, snake venom, and good husbandry such as pruning infested parts of the plant, and manual removal of pests. In addition, the national university runs a course in agro-ecology, giving students a grounding in organic alternatives, especially in relation to the use of medicinal and toxic plants. Of the many initiatives documented in the database, some examples are set out below.[45]

- One experiment involves 'solarisation' as a means of controlling soil diseases in agriculture, and this has been successful against the main diseases. Work also covers the identification and use of fungi and bacteria to control diseases biologically and the use of organic fertilisers.[46]

- A project has been researching the insecticide potential of a plant in the indigenous reserve of Kekoldi in communities near Fila Carbon, Talamanca. The plant is *Ryania speciosa*, which contains an alkaloid, ryanodina, a natural insecticide. By the end of 1990, preliminary studies on the use of this plant by the local population had been completed. Research has been carried out into the ecology of the species.[47]

- The Union of Atlantic Region Smallholders (UPAGRA) has established a non-governmental organisation, Nuestra Tierra (our land), to develop projects initiated by members. UPAGRA has used various pest control methods with the emphasis on alternative technologies such as organic production of ginger and other crops.[48] In another project in this region, members of the Community Development Associations of Gandoca, Bonife, San Miguel and Kekoldi are developing community and family organic plots, using organic compost, barriers of insect-repellent plants, and pastes of aromatic plants.[49]

- A Multiple Services Co-operative in Santa Rosa (COOPEBRISAS) has used experimental plots to compare customary methods of growing vegetables with organic agriculture practices organised by Dr. Sasaki of the Japanese Technical Co-operation programme. Methods used include organic compost, fermented wood and ground plant mix. These alternative methods have proven to be more effective pest control methods. They have also increased the yield and quality of produce when compared to other farmers in the region using conventional methods.[50]

The database also documents private initiatives by individual farmers and researchers.

- A farmer who has been growing a variety of crops for over 40 years, initially used pesticides indiscriminately. He stopped some years ago, and developed a system of production designed to promote a healthy environment. The local insects continue to exist, but he encourages ecological diversity, conservation measures, barrier plants or uses fringes of natural woodland between his crops and areas of pasture, and successfully grows fruit, cotton and other crops.[51]

- One biological product sold in Costa Rica for control of nematoid parasites in tobacco is called 'Nemout', a mixture of three fungi. This has been used on three experimental plots, with two types of organic fertilisers: fish emulsion and marine algae which provide macro and micro-nutrients and growth hormones. The three experimental plots are owned by the Tabacalera Company of Costa Rica.[52]

NGO initiatives for alternatives

Non-governmental organisations have played a significant role in supporting sustainable agriculture. In November 1991, ENDA in Senegal organised a conference for NGOs and farmers in West Africa. In February 1992, the California Institute for Rural Studies organised an organic cotton conference. Some cotton farmers in California, Texas and Arizona have switched to organic production, helped by a demand for their product and a premium on organic cotton.[53] The conference attracted nearly 100 'non-organic' farmers interested in learning about its potential. Significant initiatives in alternatives have been undertaken in Brazil.

Brazil

Gert Fischer of PAN Brazil has been documenting alternatives to pesticides practised in the country, using reports in newspapers, magazines and technical journals; direct contact with farmers; and information from researchers and officials in the universities and government agencies. In Brazil, the introduction of alternatives has been encouraged by the independent official national research network EMBRAP (Brazilian Agricultural Research Company).[54] Some examples of the alternatives include:

- In Araras, Sao Paulo State, a company called PLANALSUCAR operates a research programme looking for ways of controlling sugar cane borer using a larval parasite. Experiments began in 1978, and have been very successful. The parasites, introduced from India and Pakistan, are now bred in 30 laboratories, producing 1.2 billion a year, enough to cover 200,000 hectares of sugar cane plantations.

- Fertilisers from recycled organic waste are commercially available, as are supplies of worms to improve soil quality.

- Early warning systems have been established to keep down the use of pesticides in apples. These methods have reduced pesticides to control some pests by 40%.

- A rice farmer introduced to his farm the Moroccan duck, which eats weeds and insects as well as fertilising the soil. At a stocking rate of 52 ducks per hectare, it allowed the farmer to stop using pesticides completely, saving US$47 per hectare, and increased rice production by 201 kg per hectare, earning a further US$47.[55]

Research for pesticides or sustainable agriculture

More funds and resources are devoted to chemical pesticide use than to alternative, sustainable and less ecologically damaging methods of control. This is the case even when information is widely known and documented, such as in Costa Rica.

In Sudan, preference is given to pesticide use over other controls, such as integrated pest management, in spite of a successful FAO-run integrated pest management project in the country. An analysis of funding for agricultural research found that in 1989/90, the Department of Entomology of the Agricultural Research Centre spent £124,000 in experiments involving testing chemicals, compared to only £13,000 for non-chemical methods. These figures do not include donations provided by some chemical firms and companies. In the same season the faculty of graduate studies of the University of Khartoum paid £39,000 for postgraduate students studying for MSc or PhD degrees relating to some aspect of pesticide use, while those studying biological control received only £6,000. Of 29 reports and/or scientific papers published in the field of entomology in relation to cotton by Sudanese scientists during the last six years, only two covered non-chemical methods of control.[56]

Conclusion

The environmental impact of pesticides is relatively well-documented in industrialised countries, although the implications are not always fully understood. If the human impact is under-documented in Third World countries, the environmental impact is even less so. However, studies undertaken by academics, researchers, government departments and non-governmental organisations indicate a serious case for concern. In addition to the impact of earlier (and in some cases current) use of persistent organochlorine pesticides, problems include those of guaranteeing clean water, safe aerial spraying, effect on non-target and beneficial insects, and triggering insect resistance.

International opinion, emerging particularly as a consequence of the Earth Summit—but also from international regulatory initiatives such as the Barcelona Convention and the North Sea Conference—is demanding more resources for sustainable agriculture. At present this term can be interpreted in many ways, and does not include a specific commitment to a reduction in pesticide use. Non-governmental organisations have sought to define the term more clearly, and to go beyond integrated pest management to include organic farming, conservation and agro-ecology, and low external inputs for sustainable agriculture. These alternatives now need political and financial backing.

References:
1. See Chapter 3, Health and Safety.
2. Report in *International Agricultural Development*, March/April, 1992.
3. Kurtz, D.A. (ed.) *Long-range Transport of Pesticides*, Lewis Publishers Inc., Michigan, USA, 1990.
4. Wright, R., 'Report from Turkestan', *The New Yorker*, April 1992. Also material from Yablokov, A. and Fleurova, G., 'Summary of report on pesticides, environment and human health—the Soviet Experience', from the Committee of Ecology of the USSR Supreme Council, 1990.
5. Quoted in Bull, D., *A Growing Problem: Pesticides and the Third World poor*, Oxfam, Oxford, 1982.
6. UNEP(OCA)/MED IG2/5, Annex IV pp. 18-19, 1991.
7. Report of conference, *Pesticides News*, No. 8, June 1990, p. 16.
8. Lohse, J., Winteler, S., *et al.*, *Lindane and Other Pesticides in the North Sea: A reason for concern*, Greenpeace International, March 1990.
9. Pollard, N., 'The Gezira Scheme--A study in failure', *The Ecologist*, Vol. II, No. 1, January/February 1981, quoted in Bull, D., *op. cit.*
10. El Abjar, Dr. Z., 'Cotton and Pesticides: Sudan case', report prepared for The Pesticides Trust, 1991.

11. El Abjar, *ibid*.
12. See India country report. Also *Agrow*, No. 144, 27/9/91, p. 23.
13. Bouguerra, Prof. M.L., Faculty of Sciences, Tunis. Unpublished report on organophosphates for Greenpeace International for submission to the Barcelona Convention, covering 1987-90.
14. Bouguerra, *op. cit*.
15. See Brazil country report.
16. Gawaad, Prof. A.A., 'Ecotoxicological impact of organophosphorus pesticides in Egypt', unpublished report for Greenpeace International for submission to the Barcelona Convention, 1991.
17. Dikshith, T.S.S., Raizada, R.B., *et al*., 'Residues of DDT and HCH in major sources of drinking water at Bhopal, India', *Bulletin of Environmental Contamination and Toxicology*, Vol. 45, pp. 389-393, 1990.
18. *Ibid*.
19. El Abjar, *op. cit*.
20. Bouguerra, *op. cit*.
21. See Egypt country report.
22. See Brazil country report.
23. 'The invisible danger of pesticides', *Olho Vivo*, September 1990.
24. Study by Superintendent of Water Resources and the Environment, see Brazil country report.
25. El Abjar, *op. cit*., quoting Adil, O.M., 'Why Biological Control?', a lecture delivered at a meeting organised by the Agricultural Research Council, February 1988, 14pp.
26. 'You can't drink this water', *El Impulso*, 2/3/91, see Venezuela country report.
27. 'Hoechst blocks Philippines Government attempt to ban endosulfan,' *Pesticides News*, Issue 16, June 1992, p. 3.
28. Abdullah, Dr. A.R., see Malaysia country report.
29. 'Insects threaten agri-lifeforms', see Malaysia country report.
30. El Abjar, *op. cit*.
31. See South Africa country report.
32. See Paraguay country report.
33. The material in this section of the report is taken from El Abjar, *op. cit*. Where he has quoted other papers, these are separately referenced.
34. El Bashir, S., 'The package deal strategy for cotton pest control', in proceedings of a symposium on crop pest management in Sudan, held in Khartoum, February 1978, pp. 107-114.
35. *Ibid*.
36. Abdelrahman, A.A., 'Recent advances in the integrated pest management in cotton in Gezira and Rahad schemes in Sudan', In proceedings of international conference on pest management, Germany, Vol. 2, pp. 435-444, 1989.
37. Personal communication from Ministry of Finance and Economy in Sudan to author of Sudan report, 1991.
38. Eurostat, COMEXT, 1990.
39. van Elzakker, B., Witte, R., van Mansvelt, J.D., *Benefits of Diversity—An incentive toward sustainable agriculture*, UNDP, New York, 1992.
40. Montecinos, C. and Altieri, M., 'Grassroots conservation efforts in Latin America', in Cooper, D., Vellvé, R. and Hobbelink, H., *Growing Diversity—Genetic resources and local food security*, Intermediate Technology Publications, London, 1992, pp. 106-115.
41. Reijntjes, C., Haverkort, B. and Waters-Bayer, A., *Farming for the Future: an introduction to low external input and sustainable agriculture*, Macmillan/ILEIA, Leusden, Netherlands, 1992.
42. FAO and the Ministry of Agriculture, Nature Management and Fisheries of the Netherlands, *den Bosch Declaration and Agenda for Action on Sustainable Agriculture and Rural Development*, FAO/Netherlands Conference on Agriculture and the Environment, 15-19 April 1991, p. 8.
43. Montecinos, C. and Altieri, M., *op. cit*., and other papers in Cooper, D., *et al*., *op. cit*.
44. Garcia, J.E. Dr.Sc.Agr, 'Natural alternatives to the unilateral use of synthetic pesticides in Costa Rica' (preliminary research), 1991.
45. Trivelato, M.D. 'Alternatives to the use of synthetic chemical pesticides in Costa Rica: some actual experiences', and Garcia, J., *op. cit*., report prepared for The Pesticides Trust, Pesticides Action Network, 25-8788, Environmental Education Programme, UNED, list of current research and experiments documenting alternatives to the use of synthetic chemical pesticides in Costa Rica.

46. Vargas, E. 'Alternative methods for the control of soil diseases in agriculture', 25-0064, Phytoathology, UCR, Costa Rica, documented in Costa Rica report.
47. Ocampo, R., 'Programme for sustainable development in Central America' (OLAFO Project), UICN/ANAI/CATIE, 24-6090, documented in Costa Rica country report.
48. Hernandez, C., 21-0621, UPAGRA, documented in Costa Rica country report..
49. G.V., 33-1072, Socio-Environmental Research and Development Corporation (CIDESA), documented in Costa Rica country report..
50. Sasaki, S., Multiple Services Co-operative, Santa Rosa, Costa Rica, documented in Costa Rica country report.
51. Werner, H., 69-0444, Canas, Guanacaste, Costa Rica, documented in Costa Rica country report.
52. Albarado, J., 40-53-70, 'Experimental plots for the biological control of nematoids on tobacco', documented in Costa Rica country report.
53. *Pesticides News*, No. 16, June 1992, p. 10.
54. Fischer, G., 'Healthy Crops—alternative plots, alternatives to pesticides', Brazil, 1991.
55. Fischer, *op. cit.*
56. El Abjar, *op. cit.*

Part II
Country Reports

5. Country Report: Brazil*

Brazil is the major user of pesticides in Latin America and, with large production facilities, it also exports pesticides to other Latin American countries. One comparison showed that Brazil's expenditure on pesticides of $1,993 million in 1990[1], was half as much again as all other major users in the region put together. This puts Brazil among the world's largest pesticide consumers.

Pesticides were introduced in 1946, when BHC was applied to locusts in the State of Santa Catarana. BHC was quickly taken up to control coffee borer, substituting for previous biological controls, and used on cotton. Other highly toxic and persistent pesticides soon followed: DDT, parathion, toxaphene.

The First National Development Plan in 1972 laid down a policy of increasing agricultural productivity, and reducing pesticide imports by developing the Brazilian pesticide industry. Pesticide promotion intensified, and thousands of salesmen were employed. The plan encouraged agricultural concentration on soya, wheat and cotton, crops which require large quantities of pesticides. The government actively promoted pesticide use. Following the First National Development Plan, the Bank of Brazil began to make rural credit dependent on farmers applying 15% of the sum granted to modern technology, that is to pesticides. This, with advertising, promoted the idea that pesticides were essential. Using widespread advertising in newspapers, magazines, leaflets and television, companies promoted the idea that pesticides were indispensable to agricultural productivity and better quality foods while being harmless to man and the environment.

The scale of use is not matched by concern for the health and safety of pesticide users, particularly agricultural labourers and plantations workers.

* This chapter is based on a survey and report by Reinaldo Onofre Skalisz, a member of the State Council for the Defence of the Environment who has worked on Pesticides Policy in Parana State since 1980, for PAN Brazil and The Pesticides Trust, 1991, and material from Gert Roland Fischer of PAN Brazil and Onaur Ruano, an agronomist.

According to projections by a toxicologist from the poisoning control centre in Campinas, São Paulo, Dr. Flavio Zambroni, at least 280,000 Brazilians, 2% of the population, are contaminated by pesticides each year. He estimates that for each case registered in hospitals or clinics, there are 250 unreported victims, due mainly to the lack of doctors' toxicological knowledge. Doctors commonly mistake pesticide poisonings for food poisoning or something else.[2]

The federal government has been lax in promoting safe use, although a number of agricultural states have attempted to raise standards and implement their own regulations—frequently to be overruled by the centre.

Scale of pesticide use in Brazil

Government policies brought a major expansion in pesticide consumption, with more than 290 active ingredients, and about 800 pesticide products authorised for use. The main uses in 1989 were for soya ($282 million), citrus fruits ($117 million) and sugar cane ($109 million). Other crops widely sprayed were rice, cotton, wheat, barley, oats, coffee, corn, potatoes, horticultural crops and tomatoes.[3] Pesticides can represent a significant element in the costs of production, and the associated problems are not treated seriously by industry, government, farmers, agronomists, consumers.

The main agricultural regions, and highest pesticide users are: São Paulo State, using 27,566 tonnes of active ingredients in 1986, and Parana State using 14,835 tonnes. These were followed by Rio Grande do Sul, with 9,177 tonnes; Minas Gerais, 3,916 tonnes; Santa Catarina 2,523 tonnes.[4] Almost all agricultural production is dependent on large pesticide inputs. The State of Bahia, the sixth largest consumer with 2,255 tonnes, is near to being a monocrop economy as the major cocoa-growing region.

Figures of overall application in Parana State show a steady drop in volume applied from 64,000 tonnes in 1978, to 35,000 in 1982, 28,000 in 1988, and 19,000 tonnes in 1989. This has been brought about by the introduction of biological control using baculovirus in soybeans and growing acceptance of IPM and pest-monitoring techniques, though herbicide use has grown significantly.

Growth rates of pesticide use have levelled off. In 1988, 60 million tons of active ingredients were applied, compared to 53.8 million in 1975. The levelling off partly reflects a saturated market, and partly the lower dose rate of the active ingredients of newer pesticides. However, the value of sales has been maintained, amounting to US$1,1501 million in 1989. The fluctuations in volume and value through the eighties is reflected in Figure 5.1. Brazil uses greater quantities of herbicides than insecticides; the next major use is fungicides. Brazil is a major pesticide manufacturer and exporter, attracting subsidiaries of major agrochemical corporations. The majority of domestic production is used internally. In 1986 exports of US$83.7 million were only one-tenth of internal use valued at $836 million. In 1987 exports were US$111.2 million and in 1988 $120.8

million, compared to internal use of US$826 million and US$1,022 million respectively.

Pesticide imports remain high, and the scale of use makes Brazil an attractive market for exporters. Both the United States and Europe are major suppliers. Between 1980 and 1989, imports rose from US$254.7 million to US$377.8 million, with some fluctuations in the intervening years.[5]

Fig. 5.1

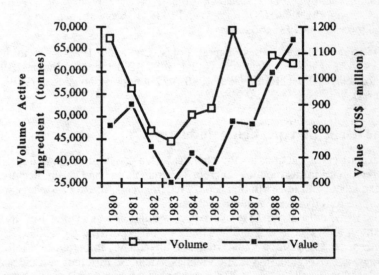

Pesticide sales in Brazil, by weight and value, 1980-89

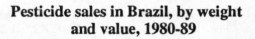

Source: Data from ANDEF, the National Association of Pesticides Companies in Brazil.

Many of the active ingredients imported were as intermediates, for example two of the largest imports in 1988 were metolachlor and cyanazine, for formulating atrazine. In 1988, 6,957 tonnes of insecticides were imported, 4,339 tonnes of herbicides, and 2,110 tonnes of fungicides. The main active ingredients in that year were:[6]

PIC and potential PIC: aldicarb, aldrin, carbofuran, methyl bromide (750 tonnes), phosphamidon

Other major imports: acephate, anilazine, benomyl, bromacil (446 tonnes), bromopropylate, captan, carbaryl (479 tonnes), cartap, chlorothalonil, chlorpyrifos, cyanazine, dalapon, dicofol (848 tonnes), dimethoate, endosulfan (629 tonnes), ethion, fenoxan, fosetyl, iprodione, MCPA, metolachlor (1,231 tonnes), metribuzin, MSMA, pendimethalin, phorate, propargite (801 tonnes), propiconazole, quintozene, tebuthiuron, thiobencarb, thiodicarb, triadimenol.

Some of the pesticides on the PIC list, and candidate PIC pesticides, imported in 1989 were aldrin, 190 tonnes, and parathion, 32 tonnes (PIC). Other hazardous imports were: aldicarb, 805 tonnes; carbofuran, 417 tonnes; dichlorvos, 10 tonnes; dicofol, 918 tonnes; endosulfan,1012 tonnes; methamidophos 15 tonnes; and phosphamidon, 138 tonnes.[7]

Some of the more hazardous pesticides have not been imported for several years, though it is not clear whether these are no longer used, or whether some may now be made in Brazil. These include:[8]

PIC pesticides: 2,4,5-T, last imported 1983 (10 tonnes); chlordane, 1980 (4 tonnes); cyhexatin, 1986 (276 tonnes) and 1987 (91 tonnes) [now banned]; dieldrin, 1980 (5 tonnes); dinoseb, 1985 (6 tonnes) and 1986 (37 tonnes); endrin, 1984, (107 tonnes) and 1985 (10 tonnes); heptachlor, 1984 (226 tonnes) and 1985 (66 tonnes).

Potential PIC pesticides: captafol, last imported 1986 (534 tonnes) and 1987 (73 tonnes); demeton-methyl, 1980, (271 tonnes); lindane, 1985 (5 tonnes); pentachlorophenol, 1980 (427 tonnes); phosphine, 1980 (15 tonnes).

The Brazilian pesticide industry

Brazil offers attractions to the chemical industry, with a large domestic market, good infrastructure, generous government tax and credit incentives, cheap labour and few pollution control requirements. Brazil is also an export platform for other Latin American markets.

In 1975, only about 35% of local consumption was synthesised in the country, and 2%, or 1.5 million tonnes was exported. By 1988, Brazil synthesised 65.3 million tonnes of active ingredients, imported 13.4 million tonnes, and exported 18.8 million tonnes. About 50 different pesticides are produced in Brazil by nearly 30 companies including the major agrochemical corporations—for example ICI has located there one of its four plants synthesising the active ingredient paraquat for internal use and export. Others synthesised in Brazil include dichlorvos, phosphine, trichlorfon, copper-based fungicides, alachlor, diuron, glyphosate, proponil, paraquat and trifluralin.[9] Exports are expanding faster than the domestic market. Six of the major agrochemical transnationals share over half the value of production, and the eight Brazilian-owned synthesisers take 15%. The others produce low-tech synthesised products and commodities.

Health impact

In 1988, 2.21 kilos of pesticides active ingredients were used for each of the 23 million rural workers.[10] Between 1986 and 1989, Brazil registered 13,277 poisonings, 16% of which were caused by pesticides.[11] This is widely asserted to be an underestimate, and a toxicologist from the poisoning control centre in Campinas, São Paulo, assessed that at least 280,000 Brazilians, 2% of the population, are poisoned by pesticides each year. In his experience, doctors frequently mistake pesticide poisonings for food poisoning or other illnesses.[12]

There is also serious concern about the amount of pesticides used in public health campaigns for example against cockroaches and mosquitoes. Between 1980 and 1988 12,305 tonnes were used for this purpose. Commonly used pesticides included malathion and temefos, and studies of blood tests in one district, Abundancia, have shown alarming levels of pesticide residues associated with public health pesticide use.[13]

Health concerns in Parana State

There are 480,000 rural properties in Parana, a major agricultural state, producing 25% of the national granary. Causes of environmental pollution and poisoning of humans and animals include application of pesticides at the wrong time; application more often than necessary; excessive doses of pesticides; use of inappropriate products; lack of personal protective equipment; massive advertising strategies of pesticides companies; lack of information about containers and their fate; contamination of foodstuffs (eg apples contaminated by dicofol, potatoes by mercury).

With the aim of getting a better picture of the effects on pesticides-exposed workers, the Agriculture Secretariat began work in collaboration with the state's hospitals, agricultural workers and the general public to research the incidence of poisonings. From 1984, the Parana Health Secretariat began joint work with the Toxicological Information Centre and health clinics throughout the state to document the health and environmental impact of pesticides. Doctors are asked to complete standard forms indicating personal details, product responsible, the relevant crop and symptoms. The state hopes to acquire a clearer picture of the extent of problems and the regions most affected. These incidents are documented in Table 5.1.

A look at overall pesticide poisoning incidents in cropping seasons includes unidentified pesticides, and shows slightly different figures (see Table 5.2). It is difficult to draw firm conclusions on trends from figures revealed through these sources. Agronomist Reinaldo Skalisz, who has worked on pesticides policy in Parana State since 1980, reports that poisoning figures fell after 1984 largely because the system for collecting information became less rigorous. In 1990, the Health Secretariat tightened procedures and the number increased again. The forms are often poorly completed. Common omissions include the product and active ingredient, and the crop. Deaths are almost always noted as suicide. PAN Brazil reports that real numbers are much higher than even these recorded numbers.

Most victims of pesticide poisonings are aged 15 to 25 years, and the greatest number of poisonings, as high as 70%, occur on cotton plantations where seeds treated with carbofuran and disulfoton still cause problems. Pesticide-related suicides are high, with 53 successful attempts (59 unsuccessful) in 1989, 94 (119) in 1990, and 70 (68) in 1991. Active

Table 5.1   Pesticide   incidents   in   Parana   State,   1982-1991.

Pesticide responsible	1982	1983	1984	1985	1986	1987	1988	1989	1990	1991
2,4 D +picloram							16	14	19	4
aldicarb	21	24	35							
aldrin	17	29	45	15	14	2	1	5		
atrazine+simazine									6	
azinphos ethyl					13		1			
BHC	14	22								
captan						2				
carbamates (not specified)								5		
carbofuran	174	60	64	18	51	6			8	5
chlorpyrifos		29	37	25	25	9	6	7	14	10
copper oxychloride										
cypermethrin						2		2		
cypermethrin +profenofos						2		2	6	7
DDT							4			
deltamethrin	20	27	56	16	15	11	6	5	16	14
demeton-S-methyl	81	135	144	72	42	24	3	19	15	12
dicofol			38	17		19	3			
dicrotophos	35	44	87	15	5					
dimethoate	13	29	52	9						
disulfoton	167	79	66	35		12	2		4	
endosulfan	18	34	74	41	36	35	9	10	22	24
endrin	167	240	76	12						
endrin +thiometon	12	25								
fenitrothion							2			
glyphosate						7		2	17	10
malathion								8	19	3
mancozeb					13			2		
methamidophos	14	16	48	40	15					
methomyl							18	10	19	12
mevinphos										3
monocrotophos	252	387	359	191	93	71	36	78	107	76
organochlorines*							3	3		
organo-phosphates*	21	44	27		5	27	27	18	55	34
paraquat	11	16	26	11	9	6	3	7	11	5
parathion ethyl	12			9	6					
parathion methyl	180	264	282	133	79	54	31	38	93	89
phorate								5	5	
profenofos	12	25	37	47	22	13	10	6	17	17
quintozene					17					

Pesticide responsible	1982	1983	1984	1985	1986	1987	1988	1989	1990	1991
sethoxydim								1		3
thiodicarb										
thiometon			33	11		12	1		5	
thiram					17					
triadimefon					5	6				3
triadimenol										
triadimenol +disulfoton									6	5
triazophos				8						
trifluralin		19	38	17	14	4		6	9	4
Total	1356	1816	1888	742	503	337	175	259	466	328

* Not specified or unclear

Source: Compiled by Toxicological Information Centre and Health Clinics, in
report on pesticides in Brazil, Reinaldo Onofre Skalisz, 1991.

ingredients used include parathion, monocrotophos and paraquat. A small
number have used demeton-S-methyl, endosulfan and profenofos. Others are
identified only as organophosphates or not known.

Animals are also affected by pesticides. A newspaper article in 1991
reported on the destruction of 101 cattle and a number of other animals
which had been contaminated with an unnamed pesticide.[14]

Although pesticides are commonly applied by aircraft in Parana State,
standards of aerial spraying have only been inspected in the state since July
1991. Farmers have been under no requirement to observe marker flags,
wind direction, and the dangers of pesticides falling outside the target area. A
number of workers remain in the field holding marker flags. An article on
aerial spraying in *Agrotécnica Ciba-Geigy* shows a photograph of aerial
spraying, in which a worker with a marker flag is discernible.[15]

Problem pesticides

In 1982 the active ingredients responsible for most recorded poisonings were
carbofuran, endrin, monocrotophos, parathion, disulfoton. Agricultural
workers were poisoned with carbofuran and disulfoton when planting cotton
seeds. The manufacturer of carbofuran, FMC, changed the formulation and
the number of poisonings fell. In 1983, an endrin formulation, Endrex 20
was responsible for most poisonings. This product was banned when the
Parana State Pesticides Law came into force, and cases fell, although cases
were recorded for a number of years while stocks were used up by farmers.

Since 1984, pesticides which can be identified as most responsible have
been parathion, monocrotophos, demeton-S-methyl, endosulfan, deltamethrin. In Parana State alone there were 466 incidents in 1990 and 328 in
1991, where the active ingredient could be identified: this is at least five

years after the FAO Code of Conduct was adopted. Those responsible for more than 10 incidents in these years are set out in Table 5.3.

Table 5.2 Pesticide poisoning incidents in cropping seasons, Parana State, 1982-91.

Incident	*1982	1983	1984	1985	1986	1987	1988	1989	1990	+1991
Poisoning	923	1875	2356	1075	840	567	534	558	1137	480
Death—Suicide	25	24	93	56	55	28	30	58	94	70
Fatal Accidents	-	1	51	20	27	11	15	3	3	-

* 1982—August to December only; +1991—January to June only

Source: Compiled by Toxicological Information Centre and Health Clinics, in report on pesticides in Brazil, Reinaldo Onofre Skalisz, 1991.

Table 5.3 Pesticides causing more than 10 incidents in Parana State, 1990 and part 1991.

Pesticide	1990	Part 1991
2,4-D+picloram	19	—
chlorpyrifos	14	10
deltamethrin	16	14
demeton-S-methyl	15	12
endosulfan	22	24
glyphosate	17	10
malathion	19	—
methomyl	12	—
monocrotophos	107	76
organophosphates	55	34
paraquat	11	—
parathion	93	89
profenofos	12	17

Source: Skalisz, report on pesticides in Brazil for The Pesticides Trust, 1991.

Incidents in other states

A study in the State of Bahia, the cocoa-growing region, in 1989, analysed occupational exposure to BHC and DDT. It was found that illiteracy was 60%; all workers returned immediately to work on the crop after application of pesticides; 73% of workers did not use gloves and 98% did not use aprons during the work. Most wore short-sleeved shirts; 31% did not wear hats, 85% did not use masks and nobody used goggles; 43%

smoked during the application or use of pesticide products; 86% ate their meals at the workplace (mainly fruits found on the same land as the crops that were being treated with pesticides), and did not have access to wash facilities. All workers used the same clothes for days or even weeks.[16]

In the Nova Briburgo region of Rio de Janeiro, where a number of small farmers have died from pesticide poisonings, it is common to meet rural workers who complain of constant headaches, stomach aches, dizziness, insomnia and other symptoms, during the periods when they are applying pesticides. They often feel too weak to work and know the cause, but are unaware of alternative pest control methods and fear losing their harvests.[17]

The Santa Catarina Agriculture Secretariat (ACARESC) carried out a survey of 7498 farmers between May 1986 and March 1990, checking the number of times they had been poisoned by agrochemicals. Over 28% had been poisoned at least once and 164, or 2%, had been poisoned more than seven times.[18]

Environmental contamination

Tests of drinking water carried out by ACARESC indicated high levels of polluted drinking water in the state. Of samples taken between June 1988 and December 1990 in 10 regions, the percent of samples polluted ranged from 68% at Blumenau to 100% in Videira.[19] Other figures included Maravilha and S.M. d'Oeste (94%), Rio do Sul (91%), S.L. d'Oeste (88.8%)

Professor Heitor Segundo Guilherme Medina of the Federal University of Parana, Faculty of Agrarian Science, carried out a study of fish from River Miranda (Mato Grosso State) and Guaraquecaba Bay (Parana) in 1988. The fish had been poisoned by the herbicides picloram+2,4-D (Tordon, a DowElanco product) in both places, with the addition of U-46 (BASF product containing mecprop+ MCPA) in the Miranda.

An investigation was carried out by the Superintendent of Water Resources and the Environment (SUREHMA) when large numbers of dead fish appeared after Tordon had been sprayed for three days. The worker applying the product, Adilson Alves Goncalves, was badly affected on his legs. Photographs taken six months after his second contact with Tordon show his legs still covered with sores and a rash. Goncalves had no training and wore no protective equipment. He received no help in seeking medical assistance.

Sheep which over a period of time drank water containing a herbicide showed flaking of the tubular cells of the kidneys. Their livers and kidneys showed signs of degeneration, with cells and membranes bleeding. Farmers apparently wash their tractors and other equipment in rivers, contributing to pollution.[20]

Fish studies in the area show disfigured and diseased fish: a white catfish captured alive in the waters of Guaraquecaba Bay showed redness of the skin, and contained fenoxiacetate;[21] cataracts and lesions were produced by unknown pesticides. A number of other mutations and internal bleeding were noted.[22]

Food contamination

Few studies of pesticide residues are carried out in Brazil, but the information available does give rise to concern. Tests on a spot-check basis from farmers' markets in several cities suggested that 2-5% of food contained residues in excess of legal limits established by the Brazilian government and/or the UN body which sets limits, Codex Alimentarius. Tests were only carried out for organochlorines and organophosphates.[23] A more comprehensive study by the Instituto de Tecnologia de Alimentos during an earlier period, 1981/82, covered 49 different widely-consumed processed foods purchased once a month in São Paulo supermarkets; 41% of the total of 1176 samples contained residues surpassing official limits. Eleven of the 49 products had illegal residues in 80% of the samples. Every sample of two different brands of soya oil was contaminated.

Dicofol was restricted to use on cotton and citrus plantations from November 1985. However, since then, products containing dicofol have been routinely renewed for another five-year period. When Parana State Inspectors apprehended tons of apples sprayed with dicofol in 1989, authorities were unconcerned, and explained that the residues were within UN maximum limits.

Legislation

State governments and NGOs have two major complaints of pesticide legislation in Brazil. Firstly that federal legislation is more sympathetic to industry than some state governments would like, and enforcement is difficult. To support industry, the government has taken bizarre steps, including changing the classification of endosulfan and chlorobenzilate from organochlorines to the esters of sulphuric acid and benzilate groups respectively.

Secondly, community and health groups, as well as state governments, believe registration requirements favour corporate needs above health and safety of users. A number of pesticides have been banned or severely restricted throughout the last 10 years. When this happens there is no corresponding action on stocks, and sales may continue for several years after regulatory action.

Federal v. state laws

The seriousness of the health and environmental impact of pesticides in Brazil, and the apparent indifference of the federal government, prompted several states to pass their own laws. Rio Grande do Sul was the first to do so, with Law 7747 of December 1982, followed by Parana with Law 7827 in the same month. The State of Parana has been exceptional for the rigor with which it enforces mandatory reporting, and in its efforts since the early 1980s to cut pesticide abuses.

These steps provoked a violent reaction from the pesticides industry, which argued in the Supreme Court that the state laws were unconstitutional. Both GIFAP and the German Federation of Pesticides Manufacturers demanded that the federal government over-rule state laws. GIFAP wrote to the Brazilian government warning about the serious repercussions the situation could have on the industry, and shortly afterwards asked the then Minister of Agriculture, Nestor Jost, to use his influence to modify the situation in favour of industry.

Some aspects of the state laws were ruled unconstitutional: specifically the articles referring to environment and toxicological data, which were said to be only within the competence of the environmental authorities and the Health Secretariat. However, some articles from these laws remain on the statute books, and Parana State Law 7827 has the following implications:

- It allows greater control by state authorities over the products sold in the state.
- It avoids trade in products not registered in the state or with the Ministry of Agriculture.
- It prevents unregistered companies from manufacturing or trading in pesticides in the state.
- It legislates that companies registering products, must inform the state of the methods they use for testing pesticide residues in food. The significance of this is that tests conducted by the state using the company's own declared methods of testing cannot then be contested by the companies.

Since this law came into force, the authorities have found that various products registered at the Ministry of Agriculture lacked information about the efficiency of the product. Now, products sold in Parana must have special labels to show they conform to the restrictions imposed.

There is a great deal of indifference from the federal government. In December 1990, registration of 116 pesticide products was up for renewal, and the President issued a decree extending the date for six months. At the end of this period all of these products were refused registration, either because the manufacturer had not provided sufficient product data, or the relevant ministry did not have the resources to carry out the work necessary for registration. The Ministries concerned were Health, Agriculture and IBAMA, the Brazilian Institute for the Environment. In spite of this decision, these three Ministries met in July 1991 and agreed to extend the registration of the products.[24] The State of Parana has to date ignored the extension and begun to ban their sale.

There are other irregularities in the registration procedures. A survey carried out in 1984/85 by the Araucaria Association for the Protection of the Environment (AMAR) found 250 pesticide products registered for use on crops for which they were not officially suited. These were criticised and Ministry of Agriculture said it would be rectified. The National Association of Pesticides Companies (ANDEF), maintained they were not incorrectly registered. However, the Parana Association of Agronomists published list of wrongly registered products and called on agronomists not to recommend these for use.

Bans fail to control sales

The government is over-considerate of corporate profits, and allows sales to continue for extended periods after implementing bans. BHC sales continued for nearly three years after notice of ban, as did mercury-based fungicides, after their ban in 1980.

There are many complaints of the slowness of the government to act. In 1990, the Ministry of Health prohibited use of the active ingredient amitraz for veterinary use because of the carcinogenicity of its impurities. In spite of complaints about inappropriately registered products amitraz was used for more than 10 years, with the authorisation of the Ministry of Agriculture, before being banned in 1990.

BHC was banned under Regulation 002 in January 1981, because of its toxic effects and its impact on the environment. But the regulation allowed sales to continue until the end of 1983, to enable companies to get rid of their stocks. Without any facilities for collection of out-of-date or banned pesticides, they often remain easily accessible and stored under hazardous conditions. Parana's Agriculture Secretariat confiscated 300 tonnes of BHC products, and storage of this waste continues to be a headache for the authorities and a threat to health and the environment. In 1991, three tonnes of BHC were found buried in the town of Apucarana, and were transferred to the toxic waste dump in Tamarana.[25]

Cyhexatin was banned under Regulation 30 in 1987, because of teratogenic effects on laboratory animals, but in 1989 cyhexatin was authorised and sold as the active ingredient in a number of agricultural products: Sipcatin 500 SC, produced by Pragro Sipcam Defensivos Agricolas, classified as low toxicity and registered for use on citrus, apples and aubergines; and Hokko Cyhexatin 500, produced by Hokko do Brasil, classified as low toxicity and registered for use on citrus, apples, peaches, strawberries and aubergines.

In 1987, agronomists of Parana's Agriculture Secretariat carried out a survey of the 265 best-selling pesticides in the state to see whether the manufacturers had presented to the Ministry of Agriculture efficacy data: there was no information at all for 120 products (45%), partial information on 142 (54%) and only three (1%) presented the necessary documentation.[26]

This prompted ex-state congressman Paulo Cesar Fiates Furiatti to ask the Federal Attorney to open an inquiry into why the Ministry of Agriculture had ignored the law to the detriment of the country's agriculture, farming community and general public, and asking the Attorney to take urgent measures to regularise the situation.[27]

Technical and label information

Leaflets and labels collected during 1991[28] which provide guidance for users showed a substantial level of misleading or wrong information. These included:

- A Monsanto technical leaflet saying that Roundup (glyphosate) is less toxic than kitchen salt, aspirin or vitamin A.
- Label of Hokko Cupra 500 recommending that penicillin should be taken in the event of the user being poisoned by the product. As an antibiotic, penicillin is not appropriate.
- A leaflet on Verdict (haloxyfop-methyl), a DowElanco product, which is registered only for use on soya, carries recommendations for use on 13 other crops, such as cotton, coffee, citrus, eucalyptus, tomatoes.
- A leaflet for the Shell product Azodrin 400 (monocrotophos), says the product should not be applied after 21 days before harvest time, but the accompanying leaflet indicates it can be applied shortly before harvest.
- A leaflet on the DowElanco product Esteron (2,4-D) says the product cannot be absorbed in dangerous quantities through the skin. Health and safety guides indicate that skin contact is dangerous.
- The accompanying leaflet for the BASF product Blazer Sol (acrifluorfen sodium) makes no reference to the need to use equipment to protect the worker and the environment.

Promotional activities encouraged by companies in the past include competitions for sales staff with prizes for those selling the most pesticides. Documentation is available of these competitions from 1988,[29] three years after the Code of Conduct began to discourage this line of promotion. It is not known whether this still continues. One company, for their product Rovrin (iprodione + thiram), include a competition for the staff where sales of 520 kilos wins a bicycle, 920 kilos wins an oven.

Labelling

The State of Parana is concerned that labels do not indicate symptoms of poisoning. A survey carried out by the Agriculture Secretariat in 1987 found that 40% of products sold omitted this information and 60% did not indicate how poisonings should be treated. Examples of contradictory information on trifluralin-based product labels include:[30]

- Hoechst and Nortox say on their product labels that there are no known symptoms of poisoning from the product.
- Shell and Fecotrigo list symptoms, though these do not coincide with each other.
- Hoechst product Cobra 21 (lactofen, a herbicide), says that no fatty materials should be taken in the event of poisoning by the product. Yet on the next line it says that a large quantity of milk should be drunk in

the event of poisoning. A correction sticker has been placed over these instructions on one side of the leaflet.

Industry influence

In 1990 Lourenco Vieira, Executive President of ANDEF, was appointed to the post of Executive Secretary of the Ministry of Agriculture. His appointment roused fears among those concerned with health and environment, who believe it could nullify advances represented by the new legislation on pesticides which came into force on 12 July 1990. Reinaldo Onofre Skalisz, member of the state Council for the Defence of the Environment,[31] points out that the Brazilian government has a record of appointing prominent members of the agrochemical industry to positions of influence. For example Golbery do Couto e Silva, President of Dow Brazil, was head of President Geisel's inner cabinet from 1974 to 1978. Nestor Host, President of the administrative council of Bayer, Brazil, was Minister of Agriculture under President Figueiredo from 1979 to 1984.

Industry in Brazil has begun to incorporate an 'integrated pest management' (IPM) approach. This includes annual contests sponsored by the ANDEF, which give prizes to agronomists for research on pesticide control methods which harmonise natural enemies and chemical, physical, biological and cultural processes. According to informed observers, these are mainly efforts to improve corporate images while holding onto or expanding current chemical pesticide markets.

Disposal

Over 10 million containers per year are disposed of inadequately in Parana, in rivers, left on plantations, thrown by the roadsides, re-used for transport of food or water or burnt without adequate controls. Some are inappropriately buried. Labels do say they should be destroyed and buried in a deep pit, but no details are provided about how they should be destroyed. New legislation covers this point, but it has not yet been implemented. It is not uncommon for containers to be dumped near rivers.[32]

A study by the Santa Catarina Health Secretariat in 1987 in two regions of the state, showed that 34% of farmers in Ribeiro Preto and 52% in Massaranduba burned or buried old pesticide containers. However as many as 21% of farmers in Ribeiro and 27% in Massarandubalarge left containers in rural areas. In Massaranduba over 30% of farmers re-used their containers, although almost none did in Ribeiro Preto. A small number sold their containers.

Local concern

The First Regional Conference on Disposal of Toxic Waste, held in Toledo in June 1991, attracted hundreds of people, including representatives from industry and local government. The conference was organised by the municipal authorities, the Parana Association of Agronomists, the state Agriculture and Environment Secretariats, and Coopagro. The conference made a number of recommendations, which included:

- Government authorities should regulate the disposal of empty containers, and industry should be obliged to collect them for re-use, recycling or destruction. Industry should consider mechanisms to encourage consumers to return containers. A community dump for containers should be established in West Parana with qualified companies involved to recycle the containers. Disposal information should be included on labels.
- The law which covers responsibility for disposal, 6938/81, states that 'those responsible for pollution are responsible for finding a solution'. This should be implemented.
- Promotional material on pesticides should only be directed at agronomists and forestry technicians. All advertisement of products in the mass media should be prohibited.

Conclusion

There is some indication that the more environmentally persistent pesticides are in less common use. But there is as yet no indication that pesticides which are hazardous to users have been substantially reduced. Given the size of the plantation and estate sector in Brazil, and the conditions of workers on these estates, it seems unlikely that there has been any reduction in the hazards posed for this rural workforce. There is no indication yet that government policies prioritise reducing or eliminating hazardous pesticide use. Although a number of progressive laws are on the statute books, the process of implementation is somewhat slower. Nor are there signs that the government has seriously considered sustainable agricultural practices which could begin to reduce pesticide use.

References:
1. Burton, and Philogene, 1988, in 'Preliminary diagnosis of the use of pesticides in Brazil and their impact on human health and the environment', Samuel, H.H. *et. al*, Brazil, April 1991.
2. Hathaway, D., unpublished report produced for Greenpeace Brazil, *Production in Brazil*, 1991.
3. ANDEF, 'Vendas de defensivos agricolas por destinacao', São Paulo, 1990.
4. ANDEF, 'Vendas de defensivos agricolas por unidades da federacao', São Paulo, Brazil, 1988.
5. ANDEF, Pesticide Imports and exports, 26 November 1990.
6. ANDEF, Pesticides Imports to Brazil, at 26 November 1990, compiled by David Hathaway.
7. *Ibid.*
8. *Ibid.*
9. *Ibid.*

10. Conference on pesticides, health and environment in Brazil, Brasilia, April 1991.

11. Henao, S.H. *et al.*, 'Preliminary diagnosis of the use of pesticides in Brazil and their impact on human health and the environment', April 1991

12. Hathaway, *op. cit.*

13. 'Pesticides contaminate residents', *Folha de Londrina*, 11/5/91.

14. 'Cabrera present at slaughter of contaminated animals', *Folha de São Paulo*, June 1991.

15. *Agrotecnica Ciba-Geigy*, No. 8, July 1991.

16. Carvalho, W.A., 'Riscos Relacionados com exposicoes ocupacionais ambientais a inseticidas organoclorados' (Risks from occupational exposure to organochlorine insecticides), Bahia, Brazil, 1990, unpublished.

17. Hathaway, *op. cit.*

18. ACARESC, State of Santa Catarina Secretaria de Agricultura e Abas-tecimento, Servico de Extensao Rural, 12 June 1991.

19. ACARESC, Drinking Water Survey, June 1988-December 1990.

20. 'The invisible danger of pesticides', *Olho Vivo*, September 1990.

21. Document 35, report for The Pesticides Trust, 1991.

22. Document 37, report for The Pesticides Trust, 1991.

23. Hathaway, *op. cit.*

24. *Diario Oficial*, Secao 1, 15177, 30 July 1991.

25 .*Londrina*, 28/2/91.

26. Skallitz, R., report for The Pesticides Trust, 1991

27. Letter from Federal Attorney's Parana office to former Congressman Paulo Cesar Fiates Furiatti informing him that an inquiry had been opened on the day of writing, 10 August 1988.

28. IBAMA, documents supplied.

29. Company memorandum setting out the criteria for promotion dated January 1988. A similar document is dated October 1987.

30. Letter to the Minister of Health, the Parana Secretary for Agriculture, Osmar Dias, 4/12/87.

31. 'Lobby das industrias de agrotoxicos chega ao Ministerio da Agricultura.' *Jornal Agricultura do Parana*, March/April 1990, p. 7.

32. 'Empty pesticides containers dumped near River Priapo', *Folha de Londrina*, 25/7/91.

6. Country Report Costa Rica*

Costa Rica is a small country whose economy is dependent on the export of cash crops, particularly bananas and coffee. The other major agricultural produce are rice, maize and sugar cane. Recent years have seen an increase in non-traditional crops such as watermelons and strawberries. Synthetic chemical pesticides were introduced in Costa Rica in the 1950s, and since then their use has become so widespread that most farmers use only chemical methods for pest control.

In spite of this, there is a history of study into natural methods of pest control in the country, dating from the beginning of the century[1] (see Chapter 4), and this tradition is developing as awareness grows of the hazards of chemical pesticides. For the first time in 1991, the Ministry of Agriculture's guide indicated natural enemies and cultural practices to control pests. For example, it recommended using a fungus for control of two pests in sugar cane, and indicated that another pest could only be controlled using biological methods.[2] There is, therefore, potential for reducing pesticide use, particularly more hazardous pesticides which are already in the PIC process, or are likely to enter the process because of their health and environmental hazards.

At the same time, other pesticides already in the PIC process are systematically recommended, including paraquat for soil preparation and methyl bromide for seed bed disinfection. There is also a significant and expanding pesticide formulation industry in the country, which has increased steadily from nine plants in 1984, to 15 in 1988 and 22 in 1991, although all active ingredients are imported.

* This chapter is based on reports compiled by Luisa E. Castillo and Catharina Wesseling, of the Pesticide Programme, (Programa de Plaguicidas: Desarrollo, Salud y Ambiente [PPUNA]), Universidad Nacional, Heredia, Costa Rica, of July 1992; with additional material on alternatives from Maria D. Trivelato, February 1992, and Jaime E. Garcia.

Scale of use

As of December 1991, 306 active ingredients (1015 products) were registered for use with the Ministry of Agriculture. This is an increase of 54% on active ingredients registered two years earlier, in March 1989. Pesticide use by the big banana companies is increasing.[3].

Roughly 75% of all pesticide imports are accounted for by a small number of products: 23 in 1989 and 18 in 1990. The major imports are mancozeb, paraquat, aldicarb, terbufos, propanil and 2,4-D, as indicated in Table 6.1.

The import of aldicarb will probably show a sharp decrease in 1992, as it was withdrawn in June 1991 for use in banana plantations after illegal residues of this compound were found in bananas exported to the US. This was the main use of aldicarb, but it is still registered for use in other crops.

Imports of chlorothalonil, a fungicide used in banana plantations, have dropped from almost half a million kg in 1987 (5% of total imports) to 131,600 and 75,300 kg in 1989 and 1990 respectively. Mancozeb imports have also diminished from 21% of all imports in 1987 to 9.5% in 1989 and 13.6% in 1990. The reduction may be accounted for by higher imports of technical material for formulation within the country, or by the application of other compounds, but it is more likely the former. Both products are formulated in Costa Rica, mancozeb in five plants and chlorothalonil in three.[4]

Increase in hazardous pesticide imports

A high percentage of the total volume of pesticides imported to Costa Rica belong to WHO Class 1 (extremely hazardous) and 2 (highly hazardous). In 1988 28% of the total volume of imports belonged to this class, 24% in 1989, and 30% in 1990 (Table 6.2). Among the 1,487 tonnes of extremely hazardous pesticides imported in 1989 were aldicarb, terbufos, ethoprop, fenamiphos and methyl-parathion. Highly hazardous pesticide imports were methyl bromide, carbofuran, methamidophos and monocrotophos.[5]

There has been a large increase in the imports of certain hazardous pesticides such as methyl bromide, aluminium phosphide and phoxim since 1989. The first two are used as soil disinfectants and post-harvest fumigants. Methyl bromide is used in some non-traditional export crops, such as watermelons, strawberries and ornamental plants, all of which have increased their production highly in the last years. Phoxim is an insecticide used in pineapples (an expanding crop) and in grains and tomatoes.

Lead arsenate was banned in 1990, and although not imported in 1989 or 1990, a 'last' import was approved by decree 20384-MAG-S in 1991, and roughly 60 thousand kilos were imported.

Table 6.1 Imports of active ingredients into Costa Rica, 1989 and 1990.

Active Ingredient	1989 imports		1990 imports	
	Tonnes	% Total	Tonnes	% Total
2,4-D	491.0	5.57	354.4	4.64
2,4-D+picloram	124.5	1.41	-	-
aldicarb	597.1	6.78	697.5	9.12
aluminium phosphide	-	-	209.6	2.74
benomyl	110.3	1.25	109.3	1.43
carbofuran	147.2	1.67	-	-
chlorothalonil	131.6	1.49	75.3	1.00
copper hydroxide	144.5	1.64	62.0	.81
copper oxychloride	133.4	1.51	-	-
coumatetralyl			70.5	.92
diazinon	329.0	3.73	93.1	1.22
diuron	160.0	1.81	156.1	2.04
ethoprop	93.3	1.06	332.6	4.35
etridiazole	149.8	1.70		
glyphosate	266.6	3.03	260.6	3.41
mancozeb	806.2	9.15	1087.3	14.23
maneb	341.8	3.88	-	-
methyl bromide	233.4	2.65	530.9	6.94
mirex	-	-	55.0	.72
paraquat	713.7	8.10	612.2	8.01
paraquat+diuron	-	-	57.1	.75
pendimethalin	157.8	1.79	132.4	1.73
phoxim	-	-	60.8	.80
picloram	134.7	1.53	-	-
propanil	537.4	6.10	391.6	5.12
propiconazole	90.2	1.02	94.8	1.24
propoxur	112.5	1.28	157.6	2.06
sulphur	-	-	61.1	.80
terbufos	578.6	6.57	431.1	5.64
terbuthylazine	107.2	1.22	74.0	.97
tridemorph	178.6	2.03	78.9	1.03
Sub-total	**6,870.4**	**77.97**	**6,245.7**	**81.72**
Total imports	**8,809.9**	**100**	**7,643.4**	**100**

Source: J. Blanco, Pesticides Program, EDECA, UNA, Heredia, Costa Rica.

In 1989 37% (3,260 tonnes) of total imports consisted of pesticides listed in the *Consolidated List of Products whose Consumption and/or Sale have been Banned, Withdrawn, Severely Restricted or not Approved by Governments* as banned or severely restricted elsewhere.[6] Of pesticides in the PIC process, chlordane, heptachlor and lead arsenate are imported, as are paraquat and methyl parathion, which are potential PIC pesticides.

Table 6.2 **Volume of pesticides imported to Costa Rica according to WHO toxicity classification, 1989-1990.**

Class	1989 metric tonnes	%	1990 metric tonnes	%
Extremely hazardous	1,487	16.9	1,775	23.2
Highly hazardous	614	7.0	556	7.3
Moderately hazardous	2,544	28.9	1,956	25.6
Slightly hazardous	4,080	46.3	3,290	43.0
Not classified	86	1.0	66	0.9

Source: J. Blanco, Pesticides Program, EDECA, UNA, Heredia, Costa Rica.

Potentially hazardous imports are set out in Table 6.4, which shows the exporting country and in some cases company, legal status in Costa Rica, and quantity imported in 1989 and 1990.

Four pesticides are registered without restriction in Costa Rica which are not registered in their country of origin, initially the US: butachlor, exported by Monsanto from the US; carbosulfan, exported by FMC from the US; haloxifop methyl, exported from Colombia by DowElanco; protiofos, exported from El Salvador by Bayer and from Germany.[7]

Formulation activities

By June 1991, a total of 22 plants were operating in the country, formulating compounds such as aldicarb, atrazine, benomyl, captan, chlorothalonil, chlorpyrifos, 2,4-D, ethoprop, fenamiphos, heptachlor, mancozeb, maneb, methamidophos, methyl-parathion, methomyl, monocrotophos, paraquat, terbufos and zineb. The pesticides formulated in Costa Rica include many giving rise to concern, some of which are in the PIC process, or are potential PIC pesticides (see Table 6.3).

There have been no recent surveys of conditions in these plants, or of related incidents of poisoning. In the past, the University's Pesticide Programme has visited some plants and observed hazardous working conditions. There is no reason to believe that the general situation has improved, although the Ministry of Health has been working in this area in recent years. In 1986, 54 poisonings of workers in formulation plants were registered at the National Insurance Institute.[8]

One of the most important formulating plants in the country, Formuquisa, which is located in the North Pacific region, formulates 40 different active ingredients. Members of the communities living in the surrounding area have repeatedly held the factory responsible for massive fish and shrimp kills in the rainy season as the source has been traced to the overflow from a disposal lagoon at the plant. The local population is worried about pollution in its underground water supplies.[9] After a plea in 1989 from community members, this company has been forced by the Ministry of Health to improve its installations.

Table 6.3 Plants formulating pesticides on the PIC list or potential PIC pesticides.

Formulation Plant	Active Ingredient
Agroquim, Rimac	paraquat
Inquisa	aldicarb methomyl methyl parathion monocrotophos paraquat
Quim, Kay	methamidophos methomyl methyl parathion monocrotophos paraquat
Chrystal Chem	methamidophos
Formuquisa	ethoprop fenamiphos phorate methamidophos methomyl methyl parathion mirex monocrotophos
Bioquimica	methyl parathion monocrotophos terbufos
Seracsa	paraquat
Import, 2005	paraquat

Pesticide sales

A total of 20 shops throughout the country were visited by PPUNA between April and June 1991. A general problem observed in all of them was the lack of ventilation. The smell of pesticides was strong at the counter and even more so in the shops' warehouses. No protective clothing or equipment were used by the employees to handle pesticides.

An identity card was demanded in only three of the shops when trying to buy a red-labelled pesticide (Class 1, extremely toxic). A general lack of knowledge on banned and restricted pesticides was observed, for example when it was pointed out in some shops that an active ingredient was banned, a different formulation was offered with the same active ingredient.

Table 6.4   Pesticides imported to Costa Rica which cause concern.

Active Ingredient	Exporting country and company*	Legal status**	1989 (Tonnes)	1990 (Tonnes)
Pesticides on initial PIC list				
chlordane	US	Ban-24/1/90	-	-
heptachlor	US	Ban-24/1/90	11.2	-
lead arsenate	Chile, Peru	Ban-2/6/90		
paraquat	Germany, Taiwan, US	Reg/NR	713.7	612.2
parathion methyl	France—Rhone Poulenc, China, Germany—BASF	Rest-10/7/87 48% Form.		
Potential PIC pesticides				
aldicarb	US	Reg/NR	597.1	697.5
captafol	Taiwan, Germany, US	48% Form		
carbofuran	US—FMC, Israel, Germany—Bayer.	Rest-10/7/87	-	-
chloropicrin	US, Israel	Not Reg		
dichlorvos	Israel	Reg/NR	32.5	19.1
endosulfan	Israel, Netherlands, US Germany—Hoechst,	Reg/NR	16.8	9.7
lindane	France—Rhône Poulenc	Rest-10/3/88	8.8	8.9
methamidophos	Germany, US, China	Reg/NR	60.0	31.6
methomyl	Israel, Taiwan, Germany—Bayer	Reg/NR	26.5	11.2
mirex	Brazil	Reg	67.5	55.0
monocrotophos	Israel, Switzerland, Colombia—Ciba-Geigy	Rest- 60% Form	36.3	36.9
pentachlorophenol	Guatemala	Ban—2/6/90		
Other pesticides considered a problem				
aluminium phos.	Germany, Brazil	Reg/NR		209.6
azinphos methyl	Guatemala—Bayer, Germany, El Salvador	Reg/NR	18.0	
brodifacoum	UK—ICI	Reg/NR	19.0	
coumatetralyl	Guatemala—Bayer	Reg/NR	53.8	70.5
disulfuron	Guatemala, Germany—Bayer, El Salvador—Bayer	Reg/NR	35.1	4.0
ethoprop	US—Rhône Poulenc	Reg/NR	93.3	332.6
fenamiphos	Germany—Bayer, Guatemala—Bayer	Reg/NR	83.8	50.9
fenthion	Guatemala—Bayer, Germany	Reg/NR	840.0	40.0
pirimiphos methyl	UK—ICI	Reg/NR	1000.0	600.0
phorate	UK—ICI, US—Cyanamid	Rest-7/10/87	19.7	17.15
terbufos	US, Taiwan	Reg/NR	578.6	-

*Where known. **Reg=Registered; NR=No restriction; Rest=Restricted; Form=Formulation
Source: Prepared by L. Soto. Pesticides Program, EDECA, UNA, Heredia, Costa Rica.

Health impact

The National Security Institute (INS) is an important source of statistics on pesticide poisonings, however their figures do not take account of mild poisonings or those occurring with small farmers who would not be covered by insurance schemes. Cases presented in hospitals are also an under-representation. A 1989 study by the PPUNA of 26 national hospitals showed that an average of 471 pesticides (requiring hospitalisation of more than one day) occurred in each year between 1980 and 1986, but a much higher percentage was registered with INS, reinforcing the point that hospitals also pick up only a small number of pesticide poisonings. About half the hospitalised poisonings were among farmworkers.[10]

PPUNA reviewed agrochemical poisonings reported at the Limón agency of the INS in the first six months of 1990, the results are set out in Table 6.5. In total, 334 cases were reported (including 41 by fertilisers), but the pesticide responsible for the poisoning was only identified in 99 cases.

Problem pesticides

PPUNA investigated details of some of these poisonings, and others from different regions. These show a number of pesticides consistently responsible for health problems.

Aldicarb: This compound has been responsible for many poisonings in the past.[11] In the first six months of 1990, 22 of the work poisonings reported at the rural agency of Límon, out of 99 for which the pesticide responsible was identified, were caused by aldicarb (Table 6.5). Even though the high toxicity of aldicarb had been repeatedly pointed out, as well as the high incidence of aldicarb-related poisonings in banana plantations, this was not the reason why the company finally withdrew it from the market. This was due, as pointed out earlier, to the danger it posed for the consumers in the US after residues over the tolerance limits were found in bananas shipped from Costa Rica and other countries.

Ethoprop: This caused six of the 99 poisonings (Table 6.5) in the poisoning study.[12]

Fenamiphos: In 1990, five women were poisoned in Sarapiqui after eating bananas that had been recently sprayed with this compound. In Pococi a banana plantation worker was poisoned after applying fenamiphos. Another 20 workers spraying fenamiphos in a coffee plantation in Grecia (in the Central Region of Costa Rica) were poisoned over a three-day period.[13]

Lead arsenate: Three incidents were reported by the sanitary inspectors.[14]

Methamidophos: This compound was responsible for 20% of the poisonings reported by the watermelon producers interviewed.[15]

Methomyl: Of the 30 poisonings reported by the 24 watermelon producers interviewed in the regions of Orotina and Parrita in the province of Puntarenas, methomyl was responsible for 46%.[16] Sanitary inspectors interviewed reported an incident after methomyl was used in corn and rice fields. A dog died after drinking water in a creek where the application equipment had been washed.[17]

Methyl bromide: A worker applying methyl bromide without protective equipment was poisoned in a watermelon plantation in 1989.[18]

Paraquat: This compound is widely used on plantations, and evidence shows that it has a severe health impact on regular users. In some countries death and suffering caused by paraquat is suicide-related, but this is not the case in Costa Rica, where 75% of hospitalised cases are non-suicidal. Further details of paraquat use in Costa Rica are set out in the box.

Terbufos: When environmental sanitary inspectors of the Ministry of Health were interviewed in one study,[19] terbufos was mentioned in several poisoning episodes and it was responsible for 27% of identified poisonings in the first six months of 1990 (see Table 6.5). In 1987, an agricultural worker suffered an acute poisoning while applying terbufos in coffee. In 1989, 18 persons were acutely poisoned after terbufos leached from a coffee plantation and contaminated a potable water system in the community of Pérez Zeledón. This community mentioned two more cases of water pollution caused by terbufos, one because of washing the spray equipment in a creek and the other because of leaching from a tomato field. In interviews with 24 watermelon producers in the regions of Orotina and Parrita in the province of Puntarenas, they reported 30 poisonings, of which 13% were caused by terbufos. Three or four employees were hospitalised and the others received attention in the emergency room.[20]

Environmental and wildlife impact

In some environmental incidents, the pesticide can be identified, though more often the source is not identified.

Carbaryl: This compound is still being used and has been associated with several fish kills.[21]

Lead arsenate: In 1987, 50% of a trout culture (10,000 fishes) in Santa Maria de Dota were killed after the application equipment was washed upstream and the leftover residues of lead arsenate were dumped in the stream. In San Ramón in 1989 an indeterminate number of rabbits died after being fed cabbage which had been illegally sprayed with lead arsenate. This product had been restricted for use on coffee only since 1982 and was banned in 1990. In 1989, also in San Ramón, a coffee growing area, the potable water system was polluted by lead arsenate because the applying equipment was washed there.

Methyl parathion: The sanitary inspectors interviewed reported a massive kill of birds when methyl parathion was applied by plane in a cotton field.[22]

Terbufos: This has been linked on several occasions to fish kills near the banana plantations. The kills have been reported to occur when it rains shortly after the application of this compound in the banana fields.[23] As noted above, this pesticide has contaminated community supplies.

Table 6.5   Agrochemical poisonings reported to the Limón Agency of the National Security Institute during the first six months of 1990

Active Ingredient	Trade name	No. of cases
Herbicides:		
paraquat	Gramoxone, Radex	36
paraquat+ametrine	Radex+Gesapax	1
paraquat+diuron	Gramúron	1
picloran+2,4-D	Tordón	1
Unidentified	-	37
Fungicides		
carboxin	Vitavax	1
carboxin+captan	Bacterol	1
Unidentified	-	2
Insecticides		
chlorpyrifos	Dursban	2
PCNB	PCNB	1
Unidentified OPs	-	1
Nematicides		
aldicarb	Temik	22
ethoprop	Mocap	6
fenamiphos	Nemacur	1
terbufos	Counter	26
Unidentified	-	14
Other unidentified		
Fertilisers and other non-pesticide agrochemicals		45
Non-identified compounds		135
Total		**334**

Source: Prepared by L. Soto, Pesticide Program, EDECA, UNA, Heredia, Costa Rica.

Portrait of a Pesticide:
paraquat in Costa Rica[24]

Paraquat is used on nearly every crop before planting, and is sprayed on a regular basis on bananas (between 8 and 12 times a year), corn, coffee, palm heart, citrus and other fruit trees. There are no restrictions on sale or use and it is increasingly used in private homes, on road sides and railways, in parks and playgrounds. Paraquat is widely used by small farmers, who call it 'the chemical machete', being easily available and cheap.

On plantations, spraying is most commonly done with backpack sprayers. Spray equipment leaks, soaking the back and genitals, or workers have to touch and repair clogging nozzles. Protective equipment is hardly ever used with paraquat, even on banana plantations with occupational health programmes. A study carried out in 1992 in Guápiles, one of the main banana plantation regions, identified 284 accident cases caused by paraquat between 1988 and 1990. These included 123 cases of systemic poisonings, burns, eye injuries and fingernail damage.[25,26] The population of wage-earning agricultural workers in the area is less than 10,000.

A review of fatal cases from the records of autopsies in the Medical Forensic Department, showed a total of 248 paraquat deaths between 1980-89. Of these, 22 were occupational accidents and two were from chemical burns because of spills. A further case was linked to dermal absorption of paraquat after treatment for body lice.[27]

There is no scientific data on chronic toxicity in Costa Rica, but an investigation of hospital records and patient interviews showed patients who suffered acute paraquat poisonings in the past refer to non-specific, chronic symptoms, such as loss of weight, tiredness, lack of appetite, loss of memory, psychological changes and chronic headaches. There were cases of chronic renal failure, psychosis and pulmonary fibrosis related to paraquat poisoning, including occupational and accidental poisonings.[28].

A pathologist at the National Children's Hospital investigated the deaths of two children under the age of two from Tierra Blanca de Cartago, a rural village with a population of about 5000, in an area of high pesticide use. The children died from ideopatic pulmonary fibrosis in 1989 and 1991. Dr. Carranza found the pulmonary lesions compatible with paraquat poisoning. Most houses in Tierra Blanca are near agricultural fields: also it is common to spray paraquat in the yards of private homes, and Dr. Carranza speculated that diapers were accidentally sprayed.

A doctor at the Guápiles hospital, Dr. Edwin Solano, a specialist in internal medicine, pointed out in an interview in February 1992[29] that he deals not only with suicidal patients, but also many accidental poisonings and occupational chemical burns. On the day of the interview a patient was hospitalised, who accidentally took paraquat in his mouth, thinking it was 'water' in a refilled Coca Cola bottle stored in the kitchen. Although stained with blue dye, the electricity was out and the room was dark.

Environmental impact of banana plantations

The US transnational Standard Fruit Company is the major banana grower in the Valle de la Estrella. Pesticides used in the plantation have been polluting rivers and underground water of the area. Evidence was presented to the International Water Tribunal in Amsterdam in February 1992.

In a preliminary study of residues in the Atlantic Zone of this region,[30] several pesticides were found in superficial and underground water as well as in sediments and in sea cucumbers. Seven of eight river sediment samples had pesticide residues; the compounds present in the samples were chlorothalonil, chlorpyrifos, terbufos and ethoprop. The highest level detected was 40 ppb of chlorothalonil.

In superficial water chlorpyrifos and chlorothalonil were the compounds more frequently found. Chlorpyrifos is used in the bags that cover the fruit in the fields and chlorothalonil is used in the control of a fungus and applied aerially. Chlorothalonil was found in concentrations as high as eight ppb; adverse reproductive effects in fishes have been reported between three and 6.5 ppb.[31]

The analysis of a sample of several sea cucumbers from the National Park of Cahuita showed residues of eight ppb of chlorpyrifos. This National Park is located on the Atlantic coast, close to the mouth of the River Estrella which crosses the banana fields.

Seven out of nine underground water samples were found positive for chlorothalonil; the highest value found was 0.98 ppb. Aldicarb, benomyl, chlorpyrifos, diazinon, oxamyl and terbufos were also analysed but not found. In the European Community the maximum limit accepted is 0.1 ppb for individual pesticides and 0.5 for total pesticides in potable water.

The case was presented to the International Water Tribunal, citing this evidence of chemical residues washed by flood waters into the river, leached into the ground water systems and contaminating wells:

> The large-scale banana production in Costa Rica causes severe chemical pollution and other related environmental damages. The use of pesticides for banana production causes contamination of the hydrographic basin and the river courses in the zone of the Estrella Valley in the Limón province. This contamination also affects existing bordering zones, such as the coral reef on the Caribbean Coast of the Limón province. ...
>
> The plantation system of drainage channels ends up in the Estrella river, and transports besides superficial water also sediment and chemical substances which are a potential danger for the population and natural aquatic environment of the zone. The contamination with pesticides severely affects the surface as well as the ground water, and causes direct severe damages to the natural aquatic environment, plus indirect damage to the health of the inhabitants of the area and to the ecosystem.

On reviewing the evidence from samples, the Tribunal upheld the complaint, and ruled that the Standard Fruit Company should phase out the use of pesticides recognised as being extremely hazardous and minimise the use of others, and that it should investigate and use environmentally friendly pest-control practices.[32]

Legislation and response to PIC

Costa Rican law provides for a registration scheme according to which pesticides are registered for use on specific crops. This practice, is however not adhered to and pesticides are used in many ways for which they are not registered.

A presidential decree in 1992 aimed to create a new category of pesticides called 'consolidated generics'. The move created a local outcry, and the decree was temporarily withdrawn, but is likely to be presented again. It is proposed to cover pesticides such as captan, diuron, paraquat, mancozeb, chlorothalonil, 2,4-D and benomyl. This would have the effect of allowing registration without presenting new information and research; eliminating the need of a letter from the pesticide manufacturer authorising the request for registration of the product in Costa Rica; releasing the applicant from the obligation to provide new data.

This is contrary to international moves to tighten controls on trade in hazardous pesticides, and to transfer more information through, for example, the PIC process. When interviewed in July 1991 about the Prior Informed Consent process, the government response was that although it might be useful for countries without a good registration system, Costa Rica would participate but would not need such a provision.

Conclusion

The report on Costa Rica provides a useful study of a country with advanced processes for registering and reviewing pesticides, and with a strong tradition of research into both the problems created by pesticides, and non-chemical alternatives. These traditions have not yet had a major impact on government policy: pesticide imports have increased, local formulation is increasing, and recent indications that the government aims to ease the registration requirements give cause for concern.

References:
1. Trivelato, M.D., 'Alternatives to the use of synthetic chemical pesticides in Costa Rica', report for The Pesticides Trust-PAN, February 1992.
2. Trivelato, *ibid.*
3. Castillo, L., Soto, L., Chacón, M., Blanco, J., Wesseling, C., 'Estudio sobre accidentes laborales e intoxicaciones por plaguicidas en el Valle de la Estrella. Informe para la Fundación Güilombé: Un caso para el Tribunal Internacional de Aguas', Programa de Plaguicidas, Universidad Nacional, 1991, 15pp.
4. Roldán, C. and Aguilar, M., 'Informe de la visita a Formulaciones Quimicas S.A. (Formuquisa)', Programa de Plaguicidas, Universidad Nacional, 1989, 6pp.
5 Blanco, J., 'Importación de Plaguicidas en Costa Rica (1970-1989),' Ponencia presentada a las *Jornadas de Toxicologia*, San José, Costa Rica, 1990, 10pp.
6. Blanco, *op. cit.* 1990.

7. Soto, L., Pesticide Program, EDECA, UNA, Heredia, Costa Rica prepared information.
8 Castillo, L., Wesseling, C., Hidalgo, C., Mora, S., Bravo, V., 'Diagnóstico sobre el uso e impacto de los Plaguicidas en América Central: Informe de Costa Rica', Programa de Plaguicidas, San José, Costa Rica, 1989, 181pp.
9 Roldán, C. and Aguilar, M., *op. cit.*, 1989.
10. Final report from Costa Rica for The *FAO Code: Missing Ingredients*, The Pesticides Trust/PAN International, London, 1989.
11. Castillo, L. and Wesseling, C., 'The FAO Code: PIC and monitoring project, final phase-Costa Rica', Report to The Pesticides Trust, Pesticide Programme, UNA, 1989. 12pp.
12. Castillo *et al*, 1991.
13. Blanco, J. and Ramirez, O., 'Costa Rica: Percepción de los Inspectores de Saneamiento Ambiental sobre la contaminación por plaguicidas. Borrador', Programa de Plaguicidas, UNA. 1992, 11pp.
14. *Ibid.*
15. Trivelato, *op. cit.*, 1992.
16. Trivelato, *op. cit.* 1992.
17. Blanco and Ramirez, *op. cit.*, 1992.
18. Blanco and Ramirez, *op. cit.*, 1992.
19. Blanco and Ramirez, *op. cit.*, 1992.
20 Trivelato, M. 'El Melón en Costa Rica: Estudio de caso de un producto no tradicional para exportación borrador', CECADE, University of Texas, 1992, 18pp.
21. Blanco and Ramirez, *op. cit.*, 1992.
22. Blanco and Ramirez, *op. cit.*, 1992.
23 Wesseling C., Castillo, L., Ruepert, C., Trivelato, M. and Roldán, C., 'Uso de los plaguicidas en la actividad bananera y su efecto en el ambiente y la salud humana,' in *Evaluación del Impacto Socioambiental de la Actividad Bananera en arapiqui, Tortuguero y Talamanca*, Unión Internacional para la Conservación de la Naturaleze (IUCN) Oficina Regional para Centro América, 1991.
24. This box is based on Wesseling, C. and Castillo, L., 'Current status of paraquat use and impact in Costa Rica', Report submitted to the FAO/UNEP Joint Expert Committee on Pesticides, 1992.
25. Vergara, A. 'Accidentes con productos agroquimicos reportados al Instituto Nacional de Seguros durante 1990, canton de Pococi y Guácimo: un análisis preliminar', Manuscrito preparado para el seminario: Ajuste Estructural: Mujer, Salud y Empleo. San José, Costa Rica, 1991.
26. Wesseling, C. and Castillo, L., 'Current status of paraquat use and impact in Costa Rica', *op. cit.*, 1992.
27. Wesseling, C., Aguilar, M., de la Cruz, E., Ramirez, O., 'Análisis de las autopsias en la medicatura forense del organismo de investigacion judicial correspondientes a intoxicaciones con plaguicidas durante el período 1980-89: un informe preliminar', Programa de Plaguicidas: Desarrollo, Salud y Ambiente (PPUNA), EDECA, UNA, Heredia, Costa Rica, 1991.
28. Wesseling, C, De la Cruz, E., Hidalgo, C., 'Estudio epidemiologico de intoxicaciones agudas con plaguicidas en Costa Rica', Escuela de Cientias Ambientales, Universidad Nacional, Heredia, Costa Rica, 1988.
29. Castillo, L. and Wesseling, C., report for The Pesticides Trust, 1992.
30. Abarca, L., Ruepert, C., 'Impacto ambiental de la actividad bananera en el Valle La Estrella: Informe final sobre análisis de residuos', Consultoria para la Fundación Güilombe, 1992, 32pp.
31. EPA. 'Pesticide Fact Sheet—Chlorothalonil', Washington, D.C., 1986.
32. *The Second International Water Tribunal: Amsterdam, 16-21 February 1992*, International Books, and judgment of the IWT jury of 21 February 1992.

7. Country Report: Ecuador*

Ecuador has immense banana, cocoa, coffee, soya, palm and tropical fruit plantations. It encompasses several ecosystems and temperature zones, and is characterised by wide genetic diversity. The Andes mountain range runs through the country. The country is rich in agricultural produce, which ranges from fruits such as apples, pears and peaches to staple crops such as potatoes, maize, wheat and barley. Major agricultural exports are bananas, coffee and cocoa. In spite of the richness of the country, the infant mortality among the population of 10 million is one of the highest in South America, mainly due to malnutrition, respiratory illnesses and basic infections, and the per capita gross national product is amongst the lowest on the sub-continent.

Agriculture has now become largely dependent on the use of pesticides, but misuse and abuse is widespread. At an OECD workshop in 1991, the Ecuadorian representative commented that:

> . . . under the economic and social conditions of a developing country like Ecuador, the proper use of pesticides is not really feasible. Therefore, the resulting health problems of direct users, and consumers in general are very serious. Although there is already an alarming record of such victims, more frightening still is the number of cases of chronic illness and death resulting from the improper use of pesticides in Ecuador.[1]

The government is committed to reducing misuse and abuse of pesticides, and in 1990 passed a law paving the way for tighter controls, including the right to refuse to register pesticides threatening health and the environment. Ecuador welcomes and is an official participant in the PIC scheme, and a measure of its commitment is the speed with which it acted to ban pesticides on the initial PIC list, which were not already restricted under previous legislation. There are still not sufficient resources to implement the law fully and to monitor pesticide misuse.

---

* Case study based on survey and report from Fundación Natura, by Ing. Agr. Mercedes Bollanos, M.Sc (MAG).

Scale of pesticide use in Ecuador

There is no pesticide manufacture in Ecuador, and all active ingredients are imported. In 1990, 6,200 tonnes were imported, at a cost of US$29 million, and in the first half of 1991 imports of 2,200 tonnes cost US$12.5 million.

Over one-fifth of the imports are pesticides which give rise to concern: paraquat is on the PIC list, and seven are candidates for the PIC list: carbofuran, dichlorvos, endosulfan, methamidophos, methomyl, monocrotophos and phosphamidon (see Table 7.1). Paraquat accounted for 6.6% of all pesticide imports in 1990, and carbofuran, the largest single import, 8%.

Paraquat comes largely from the UK; in 1990, 65% came from England, 14% from the United States and 21% from China (it seems likely the source was Taiwan, as the exporting company is Taiwanese). All endosulfan imported during 1990, 48,400 kg, came from Hoechst in Germany. Most carbofuran comes from FMC in the USA, and a small proportion (9,180 kg, 1.8%) from Bayer in Germany. Europe is a major exporter of monocrotophos: 81% came from Ciba-Geigy in Switzerland, and 15% from Rhône Poulenc in France.

Table 7.1   PIC and potential PIC pesticides imported to Ecuador 1990/part 1991.

Pesticide	1990 (kg)	To 30 June 1991 (kg)
1. PIC pesticide:		
Paraquat	407,020	70,000
2. Potential PIC pesticides		
Carbofuran	513,500	288,040
Dichlorvos	2,000	2,200
Endosulfan	48,400	21,000
Methamidophos	188,787	60,400
Methomyl	6,500	1,500
Monocrotophos	93,430	36,904
Phosphamidon	4,000	6,000
Total	1,263,637	486,044
Total imports	6,184,874	2,232,343
Proportion PIC and potential PIC imports	20%	22%

Source: Report from Fundación Natura.

While no active ingredients are manufactured in Ecuador, there are five plants which formulate or repackage pesticides, including paraquat, and two pesticides which are candidates for the PIC list, carbofuran and dichlorvos. The others formulated or packed locally are: propanil, omethoate, glyphosate, propoxur, pencazole and fenamiphos.[2] The pesticides now banned in Ecuador are:[3]

Registration forbidden under Parliamentary Resolution, May 1990: aldrin, dieldrin, BHC, camphechlor (toxaphene), chlordimeform, chlordane, DBCP, lindane, EDB, 2,4,5-T, amitrole, arsenic, mercury, lead, carbon tetrachloride, leptophos, heptachlor, parathion, mirex, dinoseb

Severe restrictions apply to: pentachlorophenol (for industrial use), DDT (for malarial control)

Additional pesticides banned, 1991: In August 1991, the government added a ban on PIC list pesticides as revised at the June 1991 meeting of the panel of experts, dinoseb, HCH (mixed isomers), heptachlor, parathion ethyl, parathion methyl, cyhexatin (never been imported), fluoroacetamide (never been imported).

Awaiting decision: paraquat

The legislation aims to facilitate refusal to register PIC pesticides, however the country is heavily dependent on paraquat and alternatives will be more expensive. The need for alternatives becomes obvious, when considering the dilemma facing the government if other pesticides on the candidate PIC list become PIC pesticides, as these account for an additional 14% of all pesticides used in the country.

Pesticides are generally accepted as necessary by farmers and indigenous peoples. One ecological organisation, Tierra Nueva, maintains that sales of parathion, aldrin and paraquat are not controlled in Ecuador.[4] This organisation believes aldrin and parathion may be smuggled into the country.

Health and environmental impact
One Ecuadorian agronomist, Antonia Kakabadse, says that 'selling pesticides to farmers in the way it is done in Ecuador is like giving strychnine to people who don't know what it is.' Only 5% of Ecuadorian agricultural workers use protective clothing when working with hazardous pesticides.

There is under-reporting in the health centres of the Ministry of Health, because the symptoms of pesticide poisoning are not easily identified by health workers and many cases, particularly of chronic poisoning, are registered and treated as some other form of ailment. There is no regular monitoring to determine levels of acute and chronic poisoning and environmental contamination. While some cases are reported in the press, it is impossible to put these in the context of overall acute or chronic toxicity while no statistical information is available. However the number of poisonings is said to have increased considerably over the last 10 years.

The most widely used pesticides are carbofuran, dichlorvos, endosulfan, methamidophos, methomyl, monocrotophos, paraquat and phosphamidon. In the absence of more specific information, the environmental group Fundación Natura assume that these are responsible for the majority of health problems.[5]

According to a report in the Ecuadorian newspaper *Hoy*:

. . . there is an alarming number of poisonings caused by using pesticides. But there are no laboratory facilities available to determine the cause of the poisoning and there are no statistics or regulations governing the use of pesticides.[6]

Many of the deaths are suicides, which are more easily traced to pesticides when this is the chosen method. Press clippings cannot pick up chronic pesticide poisonings and accidents in rural areas, and while very limited they are the only available source of information. In no case was the responsible active ingredient reported in the press. Table 7.2 documents press reports from January 1990 to June 1991.

Because of under-reporting and the lack of any structure to collect information, it is impossible to know the extent of the problem in Ecuador. Fundación Natura report the case of Carmen Miranda, now a Plant Protection Inspector, whose son was born with half an arm after she was contaminated with carbofuran during pregnancy. She told her story to Fundación Natura:

My name is Carmen Miranda, my son's name is Octavio David Median Miranda, who was born on 2 November 1985. During February of 1985, I did not menstruate, and from about 20 March I was working in the fields, handling the pesticide Furadan 5% granular (carbofuran), without any precautions. I collapsed for a minute, and the doctor warned that I would lose the baby because of the poisoning. Four months later, I was going to lose the baby, but I took plenty of rest and later my son was born without half of his arm. He is sensitive to pesticides, and cannot support strong smells, but he is in a good psychological state and has no other problems.

Carmen Miranda has tried to have a clinical analysis to check whether she is still contaminated, but has been told it is not possible to carry out this sort of analysis in hospitals in Quito.

Food contamination
It is generally accepted that residues are high, but little testing is carried out. A 1980 study confirmed the harmful effects of pesticides used on fruit.[7] One study in Quito which carried out random tests on milk, including breast milk, found that all samples had traces of some of the hazardous pesticides BHC, lindane, aldrin, endrin and chlordane. This was confirmed by a report written by the National Science and Technology Council (CONACYT), which concluded that all the country's foodstuffs are contaminated by

Table 7.2 Press reports of pesticide-related deaths.

Date	Names	Manner of death
Accidental Deaths:		
31.1.91	Serafin Erazo, teacher, and 4 children aged 12-14: Ramrio Chuquitarco, David Juez, Roberto Samaniego, Joffre Veintimilla.	Inhaled unnamed pesticide
28.1.90	Jose Alejandro Chiriguaya	Working without mask —inhaled fungicide
24.1.90	Mario Ronquillo, 40, and son Rizzo, 15.	Insecticide-contaminated rice
26.2.91	Name not given	Fumigation on banana plantation
6.4.91 (Hoy)	3-year-old child, Mercedes Moran Moran, died: three siblings seriously ill	Head lice treatment with pesticide (possibly paraquat)
Poisoned by consuming pesticide—possibly suicide:		
6.7.90	Rosendo Monroy, 94	Died—herbicide.
9.12.90	Maribel Zambrano, 20	Died—insecticide
9.6.90	Maxima Dolores Anchudia, 39	Died—insecticide
21.1.91	Narcisa Montes	Kererex and insecticides
3.1.91	Gladys Hermelinda Villacis	Insecticide
26.2.91	Luis Pomanilla	Kererex and insecticides
4.5.91	Alberto Lasso Zambrano dies	Pesticide
12.6.91	Freddy Antonio Balcazar Jimenes	Pesticide
Suicides (deaths, unless otherwise indicated):		
17.1.90	Maria Magdelena Lopez, 38	Suicide attempt
8.2.90	Gloria Holguin, 44 and	
6.2.90	Jesenia Maeicas, 16	Paraquat
3.2.90	Pedro Camacho, 20	Suicide attempt
8.6.90	Flor Jacqueline Torres, 16	
10.7.90	Maximo Andrade Villareal, 38	
4.10.90	Milenco Antonio Villao, 65	
5.12.90	Julio Cedeno, 51	
26.1.91	Hugo Villegas, 67	
20.3.91	Jesus Castro Franco	
19.4.91	Julio Eduardo Moran Mora	
18.5.91	Narcisa Heras	
20.6.91	Landy Tapuy Lara, 20 Maria Margarita Sarango Tapiar	

Source: Press reports in *El Universo*, unless marked otherwise.

pesticides. In 1986, research found that a large proportion of food and drinking water consumed in urban areas contained pesticide residues.[8]

A local authority in London (Lambeth Analytical Services of Lambeth Borough Council) which tested organochlorines in tropical produce sold in the local market in 1991, found residues in green bananas from Ecuador of beta HCH. These were noted as being at less than 1 mg/kg.[9]

Few environmental studies are carried out, but experts are concerned about falling bean yields, which they believe is due to the increasing incidence of pests and disease, as pesticides have encouraged insect resistance.[10]

Legislation

A new law, under Parliamentary Resolution No. 71 of May 1990, drawn up with assistance from the UN FAO has banned a range of problem pesticides. Although the original proposals were watered down, Article 27 allows the National Programme for Vegetal Health to 'refuse to register a pesticide or related product if there is unacceptable risk to consumers' health and/or the environment, according to the guidelines supplied by the International Code of Conduct on Distribution and Use of Pesticides'. The legislation has forbidden the registration of 20 pesticides, and placed severe restrictions on a further two.

The scale of resources available to implement the law is not yet clear. In many South American countries, model legislation has been passed without either the political will or financial resources for implementation. Under the new law, all pesticides used in the country must be re-registered. This puts an immense strain on technical and financial resources. The government has asked for help of institutions, governments and international organisations who can assist in evaluating such data as the chemical and physical details of the active ingredient and the final product, toxic content, environmental impact, efficiency and economic viability, quality control, residue analysis, benefits and risks of the use of these products. The intention is to register only those pesticides whose benefits outweigh their risks, but Ecuador lacks resources, information and alternatives to make this a reality.

In a move to strengthen its economy, Ecuador is one of the five Andean Pact countries, with Bolivia, Colombia, Peru and Venezuela, which are aiming to harmonise requirements for the register to operate similar regulations in all countries. As with other common markets, Ecuador will not be able to apply more restrictive measures than are applied to the same product in another Andean country. It is not yet clear whether this will affect Ecuador's new pesticide laws.

Industry influence

All pesticide companies in Ecuador, including two major pesticide-importing companies, Ecuaquimica and Agripac, are represented on the Ministry of Agriculture technical commission that controls pesticide imports. During 1990, two of the more important importers in Ecuador held two training courses for the Plant Protection Program. One course covered technical recommendations to control pests; the second dealt with safety measures during the preparation of the mixture, application and post-application of one pesticide. In the field, many companies train farmers, in particular emphasising safety measures in handling pesticides sold by the company.

Advertising and publicity

Agripac, one of Ecuador's main importers, promotes pesticides, such as paraquat on the early morning television programme called 'Good Morning Farmers' and sometimes uses the programme to give information on pesticides most suited to certain crops.

Conclusion

Health and environmental groups are concerned about the scale of pesticide use in Ecuador, and the lack of monitoring. Although recent legislation is laying the groundwork for tighter controls, this is a far cry from resources needed to support safer agricultural practices with reduced use.

References:
1. Report to OECD Workshop 17-20 September 1991.
2. Letter from Mercedes Bolanos de Moreno to The Pesticides Trust, 30/8/91.
3. OECD, *op. cit.*
4. Report in *Hoy*, 19/2/91.
5. Bollanos, M., in letter to The Pesticides Trust, 9/3/92.
6. *Hoy*, 5/1/91.
7. *El Universo*, 12/6/90, referring to an old study carried out in 1980 in the Pesticide Laboratories of the Plant Protection Programme, under the direction of Ing. Agr. Mercedes Bollanos, sponsored by Consejo Nacional de Ciencia y Tecnologia (CONACYT).
8. *El Comercio*, 2/6/91, referring to 1986 study by Ing. Agr. Mercedes Bollanos, M.Sc (MAG), Directora del Proyecto, 'Estudio de la contaminacion por plaguicides en alimentos basicos constituyentes de la dieta media Ecuatoriana', for Ministerio de Agricultura y Ganaderia (MAG), CONACYT, Quito.
9. 'Local authority residue testing on tropical products', *Pesticides News*, No. 13, October 1991.
10. *El Comercio*, 2/1/90.

8.   Country Report: Paraguay[*]

The present government came to power in a coup d'état in February 1989, and its agricultural strategy has been to consolidate previous policies, and to continue the process of modernisation begun in the 1960s. This means an emphasis on the export of primary agricultural products, in line with strategies of the bilateral and multilateral development agencies and the private international banking community. This has strengthened the position of the country's agro-industrial sector.

Rural workers, who were badly affected by the agricultural policies of the previous 30 years, believed the new government would respond to their demands for land, and this encouraged them to occupy private land. Landless rural workers generally occupy properties which are not being used for agriculture, forestry or livestock rearing: these properties were often wooded, and have proved productive once cleared. Officially, they are classified as unused land, and it is generally acknowledged that the State should be able to expropriate such properties and turn them over to landless rural workers. About 100,000 landless families live in rural areas, and there is no significant pool of public land the government can use for land grants to these families. Nor does the government have the financial resources to be able to buy land from private landowners.

In response to land redistribution, large landowners have sought to have their properties classified as 'productive', and have cleared it to prevent expropriation. This deforestation has happened all over the country, and since 1989 has reached an alarming rate of the order of 400,000 hectares annually.

[*]   Based on survey and report by Jorge Abbate of Alter Vida, 1991.

There have been many serious confrontations when aerial spraying contracted by cattle ranchers has contaminated smallholders land. The ranchers are only concerned with indiscriminate weed control, and in the process destroy cotton and food crops grown by the smallholders. This problem goes back to the 1970s, but one of the most grave cases to come to public attention occurred in the Zone of Guayaibi in 1990, when a rancher sprayed 2,4-D and almost totally destroyed cotton and food crops of 334 families on 200 hectares of land. By the end of 1991, compensation had still not been agreed.

National agricultural policy is centred on the export of two basic commodities, soya and cotton. The price of these products on the international market has fluctuated dramatically. Cotton-growing occupies a central place in the country's economy. It is one of Paraguay's highest-earning exports, and the area covered by the crop has increased considerably during the last eight years. According to statistics provided by the Paraguayan Central Bank, cotton and cotton products accounted for 32% of the income generated by the country's exports in 1989 and 30% in 1990.

Cotton is grown in most regions of the country and currently around 170,000 families depend on the crop for their living. This amounts to about one and a half million people out of a total population of approximately 4.2 million. An aggravating factor is that cotton, responsible for a third of the country's earnings, is going through a critical period because of the recent arrival in the country of the 'picudo' pest, *Antonomus grandis*. The country is preparing for a full-scale fight against this pest and aims to use the well-know method of applying massive quantities of insecticides. As the Minister of Agriculture has said, 'we had better get used to the idea that the picudo is here and we must learn how to fight it'.

Scale of pesticide use in Paraguay

In 1990, total reported imports of pesticides amounted to US$22.94 million, of which US$7.2 million were insecticides, US$6.8 million were herbicides, and the balance fungicides. Table 8.1 sets out the import of pesticides on the PIC, and candidate PIC list. Among the importing companies were Hoechst (carbofuran, 2,4-D, endosulfan, monocrotophos) and Shell (2,4-D, monocrotophos). Of all the imports in 1990, $18.8 million, or 82%, was for use on cotton production.

Two pesticides causing concern in Paraguay are 2,4-D, of which $64,154 was imported in 1990 from Argentina and USA, and picloran+2,4-D, with imports of US$2,195 from Panama. Other pesticides widely used in Paraguay, by 1990 figures, include:

Insecticides: acephate (US$1.3 million), carbaryl, cypermethrin, cyfluthrin, deltamethrin, fenpropathrin, fenvalerate; lambda-cyhalothrin.

The cotton crop was almost totally lost. The affected families have refused to take this matter lying down, and 300 came to the capital to protest. They want compensation of 600,000 Guaranies per hectare, 120 million in all, but the landowner is procrastinating and had not, at the time of these reports, paid anything. The families asked the Ministry to intervene.[14] Leaders of the Independent Peasant Organisation, (Organizacion Campesian Independients—OCI), which is supporting the people, said:

> We believe that this is a national problem. In the case of those affected by Sosa Gautier various attempts to talk to the Ministry of Agriculture have been made but so far they have not shown any interest in the problem.

Smallholders believe that diarrhoea suffered by many children was a direct consequence of the pesticides. The ranchers merely say that the herbicide used is not toxic. The Ministry recognises that cotton is very sensitive to this pesticide but says that 'experts' have told them it will not affect the yield.[15] The Ministry also said it was trying to intervene, but if nothing could be done the matter would have to go to the courts. Several months later, Ricardo Sosa Gautier offered 26 million Guaranies, which was rejected by the families, and member of parliament, Dr. Augusto Brun, has called for their support. The Ministry of Agriculture agreed to investigate again.

The peasants said this was not the first time they had been sprayed and their crops destroyed. They also pointed out that recently in the same region other agricultural companies have done the same thing and caused serious damage to families in Chore, Arroyo Moroti.

In a similar case, 112 people were affected when a company aerially sprayed its grazing land with herbicides. One spokesperson said 'The poisonous liquid spilled onto our cotton crop . . . It has caused illness to children and adults.' The smallholders lost between 50% and 100% of their cotton, manioc and tartago. The company concerned, Corina Campos y Hacienda S.A., offered 32 million Guaranies, which is regarded as risible by the smallholders.[16] In Republicano, 483 hectares and 176 farmers were affected by aerial spraying and 67.55 hectares of cotton was lost.[17]

This problem goes back to the 1970s. Smallholders point out that it is practically impossible to control drift because aerial spraying is carried out early in morning when it is very humid, as sun would evaporate the pesticide if it was done later. They believe the only solution is to halt all aerial spraying in the country, and that laws are urgently needed to defend peasant families and the environment.

Environment

There is no attempt by the authorities to monitor the environmental pollution caused by the use of pesticides in agriculture. The government sometimes responds when local communities denounce the problems caused by pesticides but it does not, generally, take things very far and the affected communities do not receive any kind of compensation.

However, there is evidence of environmental disturbance caused by pesticides. Many beneficial insects have disappeared and animals have been poisoned. Water has been contaminated causing the death of numbers of fish, etc. The lack of research on such phenomena means that these conclusions are based only on the evidence of people working in the cotton-growing areas.

Pesticide use in horticultural production

For the last year, Alter Vida has been carrying out research into the use of pesticides in the country's most important horticultural zone, in the Central Department, location of the capital Asuncion, the biggest consumer of horticultural produce. According to the medical toxicologist of the Tropical Medicine Institute Central Laboratory, which registers most poisonings in the country, this area is one of the worst.[18]

The interim results are detailed here. The research has not been easy to carry out, and Alter Vida has had to overcome many obstacles. In particular, it has been extremely difficult organising tests for pesticide residues in horticultural products because of the low level of concern, and the lack of laboratory facilities with the necessary equipment in both the public or private sector.

Ciba-Geigy donated a gas chromatograph to the National Agricultural Institute, in about 1989, so they could test the quality and purity of imported insecticides. The government transferred this chromatograph to the Veterinary Faculty for analysing chemical residues in meat destined for export. Alter Vida has tried on many occasions to gain access to the facilities of the chromatograph for this survey, but without success. Links have now been made with research organisations in neighbouring countries (Argentina) and samples may be analysed there.

The survey

There are 1419 households involved in a horticultural expansion project around Asuncion. A random sample of 121 was chosen for interview to ascertain details of the extent of pesticide use, practices and problems. These were from the districts of Luque, Cnia, Laurelty, Estanzuela, San Lorenzo, Itagua and Itagua Guazu. Of the 121, only seven use no chemical product, some because they know of the dangers involved, and some because the economics of pesticide use do not make sense, and they have no training in application methods.

Most of those applying pesticides were aged between 20 and 42, and of all those interviewed, only one woman was responsible for spraying, although three women (or female children) accompanied the applicator.

It appears that pesticide use has been increasingly rapidly, as most of the horticulturists in the survey, 58%, have been using pesticides for five years or less; 32% have been using them for 6-10 years, and 10% for 11-20 years. The majority, 83%, use pesticides to combat pests and diseases, while 67% use them for soil treatment and only a very small number, less than 1%, use pesticides against weeds. In all, 869 different products are used, of which 52% are insecticides or acaricides and 30% fungicides or antibiotics. Many of these pesticides are highly toxic with nearly 9% forming WHO Class I pesticides and nearly 20% Class II. The active ingredients most commonly applied are set out in Table 8.2 in order of importance.

The same active ingredients are sold under numerous labels, and as many as 49% of the formulations are mixed by local suppliers. Labels are not always those of the manufacturer. In the survey, 51% of labels on packaging were original, 42% were those of the supplier and 7% had no label at all.

Table 8.2 Pesticides most commonly used by horticulturalists in Paraguay.

Most used pesticides in order of importance	No. in sample	% using
mancozeb	—	—
copper oxychloride	—	—
methamidophos	50	53%
carbofuran	45	48%
sulphate of streptomycin+terramicin	—	—
thiophanate-methyl	—	—
methyl parathion	35	38%
aldrin	31	33%
cartap	—	—
profenofos + cypermethrin	—	—
monocrotophos	21	23%
endosulfan	15	16%
captafol	6	6%
dicofol	5	5%
methomyl	4	4%
phosphamidon	3	3%
demeton-s-methyl	3	3%
chloropicrin with methyl bromide	3	3%
lindane	2	2%

Source: Alter Vida survey.

Application

In the survey a number of questions were asked about safe use of pesticides, and a number of these are set out in Table 8.3. Generally, farmers spray their own plots, but around 26% would employ someone to spray for them. Many farmers, as many as 83%, use pesticides for prevention as well as when pests or diseases appear, although farmers sprayed by the calendar. Most farmers, about 90%, use a manual back-pack spray, which is prone to spillages when full. A small number, just under 3%, apply with a watering can.

Table 8.3. Health, safety and environmental hazards associated with spraying pesticides in horticultural production in Paraguay.

Clothes	Safety	Training	Location of homes	Mixing	Disposal
67% of farmers wear only partial clothing, and only bare feet or slip ons	5% smoke while spraying 2% chew 8% take *terere*	10% have no training 77% received training from experienced agricultural advisers	36% next to plot 21% near 38% far **Storage in relation to homes:** 26% store inside homes	38% mix product with water: directly in tank 56% mix in a separate container	41% leave on their plot. 39% bury 9% burn 24% dispose of containers in some other way: e.g. throw in streams, latrine/ sewers, ditch/ drainage channels
None of the sample wore gloves or masks The majority, 75%, always wash clothes after spraying, but 8% never do.	10% take other liquids 11% eat **Washing/ bath after spraying:** 73% always 1% often 14% at times 4% never	4% from supplier of pesticides 3% from agronomists, extension services	24% store attached to house 41% store near home 1% store far from homes 0.06% in mixed store	**Skin contact when mixing:** 53% always 4% often 30% at times 7% never	334 people who leave containers on the plots live next to the plot

Of those who keep pesticides and equipment inside their homes, many did not know the symptoms of pesticide poisoning. 'Inside home' meant not in any special storage place, and interviewees mentioned the kitchen, dining room, bedrooms or hallway. While all those interviewed kept pesticides in their original containers, there was less care taken with instruments used to mix pesticides, and 32% used any available instrument, which was then discarded.

Almost half the horticulturalists prepare pesticides near sources of water and, in addition, about one-quarter expose water sources to pesticides during spraying. The majority of back-pack sprayers and clothes are also washed in water sources.

Health

While only about half those interviewed, 54%, had a knowledge of poisoning symptoms, a very large number, 75%, of horticulturalists experienced some health problems after spraying. The most commonly identified were flu-like symptoms, 23%, followed by cold, cough, diarrhoea and fever. Other problems mentioned included headache, aching joints, stomach ache, respiratory problems, backache, 'parasitosis' (may be numbing of extremities) and kidney ache. Table 8.4 shows the number of sprayers experiencing certain symptoms, and whether this occurs frequently or occasionally. When ill, most people went to either the doctors surgery or a health centre. About 10% see to themselves. The most frequent treatment for poisoning symptoms is to take analgesics.

There have been 46 fatal cases of pesticide poisoning in the area in recent years, including suicides. Of those interviewed, 42% knew of fatal cases.

Table 8.4. Frequency of symptoms experienced during or after spraying.

Symptoms	Experienced always/often (%)	Experienced occasionally (%)
Headache	12	17
Dizziness	6	14
Sickness		5
Nausea	4	6
Trembling	1	4
Weakness	2	1
Abundant sweating	2	4
Blurred vision		5
Tightness in chest	2	5
Watering of eyes	1	6
Diarrhoea	2	4
Lack of appetite	1	1
General sense of malaise	1	1
Numbing of extremities		3
Pain in kidneys	4	10

Washing produce

This was one other area of concern, as water sources are used for washing clothes and equipment and many are contaminated during spraying. Over 66% of those interviewed also wash their produce in the same water sources, risking contamination from pesticides.

Tropical Medicine Institute Central Laboratory treats both consumers and workers poisoned by pesticides. Dr. Nidia de Mendoza of the Institute says 'poisoned people come in all the time', and she is concerned about the numbers of cases arising from consumption of horticultural products grown above ground, such as tomatoes, cabbage, lettuce.[19]

Legislation and regulation

Pesticide legislation is in hand, and the Direccion de Defensa Vegetal (DDV), the crop protection department of the Ministry of Agriculture and Livestock, was requested to present to Parliament a proposal for a Phytosanitary Protection Law, following a Special Commission set up to draft the law established by Ministerial Resolution No. 599 of 29 November 1990.

One concern of NGOs in Paraguay has been that the Ministry of Health has not been involved in drafting this law, and this has left a gap that other official bodies have not the competence or infrastructure to fill. Further, the draft law has not cited the International Code of Conduct for the Distribution and Use of Pesticides.

Until this law is implemented, the use of pesticides in Paraguay is not regulated at all. The DDV is the only body that records the use of pesticides. The DDV inspects samples of the chemicals, but there is no attempt at a chromatographic analysis of products and there is no kind of quality control.

There is thus no control over the quality of the products imported or formulated in the country. A comparison of product names and active ingredients of pesticides inspected by the DDV between April and December 1990[20] and of pesticides manufactured by BASF marketed by Paraguayan companies, illustrates the difficulty of relying on statistics in Paraguay. Only two of the 10 herbicides listed by BASF have been inspected by the DDV. Some of the active ingredients not inspected were: dalapon, tridemorph, chlormequat, vinclozolin, cycloxydim and mecoprop (dichlorpropane).

The draft Phytosanitary Protection Law, which would provide the basis for any implementation of the Prior Informed Consent procedure, covers pesticides bans under Article 34 in Chapter IV. This says:

> The DDV prohibits the import, manufacture and/or sale in this country of substances and products used on agricultural crops, such as pesticides, fertilisers or others used to fight pests and diseases, and equipment for the application of such substances, when they have not been officially registered and/or have been banned in the country of origin or have been banned by other competent national and international organisations because of their harmful effects on the crops, people, animals or the environment or because they may cause crops to become resistant to treatments applied at a later date or because they may cause obstacles to the sale of the treated crops.

On 18 July 1991, Alter Vida interviewed the DDV about the operation of PIC in Paraguay. At that time, Paraguay had not appointed a Designated National Authority to operate PIC, and as the DDV will present to Parliament the draft law on phytosanitary protection, including a regulatory code for the use of pesticides, it was the most representative institution to discuss implementation of PIC. The DDV is considering not allowing the import of any pesticide on the PIC list. However at present, there is no control over the quality of imported products, and no bans on their import. Nor are there restrictions on the formulation, mixing, distribution, marketing and use of any kind of pesticide for any crop. The Ministry of Health's National Malaria Eradication Service (SENEPA), uses massive amounts of pesticides that are among the Dirty Dozen or that are on the PIC list including, for example, DDT.[21]

There have been calls on the government to tighten up the laws relating to pesticides to protect both the agricultural worker and the consumer. Dr. Victor Duarte Pistilli,[22] specialist in occupational health and pesticides, pointed out that lack of legislation on exposure levels should be addressed by a multi-disciplinary team at both national and community levels. He believes the only solution is to begin systematic analysis, to set tolerance limits, and to introduce sanctions against offenders.

Corporate work in Paraguay

There are many links between private industry and the country's university and research centres, which create a climate for promoting pesticides rather than non-chemical methods of control of pests and diseases.

For example, Ciba-Geigy, has links with the only Agricultural Research Centre, working with the Ministry of Agriculture. The company holds courses and seminars in some of the agricultural schools in the interior. The company was recently invited by an agricultural school to hold a series of talks on the use of chemicals in agriculture. This school, located in Coronel Oviedo in the centre of the Eastern Region, is very important at a local level and attracts a regular flow of students, mainly farmers, from all over the country. It offers the qualification of Technical Agronomist. Although it was founded by the Silesian Fathers of Paraguay, it currently receives significant economic support from the United States' Agency for International Development (USAID).

A Shell pesticide sales representative, Dr. Bruno Banks, has expressed concern about the extent of poisoning in parts of the country, presumably commenting on the cases of monocrotophos poisoning and paralysis, as Shell is a major manufacturer of this active ingredient.[23] He believes these result from incorrect use of pesticides by farmers. Dr. Banks said that the incorrect use of chemical products in the treatment of cotton seeds by the Cotton and Tobacco Inspection Office (Oficina de Fiscalizacion del Algodon y el Tabaco) results in the need to make at least two additional applications of organophosphorus pesticides during the cotton period. Shell was about to launch an educational video showing the correct pesticide application methods for use by its sales representatives.

More appropriate than educational videos would be research and development into appropriate integrated pest management and alternative methods of pest control. There is little evidence of support for alternatives from the Ministry of Agriculture, which actively promotes the use of many pesticides. For example, the Ministry recommends systematic pesticide application for up to 40 days after planting cotton to forestall infestation by thrips. It is very common to find the Ministry giving such advice for all the stages of development of the crop and for all kinds of pests. This is in spite of the fact that this strategy is not proven to work.

In Paraguay, there are many instances where a close connection exists between government and the pesticide industry. There are, for example, at least five cases where professors, or highly qualified academics in agricultural departments of universities, also work for, or have an interest in, pesticide companies. One Minister of Agriculture was a shareholder in Ciba-Geigy, one of the market leaders in Paraguay, and the Minister maintains ties with the company, although the extent of these are not clear.

Conclusion

The Paraguay report provides well-documented material on issues which are sometimes difficult to substantiate. The incidence of monocrotophos poisoning, which have resulted in paralysis in a significant number of children in the country, is horrifying. These cases would never have been established if a polio eradication programme was not operating in the area. Unfortunately the incidents, which arose during cotton spraying, have not led to a change of policy in the government. With fears of the arrival of a cotton pest new to Paraguay, the 'picudo' or bollworm, the country was preparing for a full-scale pesticide war against infestation.

A survey conducted by Alter Vida of pesticide use by smallholders around the capital of Paraguay provides particular insights to problems of small farmers, even when a large number, 77%, said they had received some training in pesticide use from agricultural advisors.

Spray drift is a problem where small farmers are surrounded by large land-owners. The disregard of smallholders' rights, and failure to act to protect their crops and award compensation, is a political issue as much as a technical one of establishing and enforcing standards for aerial spraying. There are strong ties between industry and the academic research establishment and some ties between industry and government.

References:
1. Figures are supplied by Oficina Consultiva de Investigacion Tecnica (OCIT), the Technical Research Office, which is a private company. Its sources are customs records. The government records of imports are kept by the Direccion de Defensa Vegetal (DDV), an agency of the Ministry of Agriculture, which also uses official statistics. Their import figures are similar.
2. *Ibid.*
3. Interview carried out by Alter Vida.
4. 'Insecticide causes paralysis', *ABC*, 26/3/91.
5. 'Insecticides responsible for paralysis', *ABC*, 20/4/91.
6. *Ultima Hora*, 16/1/90.

7. Press report, 19/2/90.
8. *Noticias*, 30/3/91.
9. *Noticias*, 30/1/91.
10. *Ultima Hora*, 1/4/91.
11. Press reports, 13/6/91.
12. *ABC*, 6/9/91.
13. *Ultima Hora*, 29/1/89.
14. Press reports, 22/3/90.
15. Press reports in January 1990.
16. *Ultima Hora*, 17/3/90, 22/3/90, 26/3/90.
17. *ABC*, 31/1/90.
18. See Chapters 3 and 4.
19. *ABC*, 8/5/91.
20. Annexes 10 and 11 of report by Alter Vida.
21. Alter Vida, interview conducted with the Crop Protection Department (Direccion de Defensa Vegetal—DDV) of the Ministry of Agriculture and Livestock.
22. 'The country needs laws to protect against pesticides: Unjustified use of chemicals on the land', *ABC*, 9/5/91.
23. Abbate, J., Interview with Dr. Bruno B. Guggiari Banks, Shell pesticide sales representative, 1991.

9.   Country Report: Venezuela*

Introduction

Venezuela, like other countries, suffers from the improper use of pesticides. The major problems are lack of guidance and training for users; availability of hazardous pesticides; lack of regulation of the distribution and use of pesticides; insufficient research into related health and environmental problems. Increasingly, people are aware of the seriousness of these problems and this has led to a search for solutions.

Scale of pesticide use in Venezuela

There are 538 pesticides with a total of 243 active ingredients registered by 40 companies at the Venezuelan Ministry of Health and Social Welfare. Of the active ingredients, 33% are insecticides, 30% are herbicides, 25% are fungicides, and the remainder are rodenticides, growth regulators, with a small proportion of others such as nematicides and molluscicides.[1] Of the pesticides on sale, over 26% are registered as highly to extremely toxic by the Venezuelan Ministry of Agriculture, as shown in Table 9.1. In this report, the term 'highly toxic' includes both these categories.

Table 9.1   Toxicological classification of pesticides according to Venezuelan legislation.

	Class	LD50 (mg/kg)*
Extremely toxic	(E)	1-100
Highly toxic	(A)	101-250
Moderately toxic	(M)	251-1,400
Mildly toxic	(L)	1,400+

* Milligrams per kilogram. of bodyweight required to kill 50% of test animals.
Source: Ministry of Agriculture, Crop Health Department, requests for import licences, 1989.

---

* This report is based on material provided by Porfiria Mendoza de Linares, Project Co-ordinator, CIDELO, Lara, Venezuela, May 1991.

Import of highly toxic pesticides

The Ministry of Health granted import licences in 1989 for 5.8 million kilograms or litres of active ingredients. However the real figure is much higher as pesticides are smuggled into the country. Of these, just over 43%, a total of 2.5 kilograms or litres, fell into the category of highly toxic. In addition, a further 9.3 million of kilograms or litres of formulated products were granted import licences, and 2.2% of these were in the highly toxic categories. Table 9.2 sets out the pesticides classified in Venezuela as highly toxic, which were imported in 1989, together with their country of origin.

Many of the major agrochemical corporations operate in Venezuela.[2] Those whose registered products are classified as acutely toxic include: BASF Venezolana SA, Bayer de Venezuela, Ciba-Geigy, Rhône Poulenc de Venezuela SA, Cyanamid, DuPont, Eli-Lilly, Hoechst Remedia, ICI de Venezuela SA Inica, Roussel de Venezuela, Shell, Tecnica Petroquimica de Venezuela (DowElanco CA). Bayer and Shell operate a joint venture known as Plant-Agro. Companies with registered products which do not fall into the acutely toxic categories include: Monsanto de Venezuela C.A., Sandoz, Quimica Schering Ag. de Venezuela.

Pesticide smuggling

Large quantities of banned pesticides, particularly organochlorines, are smuggled into the country: they use names of other registered products and often have lower concentrations of active ingredients. The trade association (AFAQUIMA), to which companies with registered products belong, is concerned about contraband dealings, and has emphasised that, for products sold by its members, it can provide technical and scientific information and assistance. AFAQUIMA has called on government assistance to eliminate this trade, 'to avoid damaging the health of farmers.'[3] The government believes many of the smuggled products are banned in the rest of the world, and has indicated it will undertake a joint programme, with the National Guard, seeking to control and monitor this trade.[4] However, there has been discussion in the government about deregulating pesticide imports, a move which it is feared will increase the number of hazardous imports.[5]

Impact of pesticides on health

During the period 1980-88, 10,309 cases of pesticide poisonings were reported to the Ministry of Health. Of these, 5.6% resulted in death. Perhaps more worrying is the fact that these numbers increased throughout the 1980s, from 975 in 1980, to 1,553 in 1988, as set out in Table 9.3.[6] These are only the reported cases, and it is possible that records have improved during this period. However, it is impossible to determine the true picture because many people do not seek medical help, feeling the incident does not warrant reporting. In other cases, medical attention is not available. Cases dealt with in the private sector are not always reported.

Table 9.2 Highly toxic pesticides imported into Venezuela in 1989.

Pesticide	A*	B**	Quantity kg/ltrs a.i.	Country of Export
Classified as Highly toxic in Venezuela:				
azocyclotin	E		16,000	Germany
brodifacoum	E		172,000	UK
carbaryl	E		150,000	US, France, Germany, Japan
chlorpyrifos	A	-	13,739	US
chlorpyrifos+xylene	A	-	490,215	US, Argentina
copper oxychloride	E		110,480	Chile, Spain
diazinon	A		80,680	Switzerland
dimethoate	A		95,580	Germany
edifenphos	E	Ib	25,000	Japan
fenitrothion	A		100,000	Japan, US, Spain
phorate	E	Ia	120,000	Brazil
thiodicarb	E	Ib	90,000	US, Germany
triazophos	E	Ib	30,000	Germany
trichlorfon	E		175,000	Spain, Mexico
PIC or potential PIC pesticides				
aluminium phosphide	E		10,000	Brazil
carbofuran	E	Ib	200,000	US
demeton-S-methyl		Ib	100,000	UK, US
methamidophos	E	Ib	250,000	US, Germany
methomyl	E	Ib	100,018	US
parathion methyl	E	Ia	395,000	Denmark (70%), US, UK

* A=Hazard classification in Venezuela. (E=Extremely toxic, A=Highly toxic)
** B=WHO classification by toxicity.
Source: Ministry of Agriculture, Department of Plant Health, Venezuela, 1989.

More than 40% of reported poisonings are caused by organophosphates or carbamates. Gramoxone (paraquat) was responsible for most deaths—nearly 60%—followed by organophosphates, mainly parathion, which caused nearly 30%. The remainder of deaths were attributable to other organophosphates.

No published systematic research exists on chronic illness caused by pesticides poisoning in the country. A doctor working in Calabozo, Guarico State, claims there is evidence to suggest that pesticide poisoning has caused birth defects and other health problems to local people. The results of his work are set out in Table 9.4.

Table 9.3 Cases of pesticide poisoning of humans in Venezuela, 1980-88.

Year	Cases	Deaths
1980	975	66
1981	842	71
1982	1,332	65
1983	699	50
1984	966	75
1985	1,268	68
1986	1,263	60
1987	1,411	73
1988	1,553	48
1989	-	52
1990	-	92
Total	**10,309**	**576**

Source: Ramirez, M. *Toxicologia de los Plaguicidas Epidemiological* bulletins, Ministry of Health, 1989.

Pesticide poisonings accounted for 21% of all poisoning cases in the Centre West Region of Venezuela, which includes the States of Lara, Portuguesa, Yaracuy and Falcon. Out of a total of 117 deaths from poisoning in this region, 74, or 63%, were caused by pesticides. The highest number of deaths occur in the Zulia and Mérida regions, where the trade in contraband pesticides is highest.[7] The cause of poisoning is rarely noted. Examples of cases reported in the press include:

- November 1990: more than 80 workers were poisoned at the office block Centro Simon Bolivar, Central Park, when their offices were fumigated by an unlicensed firm using insecticides banned in Venezuela. Jose Felipe Aranguren, Director of Malariaology and Public Health at the Ministry of Health ordered an exhaustive investigation into companies engaged in domestic and workplace pest control.

- Pesticides used to combat malaria, chagas disease and others, show an average of 23 cases of poisoning per week.[8]

- February 1991: Richard Chavier Morillo, aged 18, was spraying crops when he collapsed and died minutes after being admitted to hospital.[9]

Cases of chronic pesticide poisoning amongst users are more difficult to trace. However one study of agricultural workers in the Andes zone found high levels of organochlorine pesticides in the workers. Some of the group also had very low levels of cholinesterase, possibly caused by exposure to organophosphate and carbamate pesticides.[10]

Table 9.4 Pesticide poisonings in the Centre West Region, 1985-90

Year	No. of cases	% of total poisonings	No. died	% of total deaths
1985	179	26.5	12	70.6
1986	188	22.4	13	72.2
1987	228	20.3	12	60.0
1988	254	21.9	15	62.5
1989	212	20.3	12	57.1
1990	174	16.6	10	58.8
Total	1,235	21.0	74	63.3

Source: Compiled by CIDELO from statistics listed in monthly bulletins on poisonings produced by the Centre West Region Toxicology Centre.

Pesticides and the environment

The environmental impact of pesticide use in Venezuela, while not consistently monitored, appears severe. Reports of polluted water and land are frequent, at times affecting drinking water and food. This goes back decades. For example, studies in the 1970s in Lara State showed excessive and indiscriminate use of pesticides in the Quíbor Valley seriously damaged the region's ecology and contaminated horticultural produce with substances such as endrin.

The head of Lara State's Agricultural Development Department announced the intention to carry out new studies in the Quíbor Valley. In April 1991, a Regional Pesticides Committee was appointed to look into the local situation. It is presumed that the Dos Cerritos reservoir is still polluted by pesticides used on the surrounding vegetable and sugar cane crops, and water and plankton sampling is underway. Many fish have died in the reservoir, which supplies drinking water to three towns: El Tocuyo, Quíbor and Barquisimeto, with a total of 1.5 million inhabitants.[11] The survey will include testing of cholinesterase in blood levels. It is intended that the health and environmental information will form the basis for an educational programme aimed at promoting the rational use of chemical products.[12]

The Regional Pesticides Commission and the Commission for Environmental Control and Quality propose environmental control in the Quíbor Valley including the supervision and control of pesticides use. Proposals include control on pesticide use through, for example integrated pest management, particularly on tomatoes.

State officials have supported polluters in Lara State. For example, in the municipality of Torres, a dairy company, Omey, owned by Onésimo Viloria, had been contaminating water supplies with animal faeces and chemicals, making water which supplies Jabón and San Pedro unfit for human consumption. In a press release, José Luis Montero, Director of the

Ministry of the Environment and Natural Resources, openly supported the company, stating its innocence.[13] The next day the company was found guilty in court.[14]

Organochlorine insecticides have caused soil and crop pollution in the River Guárico water basin. Research carried out by Fernando R. Saume at the Chemical and Technology Institute, Faculty of Agronomy, Central University of Venezuela, showed that 46% of samples analysed contained DDT and/or its metabolites; 26% contained dieldrin; and 2% contained aldrin.[15]

The indiscriminate use of pesticides in the state of Portuguesa has caused major disturbances to the region's ecology. The result has been a big increase in the number of rats and a corresponding increase in the damage caused by the rodent population to crops and humans. Since September of last year, the area of Guanarito in Portuguesa has witnessed the outbreak of a disease caused by an unknown virus carried by rats, similar to Asian lasa fever.[16] The 74 identified cases have resulted in 27 deaths.

In Guárico, parathion is used in the paddy fields to kill birds. Professor Luis Gonzalo Morales, a researcher at the Tropical Zoological Institute of the Central University of Venezuela, has studied pesticide residues in birds, and egg samples sent to the Bodega Bay Institute, Berkeley, California contained residues of DDT, DDE, mirex, endrin and chlordane. No studies have been carried out to show the extent of contamination of cereals like rice where parathion is used.[17]

Residues in food

In April 1991, there were increasing reports of pesticide residues in vegetables, grains, flours, pastas and drinking water in certain regions of the country. Concern has centred particularly on the country's cereal-growing zone, in Portuguesa state, where pesticides are extensively used. Research carried out by the State Experimental Agricultural Production Research Centre (CIEPE) found that samples of wheat flour, pasta and celery were contaminated with malathion and dithiocarbamate pesticides residues.[18,19]

The research, by Wojciech Draminski and Maria Gonzalez, two scientists from CIEPE's Food Analysis Department, concluded that while pesticide concentrations in general were not yet dangerous, the situation could deteriorate: 63% of wheat flour samples they tested contained pesticides, generally malathion and dithiocarbamates. In the Andes zone they found pesticide contamination in the environment, and residues in food.

They point out that agricultural workers do not use pesticides properly, mixing different pesticides to form a potion which they call a 'bomb'. Intervals between spraying are not respected and wastes are not dealt with properly. This research found celery had concentrations of dithiocarbamate fungicides five times higher than the maximum permitted level, although this was the only vegetable examined with dangerous levels.

All samples of a vegetable known locally as caraotas negras were contaminated with organochlorine pesticides, though this was from an unrepresentative sample as the items were taken from the same place at the same time. Among samples of flour, again not completely representative, 80% were contaminated. Gonzalez explained that fungicides are probably added during processing stages. The researchers recommended further tests.

Advertising and promotion

In 1991, CIDELO, a non-governmental organisation in Venezuela, collected a number of promotional materials distributed by the companies involved in the sale and distribution of pesticides at that time. These were examined by them in the light of the advertising laws of Venezuela, rather than the guidelines laid down by the FAO Code. The pesticides examined were methomyl, under the trade names Lannate and Methavin, aldicarb, under the trade name Temik, and paraquat, under the trade name Gramoxone.

Methomyl: This carbamate pesticide is widely used in Venezuela, which consumed 100 tonnes in 1989. It is classified in the country as extremely hazardous and is a WHO Class Ib pesticide. Concern over its use, particularly over conditions operating in developing countries, has made it a potential PIC pesticide. Methomyl is a cholinesterase inhibitor. Levels have been detected five days after spraying on barley, and up to seven days after treatments on wheat.[20] Two of the methomyl products in Venezuela are Lannate-L, Du Pont, and Methavin, BASF.

Methomyl—Lannate-L: The promotional material implies this product is perfectly safe: 'The extreme toxicity acts instantaneously on many insects either by contact or ingestion'; 'Lannate-L leaves no residues. The rapid disappearance of Lannate-L allows it to be used until just before harvest time. It will produce a good crop without leaving prejudicial residues.' The instructions refer to the use of the product on habichuela (kidney beans), a term not used in Venezuela. The literature does not warn that methomyl is dangerous to humans.

Methomyl—Methavin: The BASF literature on Methavin compares its action favourably to other pesticides such as methamidophos and monocrotophos, although all three are PIC candidates. There is no proper warning of the toxicity in the literature. Misleading statements are made about its efficiency. Methavin is said to have special characteristics that provide technicians and farmers with solutions to the management of pests. The material says: 'Powerful action against pests, even those resistant to pesticides'. It is claimed that the product: 'quickly disappears from the environment, allowing beneficial insects to re-establish themselves'. It is a 'wide spectrum pesticide that leaves no residues capable of affecting human or animal health'. It 'does not affect the plant's health' and it is 'economical to use'.

Aldicarb: The promotional material for Temik 106 does not draw attention to the extreme toxicity of the product. It gives only routine guidelines for pesticide use.

Paraquat: Although this product is highly toxic, the leaflet accompanying Gramoxone does not mention this, nor does it set out precautions for safe use.

These examples are not unique. In most of the literature that accompanies pesticides, there are generally neither appropriate directions for safe use nor warning symbols. The FAO Guidelines indicate that pesticides should be sold separately from foodstuffs. However, in Venezuela they are often stored together in supermarkets. Dr. Raúl Silvestri of the Faculty of Veterinary Sciences at the Central University of Venezuela has warned about this and pointed out the need for separation.[21]

Corporate influence

The Association of Chemical and Agricultural Products Manufacturers has been concerned about sales of illegally imported pesticides. However, as these imports also threaten the companies' economic interests, it is not clear whether the advertisements are motivated by cheaper competition, or by concern for the safety and protection of the crops, environment or human health.

In Portuguesa, CIEPE approached ICI Venezuela for funds to carry out research into pesticides in soil, water and cereal crops, following concern about the levels of pollution. The company rejected the application saying that there was no pesticide pollution in the state. It offered no data to back up its opinion.[22]

Although Venezuelan law requires manufacturers and distributors of pesticides to provide monthly production and sales figures to the Ministry of Agriculture, companies do not normally publish figures about the production and sale of their pesticides, arguing these figures would be useful for their competitors and would prejudice their sales.

Under Venezuelan law, highly toxic pesticides can only be sold if prescribed by a qualified agronomist. However, a representative of CIDELO had no difficulty buying pesticides regarded as highly hazardous from a distributor. The invoice prints a message that the purchaser has been warned of the dangers of using the product. No attempt was made to give guidance on how to use the product or on safety precautions.[23]

Conclusion

Venezuela uses a large range of highly toxic pesticides, and concern in the country is increasing. However there is still little testing or monitoring. Although environmental testing of highly polluted areas such as the Quíbor

Valley have begun, there is little sign of government support for integrated pest management, or sustainable alternatives.

References:
1. Pesticides registered at the Venezuelan Ministry of Health & Social Welfare 1989.
2. Ministry of Health Venezuela, 1989.
3. *El Impulso*, 16/5/91.
4. Galeo, Bonerge, head of the Agricultural Development Division in the State of Lara, quoted in *El Impulso*, Barquisimeto, 3/5/91.
5. 'Unregulated import of pesticides: a public health drama', *El Universal*, 18/3/91.
6. Ramirez, M. 'Toxicologia de los plaguicidas' Epidemiological bulletins, Ministry of Health, 1989.
7. *El Universal*, 18/3/91, *op. cit.*
8. *El Nacional*, 15/11/90, .
9. 'Fumigation companies investigated', *Ultima Hora*, 27/2/91.
10. *Contamination of Andes zone, organochlorinated pesticides and cholinesterase level in the blood.* [Translation as in source], in Acta Cientifica Venezolana, XL Annual Convention, ASOVAC, UDO, Vol. 41, 18-23 November, 1990.
11. 'You can't drink this water', *El Impulso*, 2/3/91.
12. 'Perishable products to be tested to determine extent of contamination', *El Impulso*, Barquisimeto, 3/5/91.
13. Minister for the Environment and Natural Resources, Press release dated 16/5/91.
14. 'Agricultural Court finds dairy company guilty of polluting water supply', *El Impulso*, 17/5/91.
15. Saume, R.F., 'Estudio prelimina sobre la contaminacion de suelos y cultivos con residuos de insecticidas organoclorados en la zona de influencia del sistema de riego "Rio Guarico"', Instituto de Quimica y tecnologia, Facultad de Agronomia, Universidad Central de Venezuela, Maracay, Edo, Aragua, SVIA, XI Jornadas Agronomicas, maracaibo 1984. Trabajo No. PV-35.
16. 'United States virologists visit the area in Portuguesa State affected by fever', *El Impulso*, 3/5/91.
17. 'Death lies in wait in the rice growing fields', *El Universal*, 27/2/91. .
18. Gonzalez, M., Draminski, W., 'Analisis de aflatoxenas y plaguicidas en harinos y pastas', Acta Cientifica Venezolana XL Convencia anual, ASOVAC, UDO, Vol. 41, 18-23 November 1990.
19. Draminski, W. and Gonzalez, M., of CIEPE's Food Analysis Department, research shows contamination of flours and pastas by pesticides, reported in *El Universal*, 7/4/91.
20. WHO/FAO Data sheets on pesticides No. 55, Methomyl, WHO, Geneva, 1982.
21. *Agropecuária Hoy*, Vol. 1, April 1980, p. 28 (Annexe 22 of report).
22. Personal conversation with Dr. Maria Gonzales, Co-ordinator of CIEPE's biochemistry laboratories in her office on 8 May 1991.
23. Receipts from three distributors, Serviagro Tocuyo CA, of 1 September 1989, and Asociacion Cooperativa Agropecuária de Servicios Multiples, Florencio Jimenez, of 1 September 1989 both in Lara State, and Agricola Tanausu CA, of 3 May 1989 of Aragua State.

10. Country Report: Egypt*

Introduction

More than 17,000 tonnes of formulated pesticides are imported annually to Egypt. More than 70% are insecticides used to control pests in cotton, which is the main Egyptian cash crop. However in recent years, intensive fruit and vegetable production has also attracted large pesticide inputs. More than 75% of pesticides are applied by aerial spraying. Health and environmental effects are inadequately monitored, even though a large number of hazardous pesticides are used.

According to recent government agricultural development plans, it appears that agricultural production will continue to intensify.[1] Many Egyptian researchers are concerned about the scale of pesticide use in the country. In proposing ways to reduce use researchers advocate, for example, more mechanical controls, better analysis of the level of insect infestation to determine whether spraying is economic, use of sex pheromones and increased support for integrated pest management.

Scale of pesticide use in Egypt

Between 1952 and 1989, nearly 700,000 tonnes of pesticides were injected into the environment, largely targeted to control cotton pests. The annual cost of these imports is high, and has risen every year but two since 1977. In 1989, the total expenditure on pesticides was US$105.48 million (see Table 10.1). Until 1973, organochlorines were the main pesticide used, but fears about their persistence in the environment brought a switch to organophosphates, which now constitute an average of about 20% of annual pesticide use. Since 1986, there has been growth in the use of synthetic pyrethroids, but these account for only about 2% of overall use (table 10.2).

* This report is based on research provided by Dr. El Sebae, prepared for the Pesticides Action Network/The Pesticides Trust, May-July 1991. Additional material is by Prof. AA Abdel-Gawaad, Professor of Environmental Pollution, Secretary of the National Society of Environmental Protection, and General Secretary of the Egyptian Society of Toxicology, from *Ecotoxicological Impact of Organophosphorus Pesticides in Egypt*, report prepared for Greenpeace International for submission as evidence to the Barcelona Convention.

Table 10.1   Cost of pesticide imports, 1977-89.

Year	Budget ($ million)		
	Public Sector	Private Sector	Annual Total
1977	$64.70	$1.3	$66.00
1978	59.34	3.45	62.79
1979	64.88	3.8	68.68
1980	73.67	4.3	77.97
1981	83.46	4.5	87.96
1982	72.18	5.8	77.98
1983	73.56	6.7	80.26
1984	75.36	7.2	82.56
1985	76.49	8.4	84.89
1986	74.41	18.1	92.81
1987	76.34	23.6	99.94
1988	74.24	26.2	100.44
1989	77.18	28.3	105.48

Source: Figures supplied by Dr. El Sebae.

Table 10.2   Quantities of pesticides used in Egypt since 1952.

Season	Total Quantity (Tonnes)	OPs* (Tonnes)	OPs* %	Pyreth-roids (Tonnes)	Pyreth-roids %
1952/53	2,143				
1957/58	8,075				
1962/63	12,550				
1967/68	28,914				
1972/73	20,910				
1977/78	28,340				
1982/83	12,786				
1983/84	15,462				
1984/85	9,516	5383.9	56.6	111.5	1.2%
1985/86	10,446	2109.7	20.1	130.5	1.3%
1986/87	17,211	4636.6	26.9	197.0	1.1%
1987/88	21,790	2723.3	12.5	263.3	.9%
1988/89	14,070	2639.3	18.7	279.2	2.0%
Total	**690,540**				

* Organophosphate insecticides.

Source: Figures supplied by Professor AA Abdel-Gawaad.

The majority of Egypt's pesticide imports originate in Europe, particularly the United Kingdom (ICI), which sold on average £13.5 million of pesticides a year to Egypt between 1987 and 1990, although this figure has dropped in recent years to £4.67 million in 1990 and £4.77 million in 1991.[2] Other major European suppliers are Germany (Bayer) and Switzerland (Ciba Geigy). The United States and Japan are important suppliers, with products particularly from DowElanco and Sumitomo respectively.

Egypt does not have any significant pesticide industry, although it has capacity to manufacture about 10% of its annual consumption of dimethoate and malathion. This capacity was established in the early 1980s with help from the United Nations Industrial Development Organisation, using second-hand equipment bought from an Italian company for $US10 million. Insecticides produced in 1989-90 were valued at $21 million.[3]

However, at current international prices, the cost of the locally formulated product is higher than the cost of importing it ready formulated from abroad. In addition, a small but increasing proportion of pesticides is imported as technical active ingredient, for local formulation: between 1984 and 1988 this increased steadily, as shown in Table 10.3. Of the five formulation plants, two are government-owned and three are private, with the latter all part-owned by a multinational. Under Egyptian law the majority shareholding must be held through a local business.

Table 10.3 Annual formulation and production in Egypt— (metric tonnes)

Year	Total annual formulation	Annual production dimethoate	Annual production malathion
1984	6,824		
1985	1,945		
1986	15,779	80	100
1987	15,791	120	170
1988	16,719	130	180
1989	N/A	140	185
1990	N/A	140	189

Source: Figures supplied by Professor AA Abdel-Gawaad.

Health impact

There is surprisingly little work in Egypt on the health impact of pesticides, given the scale of use of organophosphorus and other pesticides hazardous to health, and potential for exposure. Pesticides on the PIC list are widely used, in particular chlordane and paraquat. DDT is still used for public health purposes, for example as a larvicide in Aswan lake. A larger number of PIC candidates are still widely used. These are aldicarb, amitrole, carbofuran, dichlorvos, dicofol, endosulfan, methamidophos, methomyl, methyl bromide, monocrotophos and phosphine (aluminium phosphide). In addition, nitrofen, a pesticide thought to be no longer in use, has been used until recently and may still be in use. Interestingly, some of the more hazardous pesticides, particularly parathion and methyl parathion in general use elsewhere, have not been used in Egypt for the last five years.

About 1.26 million workers are potentially exposed yearly to pesticides during aerial application, either through working as spray operators, or as workers in the sprayed field. No data is available on exposure under field conditions, yet it is known that the application of hazardous organophosphorus pesticides is high.

A study of 1,154 patients admitted to Tanta University with acute poisoning during 1988 showed that one-third had been poisoned with insecticides. In general, amongst poisoning cases admitted to hospitals, a high proportion are attempted suicides. More chronic cases of pesticide exposure are not picked up through such hospital sources.

In the summer of 1990, the Ministry of Irrigation treated an outbreak of water hyacinth in the River Nile and its irrigation branches with the herbicides acrolein and ametyrene as aquatic weed herbicides. This was applied in a large-scale aerial application programme. A large number of fish died, people were hospitalised, and drinking water was polluted. The incident was criticised in the newspapers and in Parliament. The Minister of Irrigation promised to rationalise the use of aquatic herbicides.[4]

Cancer increases

In Egypt, cancer deaths were recorded for the first time in 1964, which is almost eight years after the start of excessive use of pesticides. However, the cancer death rate has increased steadily, and increases have been greatest in governorates where pesticides are widely used. The death rate from cancer is also higher among villagers than town dwellers in the same governorate, which could indicate higher death rates among those occupationally exposed to pesticides. This could be reinforced by the fact that the cancer death rate was higher among males than females—however male villagers are also more exposed to bilharzia, and there is a relationship between this disease and bladder cancer.[5]

Exposure in formulation plants

Some information is available on workers in formulation plants.[6] A health survey and biological monitoring on 100 workers whose job involved packing organophosphorus, carbamate and synthetic pyrethroids, indicated that workers displayed prominent signs of a range of pesticide-related symptoms, including nervousness and irritability, polyneuropathy, dyspepsia and bronchial problems.

Environmental impact

Water pollution

The major environmental impacts arise from the continuous aerial spraying on cotton, covering about 1-1.2 million feddan a year. Because of the special canal irrigation system in Egypt, all the water sources—which include the Nile River, canals, ponds and the water table—are polluted. Apart from direct aerial spraying, pollution is caused by leaching of pesticide residues, washing hands, bodies and pesticide containers. Organophosphorus pesticides detected in underground and surface water varied between 3 ppb and 19 ppb, depending on the type of water source and the time of spraying. Higher concentrations are found in canals and branch canals which are directly sprayed; lower rates in Nile River water; and traces in underground water.

In some areas, pesticides as well as other toxic pollutants, have had an impact on fish production, which has declined particularly in Lake Karoon, Lake Manzallah, Lake Mariut and Lake Burullus. First identified in 1986, the losses are increasing.

Insect resistance

Methomyl and methamidophos are both sprayed aerially on cotton. The massive use of these and other products has helped build up resistance in the pink bollworm, white fly and aphids and as a result cotton yields have deteriorated.

Soil fauna

A number of local studies have examined the side effects of organophosphates on soil fauna, and identified some pesticides which have reduced natural enemies of pests, and affected soil fertility. The studies concluded:

• Triazophos, dimethoate and profenofos decreased the total number of natural enemies of pests; triazophos and dimethoate completely eradicated predaceous mites after a few weeks.
• Chlorpyrifos had a slight impact on soil fertility.
• Triazophos inhibited nodulation in broad beans, dimethoate and profenofos decreased nodulation in cowpeas.

Poor storage

Poor storage has led to the deterioration of some active ingredients and their formulations. In some cases this reduces efficiency, and in others pesticides have converted to more toxic forms. Malathion was recorded as having converted to the more hazardous iso-malathion, and diazinon to the more hazardous sulfotep.

Food contamination

As a result of the free market in pesticide sales, subsidised cotton insecticides have been misused, and appear to have been sprayed on fresh fruits such as grapes, prunes and watermelon. Widespread cases of diarrhoea have been common for the last 20 years, and these have been associated with eating fruit contaminated with toxic compounds not recommended for use on vegetables or fruits such as ekatin, triazophos, phosfolan, methamidophos and monocrotophos.

Since 1986, there has been a very large increase in the production of vegetables grown under plastic houses and in tunnels. This has been accompanied by an increase in incidents of poisoning due to heavy residues from frequent applications of pesticides, and not observing a safe interval between the final spray and harvesting. Some of the pesticides involved have been methomyl, methamidophos, dimethoate and monocrotophos. Although fatal cases are reported every season, the Ministry of Health has never carried out thorough investigations.

Residue survey

A food monitoring survey carried out by the Faculty of Agriculture sampled food in all governorates in Egypt for residues of DDT, lindane, dieldrin, endrin, methoxychlor, malathion, pirimiphos methyl. The results were alarming showing residues in all areas, in between 25% and nearly 90% of the samples. The results are shown in Figure 10.1.

Fig. 10.1   Food residue sample in Egyptian governorates.

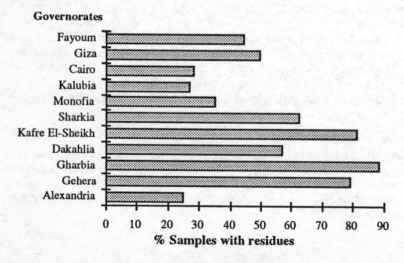

Source: Survey reported by Professor A.A. Abdel Gawaad.

In a random sample of the diet of Cairo residents, more than 23 pesticide residues and their degradation products were detected, mainly endrin, dieldrin, lindane and DDT. High quantities of drinking water and bread are eaten by Egyptians daily, and these are the main sources of pesticide intake: bread was the source of more than 50% of the daily pesticide intake.

Conclusion

Egypt is a major pesticide user, but there is little work on the health or environmental impact, in spite of indications of problems. Studies of food residues indicate widespread misuse through spraying pesticides intended for cotton crops on food, or non-observance of intervals between harvest and market. Researchers are concerned, although have said that in recent years pesticide companies have begun to take more responsibility for creating public awareness by organising workshops and issuing pamphlets on safe handling. Nevertheless, the scale of use requires more than a public education scheme, and researchers have proposed improvements in agricultural practices, the need to use less hazardous alternatives, and to pursue means of reducing pesticide use, such as through integrated pest management.

References:
1. El Sebae, Dr. A.H., 'Fate and undesirable effects of pesticides in Egypt', in *Ecotoxicity and Climate*, SCOPE, John Wiley & Sons Ltd, 1989.
2. *Agrow*, No. 162, 26/6/92.
3. *Ibid.*
4. Press clipping in Arabic supplied.
5. Abdel-Gawaad report.
6. Abdel-Gawaad, *op. cit.*

11. Country Report: South Africa*

Introduction

In 1992 the pesticide market in South Africa was valued at more than R500 million (approximately $160 million).[1] The country both imports and manufactures pesticides, which are widely used on all major food crops, particularly cereals, and in orchards and forestry. Public health still depends on DDT, and the Department of National Health annually sprays 150-160 tons of DDT to control malaria in KwaZulu in Northern Transvaal. In 1991 government policy initiated a herbicide-spraying campaign in Natal to eradicate dagga (marijuana).

Laws governing pesticide sale and use reflect those in Europe and North America, however there is virtually no infrastructure for monitoring or enforcement or controls on farmer use. Training is not widely available, although public sector sprayers may receive more and the industry association began courses recently. Information on the health of pesticide workers and the environmental impact of pesticides is scanty.

Apartheid laws have fostered an abuse of farmworkers compounded by their exposure to hazardous chemicals. There are approximately 1.4 million farmworkers, including regular, seasonal and migrant workers, with five million dependants. Illiteracy is high, and farmworkers have had few rights: for example, protective equipment and training have not been covered by basic labour legislation. Apartheid laws and racial prejudice have allowed farmer negligence, violence, evictions and unfair dismissals to operate with impunity. As farms are spread out and isolated, it is difficult for farmworkers to organise against their conditions. Against this background, pesticides pose a specific risk to certain farmworkers in South Africa.

Sections of South African agriculture are among the most modern in the world, particularly the large cereal farms owned by white farmers. But farmers are often ignorant of the chemicals they are instructing their workers

* The material for this case study was prepared by Kate Emanuel of the Environment and Development Agency, and Group for Environmental Monitoring, Johannesburg, 1992.

to use. They have little knowledge of safety laws. Of 180,000 accidents paid out by the Workmen Compensation Act's accident fund in 1988, over 10% occurred in agriculture or forestry, making these the third highest in a grouping of 24 industries. Farmworkers in the fruit and vegetable-growing regions in the Western Cape seem to be particularly at risk, because of higher pesticide use in the region and more manual spraying.

Small-scale growers increasingly use pesticides because of economic pressures and to conform with chemical-dependent farming practices. Traditional and natural methods of pest control are being abandoned. However in the black areas there is little or no instruction or information given to farmers switching to chemicals. In KwaZulu, for example, there are no agricultural courses or marketing resources. The small number of extension officers in the area lack practical experience and the ability to train. The health level is already low, and pesticide-related symptoms are difficult to distinguish from others.

South Africa has been suspended from the United Nations, however the industry association, the Agricultural and Veterinary Chemicals Association (AVCASA) which represents over 90% of the agrochemical companies in the country follows the FAO Code. A condition of membership states that 'Members will be bound by the FAO/GIFAP International Code of Conduct on the Distribution and Use of Pesticides'. No members have been monitored or challenged on their practices.[2]

Scale of use

Over 15 international companies and a number of local chemical companies operate in South Africa, responsible for Rand 500-600 million in pesticide sales yearly. They manufacture, formulate, package, distribute and sell over 900 commercial products. The market is dominated by Ciba-Geigy, ICI, Bayer and a local company, Sentrachem. Pesticide sales have dropped in 1991, partly brought about by political uncertainty over potential land reform, and partly by the drought, and this may prompt a number of mergers and takeovers. The scale of manufacture in the country is not clear, but local industry exports to neighbouring countries, Zimbabwe, Zambia and Malawi, and business observers believe this to be a potential growth area for South African-based multinationals.[3]

The major use in South Africa is for herbicides, accounting for 42% of the market, mainly for cereal use. Insecticides account for 31%, fungicides 18% and the remaining 9% is split between plant-growth regulators, industrial and amenity use. Actual tonnages have not been published since 1978. As much as 60% of farmers' herbicide costs are for atrazine, mainly made by Ciba-Geigy.[4] Atrazine application is primarily for large-scale maize production and would be largely tractor-sprayed, only once or twice a season. The lower water table in South Africa means that residues in ground water have not been observed.

In some areas of food production, pesticides are a major component of the cost. According to an economist, David Hobkirk,[5] pesticides comprise 20% of the total direct costs for an apple grower in the Elgin area of the Western Cape. His calculations show that out of total annual outlays per hectare of R15,000 for labour, machinery and spray materials, the latter account for R3,000 per hectare.

Some of the more hazardous pesticides have been banned or severely restricted. Of the Dirty Dozen pesticides, paraquat and parathion are in general use, though a number are still registered for restricted use. Pesticides on the PIC list which are registered for use are: aldrin and chlordane—for use as a soil treatment under buildings only; cyhexatin; dinoseb; DDT—for public health only; EDB.

Other pesticides which have been identified as candidates for PIC, and are found to cause widespread problems under certain conditions of use, are registered. These are aldicarb—restricted for use to control pests on sub-tropical and citrus fruits, grapes, cotton, sugarcane; carbofuran; dichlorvos; methamidophos; methomyl; monocrotophos; omethoate; phosphamidon.

Health

Some distinction needs to be drawn between the large, modern maize farms, and the plantation sector, particularly cotton, fruit and vegetable crops. In the latter, South African farmworkers are issued little or no protective clothing, and the climate in summer can make use of protective equipment hot and uncomfortable in any event. The inequitable racial relationship between farmers and labourers has created a situation where farmworkers are exploited and largely uneducated. Farmers themselves do not perceive pesticides as a health problem.

In 1991 a farmworker in Montague using pesticides without protective clothing died shortly after spraying.

Mr. Andries Sefoor, 46, collapsed on the farm Helpmekaar outside Montague on January 4, 1991 after spraying pesticides for three days. An artery burst after he had inhaled poisonous substances. His wife, Mrs Marta Sefoor, said he came home two days earlier complaining of blurred vision and a blinding headache. 'He had been working for years with poisons and had never been given protective clothing or a mask,' she said. 'He told me he had complained about his headaches to the farmer, Mr. Hermie Kriel, who insisted that he return to work.'[6]

On August 8, 1991, Martin Januarie, a 15 year-old coloured farmworker was poisoned in the field on a farm in Swellendam. He was responsible for the mixing of poisons and inhaled some pesticide dust. Symptoms included gagging, thirst, convulsions and shuddering. No first aid was given. The victim was taken to the doctor, admitted to hospital and released the next day.[7] (Department of National Health, Western Cape)

Dozens of similar incidents are reported each year, most involving 'coloured' farmworkers. Although recognised as a problem, no formal study has been undertaken in South Africa to determine the national rate of poisonings among farmworkers.

Pesticide poisonings are notifiable under the Health Act 63 of 1977, to the Department of National Health and Population Development. However, reported poisonings do not reflect the full problem. From 1971 to 1986, 1,261 cases were recorded, including 129 deaths. For 1990, 105 cases were reported, including seven deaths. These are thought to reflect less than 10% of the actual cases. It is also likely that many of those reported and registered are suicide attempts. Table 11.1 sets out a comparison. This indicates the extent of under-reporting of pesticide-related incidents. However, many incidents do not even get to a doctor or hospital. There is no course or registered specialised field in clinical toxicology at any of the country's universities.

In most cases it is not possible to identify the pesticide, but organophosphates as a group are responsible for most occupational poisonings and deaths. Between 1986 and 1987 in the Western Cape region, organophosphates were responsible for 51% of the agricultural poisonings and 66% of the suicides.[8] In 1990 organophosphates were responsible for 66% of the cases reported to the Department of National Health and Development.[9] In 1985 organophosphate poisonings were the second most common reason for admission to Tygerberg Hospital's Intensive Care Unit.[10] Pesticides are freely available in South Africa, and are widely used to commit suicide. Many of the official statistics on pesticide poisonings are suicide cases as these are more likely to be reported to the Department of Health than occupational cases. In 1989, 42% of reported cases were suicide attempts and in 1990, 31%.[11]

Accidental cases frequently involve children or user ignorance as the Health Inspectors' reports show:

Dieldrin poisoning: On February 27, 1989, 4-year-old Dawid Jansen obtained the organochlorine dieldrin and accidentally ingested the solid matter, believing it was powdered milk. As soon as symptoms appeared—cramps and vomiting—the boy was taken to the hospital where he was treated and subsequently released. As dieldrin's registration has been banned since 1980, the chemical (FBC Holding's Killdrin) was presumably obtained by the previous farm owner who gave it to the occupiers of the house. The Health Inspector's recommendations were an order to the owner 'to ensure that workers do not possess poisons'.

Organophosphate poisoning: On May 19, 1990, Liza Barends, a 34-year-old farmworker on a fruit farm in Worcester was involved in a non-fatal organophosphate poisoning. The victim obtained the chemical, omethoate (Bayer's Folimat), from the site where spraying pumps are filled. The worker wanted to kill bed fleas and sprinkled the poison over her bedding, closed the windows and then slept. The following day, the victim began to display acute organophosphate poisoning symptoms—nausea, headaches, dizziness. Two days after the initial exposure, the victim was hospitalised. The Health Inspector made no recommendations.

Table 11.1 Comparison of pesticide poisonings from identified sources with official notifications of pesticide poisonings.

Institute recording poisonings	Year	Notifications	
		Cases	Deaths
Official notifications: Pesticide Poisonings reported to the Department of the National Health & Population Development	1985	132	9
	1986	78	5
	1987	178	11
	1988	162	5
	1989	137	7
	1990	105	7
	1991 (8 months)	99	9
University of Cape Town, *The Epidemiology of Pesticide Mortality in the Western Cape*, G.J. Coetzee[12]	1977 —1980	**104 deaths:** Representing only 5% of cases notified to Department of National Health	
Tygerberg Hospital Intensive Care Unit[13]	1986	**39** cases treated, only three notified	
Groote Schuur Intensive Care Unit[14]	1986	**5** cases treated, only one notified	
Orange Free State University Pharmacology Department[15]	1982 —1985	**410** cases of pesticide poisonings were registered in the Bloemfontein area. In the same four years, only 487 cases notified nationally	
Johannesburg Poison Information Centre[16]	1990	**573** calls relating to pesticide poisonings, but only 105 cases notified for the whole country in 1990.	
Eben Donges Hospital, Worcester in Western Cape: pesticide poisoning treated[17]	1989 1990	60 cases treated 30 cases treated These cases should be reported and appear in local authorities statistics. In 1989 only five cases were reported to the authorities, and in 1990 four.	

Source: As referenced in table.

Protective clothing

Farmers are required to provide employees, whether seasonal, migrant or full time, with safety equipment for spraying, including protective helmets, goggles, gloves, overalls, chemical-resistant clothing and boots. A survey conducted in 1989/90 by the Farmworkers Research and Resource Project (FRRP) revealed that of 39 workers spraying pesticides surveyed, only four were supplied with sufficient protective gear. The rest were either given nothing or overalls. Farmworkers in the surveys were mainly from maize farms in the Transvaal, Northern Cape, and Northern Orange Free State.[18] One farmworker, said:

> No, they have never given us masks . . . If I hadn't spoken about gloves, they wouldn't have even given us that . . . We scoop the poisons like that, without gloves . . . you put your hand into the container and when you pull it out, the poison is there on your hand . . . they don't tell us that we have to use masks. [19]

In FRRP's survey of 39 interviewed workers only one knew the name of the chemical used. Training and protection may be higher among local authority and other public sector sprayers, employed for pest or weed control on roads, railways, parks and for other public services.

Health hazards in manufacturing plants

Working conditions in South Africa's manufactures plants are questionable. James Xala, a worker at the chemical manufacturer Robertsons which makes a range of products to kill flies, ants, fleas and cockroaches, said:

> Sometimes you've got to look closely to see if the level is okay and so your face is very near to the chemicals . . . I have never seen any one of the manufacturing employees using masks. . . . People are sick everyday with headaches, flu, fever and coughing. Paper masks are given every five days, but workers ask for new ones every day because masks get dirty and wet after one use. If we are not forceful, we do not get our request. [20]

Health hazards from empty containers

Under the Hazardous Substances Act 1973, empty pesticide containers and the remaining contents must be disposed of in a responsible manner—either punctured and flattened or buried. But in fact drums are generally left in the fields or orchards and not properly destroyed. In April 1989, 50 migrants from the Transkei employed on a potato farm in the Orange Free State were poisoned after drinking water from a disused drum which had contained monocrotophos. A three-year-old girl died and eight people became critically ill.[21]

In a study of 27 farmers in the grape-producing Hex River valley of the Western Cape, 51% of the farmers claimed they had a problem with the disposal of empty containers and unwanted chemicals, 18% had unwanted chemicals which they could not dispose of, and 70% of the farms had empty containers lying around. Only 7% of the farmers knew of companies that dispose of chemical waste.[22]

Philip Masia of the South African Farmworker Education Project pointed out that there may only be one communal tap on a farm, or people may have to obtain their water supply from a nearby stream: 'You're talking about people who earn so little that they can't even afford a bucket, so they use whatever container will hold water.' [23]

During a visit to Rainbow's End Farm, Western Cape, the researcher found two recently used drums of the pesticide DNOC lying in the apple orchard, and another outside the labourers' living quarters. Other drums were in the field, including two containing remnants of chlorpyrifos.

Training

Little training exists in pesticide use, though a small number of courses have been initiated in recent years. ICI in the Western Cape does periodic training, but they have only two technical advisors in the Cape. FBC Holdings in Western Cape offers free workshops to their customers, comprising a one-day workshop. A survey of tractor operators in the Hex Valley found that only 14% had any formal training in the application of poisons and 13% had no education.

In 1989, AVCASA, the industry association, initiated a training scheme for chemical sales representatives to qualify as pesticide advisers on farms, and had trained over 320 marketing employees by early 1990.

Environment

Tala Valley

The Tala Valley controversy has been widely publicised. Until 1987, hormonal herbicides, including 2,4-D, 2,4,5-T and MCPA, were used extensively in the Natal sugarcane fields to kill broad-leaf weeds. But the spray drifted over five kilometres, killing broad-leaf vegetables and crops, causing millions of rands in damage to local farmers.

In December 1986, all but two sugarcane and timber farmers in the Valley agreed to a voluntary ban on these herbicides, and in 1989 the Ministry of Agriculture instituted a temporary province-wide ban. Produce farmers lost a great deal of money. They took legal action against the manufacturers, but in June 1990 the judge ruled that the farmers' action should have been directed at the users. Farmers were ordered to pay one million rand costs, and received no compensation for damage to their crops.

The 17 chemical companies involved in the case then offered the farmers a 'deal'. If the Natal Fresh Produce Grower's Association, which represented the farmers, endorsed a newspaper campaign in support of hormonal herbicides, issued a public apology, forfeited their rights to take any more legal action and stopped their public campaigns, the companies would waive the one million rand legal costs. Farmers pointed out that this was blackmail and bullying and were incensed by the offer. Plant pathologist Mark Laing commented that

> A disturbing issue which has emerged from the Tala Valley case is that there appears to be no effective mechanisms in our current society to tackle and resolve environmental issues without resorting to the frighteningly expensive, confrontational and essentially destructive process of lawsuits . . . There is no medium through which the public

can articulate their feelings and wishes on environmental issues at the level of decision-making.[24]

The health impact of the Tala Valley affair has been largely ignored: on both the legal side and by farmers themselves. Two groups have been started by wives of vegetable farmers, and the women report high rates of asthma, birth defects, allergies and other physical complaints conveyed to them by hundreds of citizens.[25]

Locust control

The Department of Agriculture locust control team is intended to operate when necessary. The last outbreak occurred in 1985-86, and farmers were very critical of the team's operations and record in terms of keeping abreast of environmentally-acceptable methods of control. BHC was used extensively in the 1985-86 locust swarms in the Karoo, although it had been restricted in 1970 and subsequently withdrawn. Its use for killing brown locusts was prohibited in 1974. However the Department of Agriculture had stockpiled 5000 tons of BHC which were used in the outbreak, along with diazinon, fenitrothion and fenvalerate.[26]

Farmers noted that no protective clothing was worn during spraying; stocks were old; spraying was started too late; the necessary equipment had not been kept in a workable condition, and needed days of work before use; applicators were not aware of the dangers of the pesticides they were handling. The overall cost of the operation was R7.4 million.

Food residues

There is no established residue-monitoring programme for the local market, though testing is done on an ad hoc basis. Some municipalities, particularly Cape Town and Johannesburg, test on a limited basis. The Johannesburg Municipality Laboratories take approximately 500 samples of mainly fresh vegetables per year. However little information is available on residues found. As a major fresh food exporter, more emphasis is devoted to this produce, which must meet minimum standards. Samples are taken at export points, and the Department of Agriculture laboratories in Stellenbosch and Pretoria analyse approximately 25-30,000 samples a year.

Legislation

South Africa's legislation governing the use of pesticides is comparable to countries such as the US or UK. However, there is no infrastructure for monitoring or enforcement. It is widely agreed that the biggest shortcoming of pesticide legislation is that farmers do not have to be licensed to use or purchase pesticides. Under Act 36, commercial pest-control operators must complete training and be licensed. The Minister of Agricultural Development, Dr. Kraai van Niekerk, has noted this loophole: '. . . pest control operators have to conform to strict rules, but farmers virtually have a free hand in the use of these chemicals . . . we obviously had to give further attention to the matter in terms of law.'[27] The government is now attempting to redress the balance, and a trial scheme will be introduced in Natal whereby to use Class 1 poisons, farmers will need to be trained and registered as applicators.

A further amendment has been introduced stating that if an 'agricultural remedy' is used contrary to label instructions, this will be considered an offence. If convicted, the owner of the pesticide can be fined and face two years' imprisonment.[28] However the potential of farmworkers to challenge farmers in the courts is remote.

Until recently, farmworkers were excluded from most labour laws. They are, however, protected regarding health and safety. But these laws are rarely enforced. Act 36 is enforced by the Department of Agriculture's 19 chemical inspectors, but there are 30,000 outlets for agrochemical product sales. Inspectors are responsible for checking these are properly labelled, in suitable containers and registered. They must also regulate farm feeds, fertilisers, stock remedies, pest control operators and products intended for export. They should also carry out routine inspections on some 128,000 farms.

Labelling

By law, labels must be printed both in English and Afrikaans. The Department of Agriculture is currently revising their labelling standards and requires the use of pictograms and colour coding. However it is estimated that eight out of 10 farmworkers cannot read or write and, in addition, 20 different languages are spoken in the country. At present the only pesticide label printed in another language is the Shell product, alphamethrin, a synthetic pyrethroid used on cotton. There are additional dangers here. On the Zulu label, the chemical is called 'Umshanyelo' which means broom, or 'sweeps everything away'.

High illiteracy and low levels of education mean reading labels is impossible, or the technical language is overwhelming. One rural advisor in Natal said:

> In some ways, there is too much on the label—farmers take one look at it and you can see the doubt on their faces. . . there are so many complexities in using pesticides legally that I seriously doubt their appropriateness for people who can't read labels. [29]

Conversions to liquid millilitres are also difficult if a grower does not have a scale, and farmers tend to approximate, often wildly. While good labelling and detailed information is essential, it is impossible to expect farmworkers—and even many farmers—to understand detailed information. For the overwhelming majority of farmworkers, it is impossible to use a product, and observe safety precautions, according to label instructions. For example on the product Lorsban (chlorpyrifos) the label states:

> If you get it on your clothes, change and wash them.

Wear rubber gloves, if you get it on your skin, wash it off at once.
Notify all inhabitants of the immediate area to be sprayed and issue the
necessary warnings. Do not spray over or allow drift to contaminate
water or adjacent areas.

Workers do not have gloves or access to clean water and are rarely able to
simply leave the field and change clothes. Labels commonly read, as does
one Shell product: 'In case of poisoning call a doctor and make label
available to him.'   On an isolated farm, transport to a local clinic or
hospital may be very difficult for a farmworker to secure, telephones remote
or non-existent, and the label is likely to be on a drum.

Alternatives

Biological control and IPM is now used to control red-scale disease in five
million citrus trees, following a disastrous attempt to control with a range
of pesticides which had resulted in the pesticide treadmill syndrome. In the
1970s damage to trees and crop losses almost brought some growers to
bankruptcy due to the high pesticide applications needed to control red-scale.
Widely used were parathion, DDT, temephos and malathion. However these
killed red-scale's natural enemies, and orchards experienced a resurgence of
the resistant red scale.

Biological control techniques have been particularly successful in South
Africa in controlling exotic or invader plants. More than 700 problem
plants have been introduced to the country. Over the last 30 years
entomologists have introduced some 40 species of insects to attack
problematic invader plants. For example, prickly pear once infested 900,000
hectares: 80% control has been achieved using biocontrol techniques, where
the cost of herbicide treatments would have reached R25 million, with
repeated treatments over eight to 10 years.

Conclusions

South Africa is a major pesticide user and also a manufacturer and
formulator, exporting to surrounding countries. Much of the farming in the
country is large-scale and intensive, similar to large farms in Europe and
North America. There have been serious spray-drift incidents caused by
aerial application on some larger farms, most notably in the Tala Valley
area of Natal. Because of the history of apartheid, the majority of
farmworkers in the country are black and have few rights to health and
safety protection. For those working on the more isolated farms their
existing rights are further undermined by the level of poverty and illiteracy
and the legacy of apartheid laws. Farmworkers particularly at risk are those
in the fruit and vegetable sector, where application is frequent and exposure
greater. Little information is available on pesticide use and practices in the
'homelands'.

References:
1. *Agrow*, quoting data from Schering, No. 161, 12/6/92, p. 22.
2. Interview with Piet Wessels, Technical Director, ACVASA, 1991.
3. *Agrow, op. cit.*
4. *Agrow, op. cit.*
5. Interview with David Hobkirk, economist, Western Cape, 17 September 1991.
6. *South*, 12-23 January 1991.
7. Department of National Health records, Western Cape.
8. Marshall, R.A.S., 'A report on the notification of agrochemical poisoning in the Western Cape Region for the period 1 January 1986 to 31 December 1987', Community Health Department, University of Cape Town, Cape Town, 3 September 1988.
9. Interview with Dr. Adam, Department of National Health and Population Development, 29 April 1991.
10. Bardin, P.G. 'Intensive care management of acute organophosphate poisoning: a 7-year experience in the Western Cape', SAMJ, Vol. 72, 7 November 1987, pp. 593-597.
11. Department of National Health and Population Development, Western Cape Region, 'Pesticide Poisonings in the Western Cape 1989 and 1990', Belville, April 1991.
12. Coetzee, G.J., 'The epidemiology of pesticide mortality in the Western Cape', Department of Community Health, University of Cape Town, undated.
13. Marshall, R.A.S., *op.cit.*
14. *Ibid.*
15. Weis, O. *et al*, 'Epidemiologiese studie VanVergiftigings in Bloemfontein en omgewing', SAMJ, 4 July 1987, pp. 24-26.
16. Interview with employee at Johannesburg Poison Information Centre, 4 November 1991.
17. Emanuel, K., survey for this report, 1991.
18. Farmworker Research and Resource Project Farmbase Surveys: designed to identify some of the problem areas that face farmworkers and compare trends across the country. Conducted by rural advice employees and fieldworkers from 1989 to 1990.
19. Interview with Willem Botha, Rainbow's End farm, Banhoek, Western Cape, 5 September 1991
20. Interview with James Xala, chemical worker, Germiston Chemical Workers Union Meeting, 1 October 1991.
21. Koch, E., 'A mass poisoning highlights flaws in farm health codes', *The Weekly Mail*, 7-13 April 1989.
22. Reed, Dr. A., 'A descriptive study of accidental agricultural chemical poisoning in the Western Cape', Child Health Unit, June 1991.
23. Personal interview with Philip Masia of the South Africa Farmworkers Education Project, 30.4.91.
24. Laing, M., 'Jekyll-and-Hyde Herbicides', *Indicator SA Issue Focus*, April 1990, University of Natal, p. 41.
25. Interview with Molly Kudla, Gill Ashmead, Kat Channing-Pearce, 21 August 1991, 18 January 1991 and 4 December 1991 respectively.
26. Barlin-Brinck, M., *Pesticides in Southern Africa - an assessment of their use and environmental impact*, The Wildlife Society of South Africa, Durban, 1991.
27. 'Strict farm law for use of chemicals is on the way', *Farmer's Weekly*, 10/8/91.
28. *Government Gazette*, No. 13424, No. R. 1716, 26 July 1991.
29. Interview with Thelma Trench, Farmer Support Group, Pietermaritzburg, 1 September 1991.

12. Country Report: India*

The Green Revolution turned India into a major pesticide consumer, and government policies to promote industrialisation encouraged domestic pesticide production. India now manufacturers most of its pesticide needs, through production or active ingredient import for local formulation, and also exports to countries in the region. Pesticides are produced by Indian companies, and subsidiaries of transnational corporations, such as ICI.

International efforts to restrict hazardous pesticides have focused on export trade. The Indian experience poses the question: how to reduce hazardous pesticide application when production and use is internal, or regional? Pesticide production is increasing in Third World countries, and may be encouraged by export controls which dispose transnationals to set up production facilities closer to markets where a demand for these products continues. Many of the older, more hazardous pesticides are cheaper to produce, or out of patenting control, making them attractive to Third World countries. The standards of production are a cause of concern, borne out by the Union Carbide plant at Bhopal, producing pesticides for use on cotton. A leak of poisonous methyl isocyanate from this plant in 1984 has caused over 3000 deaths to date.

Scale of use

Pesticide use has increased rapidly over the last two decades, at the rate of 12% a year. Between 1990 and 1995, the government plans to further increase annual pesticide consumption from 80,000 tonnes to 100,000 tonnes by increasing the area under cultivation from 90 to 100 million hectares.[1] Rice and cotton production alone account for two-thirds of pesticides used in agriculture, while about 30% of all use is for public health projects. The Green Revolution strategies have concentrated use in the most fertile regions, only 75 out of approximately 400 districts or 7.2% of all farmland. One-third of all use is concentrated in Andhra Pradesh, followed by Karnataka (16%), Gujarat (15%), Punjab (11%), Maharashtra (5%). Yet 'modernised' agriculture accounts for less than 20% of India's food-grain production.

* This report is based on material from Dr. Daisy Dhamaraj of PREPARE Madras, with additional material from Dr. A.T. Dudani and Sanjoy Sengupta of Voluntary Health Association India, Delhi.

With 5% of cropped area, cotton uses 52-55% of pesticides. Rice, with 24% of cropped area, uses 17-18%. Chillies, vegetables and fruit, with 3% of cropped land, uses 13-14%; and the plantation sector, with 2% cropped area, uses 7-8%. Others, including sugar cane with 8% of cropped land, use 3-5% of pesticides. By contrast, cereals such as millet and oilseeds, with 58% of cropped land, use only 6-7% of pesticides.[2]

According to government statistics, DDT, lindane (HCH), malathion, endosulfan and parathion are the most widely used insecticides in India, accounting for about half the country's application (including public health use).[3] They are cheaper than most others, easy to handle, and attack a wide range of pests.

India produces and exports pesticides

India has the capacity to produce over 50 pesticide active ingredients,[4] either through domestic companies or subsidiaries of transnational corporations. With over 50 pesticide factories and 800 formulation plants operating, it produces about 98% of its domestic pesticide consumption[5] (see Table 12.1). In 1985-86, production was 54,919 tonnes, and in 1991 this had risen to 63,800 tonnes (including 19,900 tonnes of lindane, 7,000 tonnes of DDT and 3,100 tonnes of malathion),[6] although this was down on the previous year's total of 69,600 tonnes. This is only about half the country's production capacity, and the government wants production stepped up so the country can export more pesticides. At present, India exports pesticides to the value of about Rs. 1.550 million.[7] According to figures for the years 1984-85, 1985-86 and 1986-87, the main exports were endosulfan, aluminium phosphide, zinc phosphide, nicotine sulphate, aldrin (1985-86 only), quinalphos. Many of the pesticides produced in India have been banned or restricted elsewhere, notably DDT.

Cotton—high use induces resistance

Cotton is an important commercial crop in India, being grown on about eight million hectares, of which only 10% is irrigated. Cotton production now stands at around 10 million bales, though new hybrid varieties may push this up to 12 million bales. New strains produce long staple varieties which are equal to or better than Egyptian cotton. This has not yet been reflected in the price for the high-grade Indian cotton.[8]

Over 50% of India's pesticide consumption is directed against cotton pests, costing about Rs.3,000 million every year. Studies have indicated that farmers use way above the levels recommended by the agricultural department. Far from dealing with pest attacks, insect resistance has now increased to worrying levels.

The high pesticide input to cotton is frequently dismissed as less problematic in a fibre crop, as compared to food crops. However, cotton is grown for seed oil, and seeds are used for cattle feed. In India, the cotton stalk is used for particle boards and pulp and paper. Most farmers sell harvested cotton unginned.

In 1990 Punjab farmers lost 20% of their standing cotton crop in attacks from the American bollworm which has developed resistance and immunity. The neighbouring Haryana reported a similar scale of loss, and losses are high in Andhra Pradesh, Maharashtra and Gujerat. Damage to late sown cotton is higher. Loss is estimated at 492,000 bales, down to a yield of perhaps 1.96 million bales—in financial terms the loss is estimated at $500 million a year. Some farmers will lose 90%, while some may lose none.[9] In Andhra Pradesh, where cotton growers' losses have been high, the economic ruin resulted in many farmers committing suicide in 1988.[10]

Table 12.1   Pesticides produced or formulated in India including those which are, or may become, subject to the Prior Informed Consent procedure.[11]

PIC Pesticides	Other pesticides formulated in India	
BHC	2-40	fenthion
DDT	anilophos	fenitrothion
parathion	butachlor	fenvalerate
methyl	calixin	fluchloralin
	captan	isoproturon
	carbaryl (ex-Bhopal)	malathion
	carbendazim	mancozeb
Potential PIC	copper oxychloride	metasystox
	copper sulphate	nickel chloride
captafol	coumachlor	nicotine sulphate
endosulfan	cuprous oxide	oxydemeton-
lindane	cypermethrin	methyl
methyl bromide	dalapon	phenthoate
monocrotophos	DDVP	phorate
organo-mercury	decamethrin	phosalone
fungicides	dichlorvos	quinalphos
paraquat	dimethoate	thiocarbamates
phosphamidon	diuron	thiram
phosphides,	ethylene dibromide	tridemorph
aluminium and	ethion	warfarin
zinc		zineb
		ziram

Sources: Department of Chemicals and Petrochemicals, Government of India, 1989-90.

Pyrethroids have caused much of the problem. Farmers have been using these 10 to 16 times out of 15 to 30 pesticide applications. Cypermethrin has been found to induce high populations of aphids and moderate population of white flies.[12] Scientists say that pyrethroids should not be used more than two or three times during a season, and should be alternated with other groups of pesticides to avoid adverse affects. In Andhra Pradesh white fly resistance to insecticides used on cotton led to excessive applications which exacerbated the problem.

One of India's leading entomologists, from the Indian Agricultural Research Institute, asked the government to pass a law restricting the use of pyrethroid insecticides on cotton. He says that the incidence of pyrethroid resistance increased at least 100-fold over two years. However, the alternative insecticides suggested by the Institute are hazardous substances such as endosulfan.[13]

Table 12.2   Pesticides imported for use on cotton 1988-89 and 1989-90.

Pesticides imported for use on cotton	1988-89		1989-90	
	Qty Tonnes	Value (Rs.000)	Qty Tonnes	Value (Rs.000)
acephate	39	3968	34	3,989
aldrin	57	5,850	26	3,040
carbaryl	230	12,417	29	1,863
carbendazim	4	363	7	732
carbofuran	22	3,336	72	12,325
chlordane	2	139	12	866
chlorpyriphos	68	9,736	34	5,378
dichlorvos	22	892	32	1,420
dicofol	-	-	150	11,240
dimethoate	20	1,129	8	470
diuron	15	1,135	12	1,249
fenvalerate	84	26,072	-	-
fluvalinate	11	10,019	-	-
heptachlor	42	2,551	62	5,150
methomyl	71	23,421	-	-
monocrotophos	655	45,997	81	7,144
paraquat dichloride	13	717	32	1,846
parathion methyl	97	3,121	128	4,589
phenthoate	15	1,114	34	3,293
Total	**1467**	**151,977**	**753**	**64,594**

Source: Figures compiled by PREPARE.

In response to the problem government authorities have banned dealers in Andhra Pradesh from stocking synthetic pyrethroids before September. The Indian Council of Agriculture has proposed biological control measures and has started mass production in 11 states of both the parasitic wasp, *Trichogramma*, and of the nuclear polyhedrosis virus.[14] Other measures could include the purchase of insect-resistant cotton seed, such as that produced by Monsanto. The company has offered to sell its patented cotton seeds to India for $9 million. This has raised some consternation in the country, as commentators have asked for details of the origin of the gene. Monsanto was not willing to divulge this information.[15]

Other hazardous pesticides are used with apparent lack of awareness. Pesticide industry sources say that Punjab could be heading for disaster, as rich farmers liberally use pesticides like monocrotophos, which could induce resistance, when less potent remedies would have sufficed.[16] Without protective measures, monocrotophos is hazard to applicators. Many of the pesticides used on cotton are produced domestically, those imported during the years 1988-89 and 1989-90 are set out in Table 12.2.

Where possible, farmers employ labourers to spray, and their exposure levels are high. PREPARE interviewed farmers and labourers in part of Andhra Pradesh, the major producer of cotton, and the results are set out in the box on the following page.

Health

Under Section 26 of the Insecticides Act 1968 pesticide poisonings must be registered. Details of pesticide-related deaths are missing from some states, which may partly reflect more deaths in states where pesticide use is high. Figures provided by states which reported pesticide-related deaths and poisonings are set out in Table 12.3 and show vast variations. In Madhya Pradesh, for example, there were reports of 772 cases including a number of deaths, from 1986 to 1988.

In response to a parliamentary question on deaths due to pesticide poisoning, the Ministry of Agriculture said that there is no breakdown available of deaths due to pesticides in foods and occupational health hazards. The records are not required to cover these areas, and there is thus no record of occupational health hazards for workers and sprayers.[17] Yet there are indicators of cause for concern.

The official figures do not tally with other information. Aluminium phosphide is responsible for a number of reported deaths, both accidental and suicide. In December 1991, three children and their mother were killed when aluminium phosphide tablets were used in the home to kill rats. The chemical reacted with water and engulfed the small house with thick fumes. The father and two neighbours were also affected. According to one report, a single hospital in Rohtak (Haryana) has registered 418 aluminium phosphide deaths, of which 286 were suicides.[18] Social workers have for some time been concerned about the use of aluminium phosphide for suicide, and have argued for stricter controls.

Pesticides and their effect on workers in Andhra Pradesh

Andhra Pradesh consumes the largest quantity of pesticides per acre in Asia, and is the country's major cotton producer. This report covers 10 villages in the Guntur District, and is based on interviews with five peasants from each village.

The respondents are agricultural labourers ('coolies') belonging to harijan communities ('untouchables' or lowest in the Hindu caste system). Among these, 46 own some land, and their houses have some water and electricity. The men spend most of their time working as labourers in the cotton fields, and the women are responsible for the home, leaving pesticide application to men. Cotton is sown once a year, from July to March. Secondary crops are rice, groundnuts, chillies and vegetables.

One-third of the men interviewed earned less than Rs. 5,000 per annum, and they are paid on the basis of a daily wage, which varies according to the work available during the season: soil preparation, planting, manuring, pesticide spraying or plucking. There is no clear-cut bonded labour in the area, and most men remain employed, or are out of work in the lean season. During this period, they look after their own crops, and recoup their health for the next cotton season. A small number take labouring work on construction sites in nearby towns.

During the years 1988-90, the most common pests were aphids, thrips, jassids, drilling insects. Greenworm and white fly were irregular pests. Selection of pesticides is largely influenced by the experience of neighbouring farmers, dealers and government extension workers. Among the pesticides popular in the area are endosulfan, monocrotophos, endrin and parathion.

Parathion and endrin are frequently used in combination and sprayed regularly on cotton by most farmers in the state. They are aware of the high toxicity of both these pesticides. In season, farmers spray once every four days. The amount sprayed varies from .25 to 1 litre per acre. They often experiment with pesticide combinations, on advice from other farmers.

When spraying, the men wear long-sleeve shirts, head gear and dhoti (loincloth) tied up above their knees. They use a cloth round their mouth but complain that this gets wet with pesticide spray and increases the chance of inhaling and swallowing the pesticide. A pump sprayer is the common application method. These are light and made of plastic, and often leak because of pressure from pumping, however this model is cheaper than others and easy to handle.

While mixing, they pour an estimated amount into a bucket, without measuring, and use sticks to mix. One labourer is responsible for filling tanks, and as soon as a tank is empty the applicator goes to this spot for a refill, which is done without removing the pump from his shoulder. A usual work day is eight hours, covering 2-12 acres. All washing is done only after the work is complete.

Since 1987, cotton pests have become resistant, and plantation owners and their families could not pay back debts: many committed suicide. Labourers were not so badly affected, and sought jobs elsewhere.

In their own fields, agricultural labourers generally do their own work, though adult women may help in irrigation. Young girls between 10-15 years old are at a greater risk, as they are employed on a daily basis to pick worms after the field is sprayed. They pick with their bare hands, and are paid .20 paise for a small basket of worms. There is no bar on entering recently sprayed fields.

Falling mildly sick due to pesticides is frequent, and work is resumed immediately after a drink or smoke. Those who fall seriously ill from pesticide poisoning (or those who attempt suicide with pesticides) are taken immediately to the nearest Registered Medical Practitioner's clinic. First aid is rarely applied, as farmers do not find home remedies effective. Workers feel that pesticide-induced illness is not very serious. They use their savings, or borrow from friends to treat serious cases. They feel land owners should provide effective spraying equipment, and pay more to help meet hospital expenses.

The majority of labourers are illiterate. They are nevertheless aware of the dangers of pesticides, but believe they must use ever larger quantities to ensure a good yield. All appeared to think that IPM methods would be non-profitable.

Table 12.3 Reports of pesticide-related deaths notifiable under the Insecticides Act 1968 (excluding occupational health hazards and illnesses which are not recorded).

State	1987-88	1988-89	1989-90
Andhra Pradesh	Nil	n/a	34
Haryana	3 (animal)	6	10
Himachal Pradesh	n/a	n/a	n/a
Kerala	Nil	n/a	237
Madhya Pradesh	772 cases of pesticide poisoning, including a number of deaths, were reported from 1986-1988 in the zonal conference: figures for 1989-90 are not available.		
Orissa	2	Nil	2
Punjab	126	n/a	149
Tamil Nadu	4 (animal)	n/a	1
Uttar Pradesh	54	78	100
Pondicherry	Nil	108	131
Total reported deaths	**182+**	**192+**	**664+**

Source: Indian Government answer to Parliamentary Question on 4.1.91.

Chronic ill-health

Dr. K.T. Shenoy of the Thiruvananthapuram Medical College pointed out that in Kuttanad, with 52,000 hectares of paddy fields, where pesticide consumption has shown a steady increase from 1,200 tonnes in 1972 to a peak of 13,400 tonnes in 1980 (it has since stabilised at 4,000 to 5,000 tonnes a year), cancer of the lip, stomach, skin and brain, leukaemia, lymphoma and multiple myeloma, are common among farmers.[19]

An environmental toxicologist, Dr. P. Muthu, who has conducted research on the health impact of cancer, has expressed concern over his observations of pesticide use in Tamil Nadu where, he says, pesticide sprayers are usually illiterate labourers. Poor people live in one room only, so they keep the pesticide in the room where they live, cook and eat. The powder is in the air. When they spray crops, the spray sometimes drifts into the house and children are exposed. Toxic pesticides are easily available, there are few controls on their sale, and recommended safety precautions are highly unrealistic. In Tamil Nadu, where the local language is Tamil, safety instructions on pesticide containers are in English and Hindi. Dr. Muthu points out that illiteracy and poverty mean that few pesticide users are able to follow directions for the safe application of pesticide.[20]

Researchers at the King George Medical College of the Industrial Toxicology Research Centre in Lucknow carried out a series of tests on workers spraying DDT and malathion regularly. At least half of the workers developed psychological symptoms like anxiety, sleep disturbance, depression, severe headaches. One out of five had impaired memory and performed simple drawing tests clumsily. Some suffered retinal damage, blurred vision and saw flashes of light and black dots in front of their eyes.[21]

In one cotton-growing area, South Arcot in the district of Tamil Nadu, villagers work spraying 800 acres under cotton with pesticides such as parathion, DDT, BHC, dimethoate, carbaryl and endosulfan. This is thought to have claimed lives, and to be associated with symptoms which many villagers in the area have shown, including paralysis and convulsions.[22] In a study of organochlorine residues in 36 village farms in Andhra Pradesh by gas liquid chromatography, BHC was detected in 20 of the farms surveyed at amounts ranging from three to six ppm.[23]

PREPARE believes there is a great deal of ignorance among farmers on basic health and safety although, at the same time, poverty and illiteracy put basic precautions beyond their reach. PREPARE ran a two-day training programme in 1991 on safe use of pesticides and alternatives, aimed at women from the villages in and around Irumbedu, Vengadu, Vallarai, Kulathur and Gunduperimbedu.[24] They showed videos, discussed the dangers of pesticides and recorded the experiences of women. Although women were aware of the hazards impotence to change made them fatalistic (see box).

Pesticides in India
Views from Madras villages

In September 1991, over a two-day period, the health group PREPARE organised a training programme on Safe Use of Pesticides and Alternatives for women from five villages, and recorded the experiences of women. About 30 women attended the meeting, which was held during the off-season for agriculture. Most women were well aware that pesticides were dangerous, and told of many cases of pesticide-induced unconsciousness and vomiting, as well as their impact in eroding traditional agricultural practices. They had also developed a range of methods of treating pesticide poisoning. The main problems they noted were:

1. Earlier rice crops like sambar and pisini were being replaced by newer varieties like the IR8, IR20, IR30 and others.
2. The soil was previously more fertile and contained earthworms and insects which helped control rice pests. Pesticides have reduced the numbers of the natural predators, and the rice pests have increased.
3. Farmers are forced to adopt newer hybrid seeds because rice is harvested within three months rather than six months. They have to compete with their neighbours and do not want to lag behind, for economic reasons.
4. Natural pesticides they cited as effective include: cowdung water, vepam, punacca, odu pair, intercropping with cereals/plants such as kollu, karamani, pachai payeru. This ensures fresh vegetables throughout the year and keeps down the pesticide menace.
5. They say the new types of rice cannot satisfy one's hunger as well as the older varieties, but the Government does not encourage traditional rice production.

Unsafe practices and their after-effects
1. The sprayers usually mix pesticides with their hands and sometimes even taste it to ensure the right consistency before spraying.
2. Sprayers spray in the direction of the wind so that it is not blown against their faces.
3. Sprayers wear only shorts and do not wear any cloth around their mouth, hands or legs. Even if men wish to do so, they cannot wear full clothes as landlords do not like their labour well-dressed, seeing this as a mark of power and disrespect.
4. Pesticide containers are thrown in the kalani (water-logged field areas).
5. Some women sell empty containers to the tin collector for a small sum.
6. Some use containers for food after washing.
7. After spraying, their men come home and bathe thoroughly with coconut oil, water and soap to remove the pesticides, but the clothes used for spraying are rarely washed, and are dumped in a corner to wear when spraying again.
8. The men spray from 4-20 areas per day to earn extra cash.

9. The men often fall sick after spraying. They usually complain of burning of eyes, giddiness, headache, vomiting and fainting.

10. In many villages, women embroiderers mix paint with pesticide powder and apply it with their hands as dyes: other women are very concerned and believe this is dangerous.

Poisoning

Cases of poisoning, both accidental and deliberate, are common. Some recent cases include:

• In Vengadu, in 1988, a 27-year-old man drank pesticides and died (suicide).
• 27-year-old machine sprayer, Umapathi, died in 1990.
• In Irumbedu, a 15-year-old, Segar, while machine spraying, fell ill, became unconscious, vomited blood and died.
• Two women died by drinking pesticides (suicides).
• In Vellarai, men fainted while spraying, vomiting blood.
• In Kolathur, one woman mixed water in half empty pesticide container and drank it (possible suicide).

The women have noted other effects of pesticide poisoning: they say the hands become weak and covered with rashes, eyes burn and deepen, legs become paralysed and sometimes the person becomes too weak to carry on normal activities. When affected, the men's teeth are sometimes tightly clenched. Frothing occurs at the mouth, with a little blood sometimes.

Treatment

In bad cases, they rush the affected sprayer to a hospital or a private doctor. Women pledge their jewels, and any other valuables, to meet the medical expenses, but it is difficult to get proper medical treatment. A range of remedies using local herbs and foods are tried. These include:

• mixing tamarind and water (puli karichu) to drink;
• crushing local crabs and mixing with water to drink—believed to remove the poison;
• a mixture of salt and water, or even coffee, to induce vomiting.

How pesticides are sold

Pesticides are sold loosely or in sacks. Richer farmers buy them in bulk from the Government. Poorer farmers have difficulty affording pesticides but suffer as a result, as they still grow the newer varieties of rice which need pesticides. The women say the dealer is only interested in selling the pesticide, but does not warn men of the danger. He simply says: 'This is new, try it, use larger quantities and mix and apply in the mornings.' No other warning is issued. Women feel their men resort to mixing different pesticides (regardless of their ill effects) in strong concentrations to ensure a good yield. This, say the women, has resulted in the soil being filled with 'salts', killing natural earthworms and insects and predators. Only the crabs used to 'treat' pesticide poisoning survive in the fields.

Food contamination

In a Global Environment Monitoring Programme sponsored by the UN, India was among the 10 nations chosen for studying pesticide residues in human breast milk. Studies of 50 lactating women showed DDT and BHC residues at least four times higher than those in other countries. In at least one instance, residues have accounted for large numbers of deaths: in 1990, 150 people in a village of Rajpura in Uttar Pradesh died after eating food contaminated with lindane served at a village wedding.[25]

Dr. Muthu points to problems of high pesticide residues commonly present in Indian food, and high residues of persistent organochlorine pesticides found in the blood of Indians, including high levels of DDT and BHC residues in breast milk. A study was carried out of aldrin and dieldrin in breast milk and maternal serum in 25 women permanently resident in Delhi, who were tested three days after giving birth. The average dieldrin content was 0.13 in milk, 0.09 in maternal serum and 0.04 ppb in cord serum.[26]

One Government study detected pesticide residues in a major share of vegetables. Seven out of eight samples of chillies investigated contained 100 to 160 times permissible levels of malathion and other pesticides. The same article quoted another study, which found that of 204 samples of cereals, pulses, milk, eggs, meat and vegetables analysed, 108 contained pesticides: 88 contained more than one and 69 had residues above the permissible limits. Another Government study detected pesticide residue in a major share of vegetables. Seven out of eight samples of chillies investigated contained 100 to 160 times permissible levels of malathion and other pesticides. The average daily diet of an Indian contains 0.27 mg of DDT.[27] A paper by researchers at the College of Agriculture, Vellayani said that HCH and DDT residues are the most persistent chemicals in the human system, quoting reports from all over the country.

A small number of studies on food residues were taken during the early 1980s, but there is no systematic study of the entire country, and no more recent studies are known. Some examples of the pesticides and products where the incidence of residues occurred were:[28]

- cereal and cereal produce in Punjab, Haryana, Utter Pradesh, Delhi, Bombay and Andhra Pradesh: DDT in 53% of 1651 samples;
- pulses in Punjab and Andhra Pradesh: DDT in 25% of 171 samples;
- vegetables in Punjab and Andhra Pradesh: DDT in 27% of 2154 samples;
- fruits in Andhra Pradesh and Punjab: DDT in 14% of 90 samples, lindane in 3%, endrin in 12%;
- meat in Delhi, Punjab, Andhra Pradesh, Utter Pradesh: DDT in 96% of 134 samples, HCH in 90%;
- milk in Delhi and Andhra Pradesh: DDT in 95% of 980 samples, HCH in 90%, dieldrin in 1%;

- infant formula in Punjab, Gujarat, Bombay: DDT in 100% of samples (only four samples tested);
- desi-ghee in Andhra Pradesh, Rajasthan, Punjab and Utter Pradesh: DDT and HCH in 100% of 10 samples.

Training and safe use

Some efforts have been made to create hazard and risk awareness in India. The Association of Basic Manufacturers of Pesticides (ABMP) has developed cheap versions of aprons, masks and other safety gear designed for tropical climates for Government workers who train farmers. It has distributed medical kits, with antidotes and other medication required to treat pesticide poisoning, to key primary health centres. However, the Voluntary Health Association of India (VHAI) questions whether industry can distribute, and farmers can afford to buy, safety equipment, and points to the discomfort of wearing protective clothing in India's climate.[29]

In 1991 ABMP ran a five-day programme on 'Safe and effective use of plant protection products' in three villages in Pune district. This was held in association with the GIFAP, and the Maharashtra department of agriculture. Two earlier training programmes were held with GIFAP in Hyderabad and Anand. The chairman of ABMP said: 'We subsequently monitored the training programmes conducted by the trainees and we are now convinced that there has been a multiplier effect.' In view of the scale of use in India, this appears somewhat optimistic.

The World Bank indicated it would extend assistance under its 'training and visit programme' to include training for government extension workers in safe use of pesticides in more states. Some Indian groups, notably VHAI, view this as misdirected and would prefer that the World Bank concentrate on support for the development of alternative technology such as botanical pesticides, biological control methods and help sustainable agriculture.[30]

VHAI comment on measures to train doctors in emergency treatment for pesticides poisoning, which they welcome, but add:

> Knowing as we do the prevailing pathetic conditions of many a health delivery centre, with no medicines and medical personnel, one wonders how this idea is going to work. Added to this problem is the non-existence of antidotes for many of the pesticides presently sold in the country.

Alternatives

The Association of Basic Manufacturers of Pesticides point out that crop scientists have estimated the impact of a withdrawal of crop protection over crops like rice, wheat and cotton, would result in serious losses. Rice production would fall from 73 to 53 million tonnes; wheat from 53 to 45 million tonnes; and cotton from 13 million bales to nine million bales. However, work is also underway in India on non-pesticide alternatives.

Scientists at the Pantnagar Agricultural University have isolated a fungus from soil which can control several soil-borne plant pathogens and could play a major role in controlling diseases in pulses, controlling root rot and wilt in chickpea and lentil production. This disease has affected farmers to such an extent that in some parts of India they no longer cultivate these crops. Chemical controls have been ineffective. A fungus called *gliocadium virens* has been isolated in the soil, and using a technique developed as part of a Department of Biotechnology project, can coat seeds with the fungus. This has been successful in experimental conditions, as well as in farmers' fields.[31]

There is work on alternatives in Tamil Nadu, under an all-India project sponsored by the Department of Biotechnology, Agricultural University of Tamil Nadu, to demonstrate the effectiveness of biological control agents.[32] The project is promoting biological control agents in a tiny village in Dindigul-Quaid-e-Millet, where villagers are learning about friendly insects, and being trained to produce biocontrol agents on their own. The cost is favourable: Rs. 50 per acre using natural control agents, whereas pesticides cost five times more. The University believes it could be taken up as a small-scale industry in villages. They will provide the funds as well as help the farmers set up manufacturing facilities through loans from financial institutions. One farmer whose field is part of a demonstration plot says: 'We used to spray pesticides four or five times for the rice crop. Now we do so only once and resort to natural methods. The yield is better.'

Conclusion

Indian agriculturalists range from the technologically sophisticated producer and exporter to the agricultural labourer, spraying eight to ten hours a day. In spite of the large scientific community, and an active environmental movement, the work on alternatives to pesticides is limited, as the government backs pesticide use and is still planning for further annual increases in pesticide consumption and an increased area under cultivation to industrial agriculture—at present, over 50% of pesticide use is on cotton.

Many of the pesticides produced in India are hazardous, and no longer produced elsewhere. Some of these, notably aluminium phosphide, are responsible for a considerable number of accidental deaths, as well as being used as suicide agents. Pesticides are freely available in small shops and stores throughout the country. Although labourers working regularly are aware of a health impact, particularly nausea, headaches, eye complaints, vomiting, most are in no position to change their situation, and they are fatalistic. Health hazards from pesticides are vastly under-estimated by the Government, as occupational health problems from pesticides are not recorded.

References:
1. Muthu, Dr. P, 'Assessment of the occupational hazard: carcinogenicity in farmers as a result of pesticide usage, and their education in the scrupulous use of pesticides (Thanjavur District, Tamil Nadu, India)', report submitted to Ashoka Innovators for the Public, July 90- June 91, p. 8.
2. *Pesticides Information*, Vol. XI, Oct-Dec. 1985, India.
3. 'Concern over pesticide residues', *The Hindu*, 11/3/91.
4. Department of Chemicals and Petrochemicals, Government of India, 1989-90, quoted in Dudani, Dr. A.T.. and Sengupta, S., *Status of Banned and Bannable Pesticides*, Voluntary Health Association of India, 1991.
5. Answer to parliamentary question of 24 July 1991.
6. *Agrow*, 7/8/92.
7. 'Indian pesticide production in 1991', *Agrow*, 7/8/92.
8. Murthy, R.C. 'India to Import cotton', *Financial Times*, London, 19/2/92.
9. *Economic Times*, India, 3/12/90.
10. Menon, A.K., 'Death harvest: crop failure leads to suicides', *India Today*, 31/3/88, pp. 19-20, and Sawicki, R.M., 'Report on the control of cotton pests in central and southern India', unpublished report, The Royal Society, London, 1988.
11. Department of Chemicals and Petrochemicals, Government of India, 1989-90, quoted in Dudani, *op. cit.*
12. *Business & Political Observer*, India, 12/12/90
13. *Agrow*, No. 144, 27/9/91, p. 23.
14. *Ibid.*
15. *Business & Political Observer* 4/3/91.
16. *The Economic Times*, India, 7/5/91.
17. Parliamentary question answered on 24 July 1991
18. *Indian Express*, New Delhi, 2/2/92. See also reports in *Pesticides News* No. 15, March 1992 and No. 16, June 1992.
19. 'Concern over pesticide residues', *The Hindu*, 11/3/91
20. Muthu, *op. cit.*
21 'Pesticide poisoning', *India Today*, p. 74, June 1989.
22. Babu, S., *The Hindu*, 29/3/89.
23. Kumar, R.V. Nanda, *Chromatographic and Enzymatic Methods in Andhra Pradesh*, 1987.
24. Report of a workshop held by PREPARE, September 1991.
25. Thomas, C., 'Misuse brings harvest of death to India', *The Times of India*, 19/4/90, and *Agrow* No. 110, p. 21.
26. Dureja, P., Amit, N., *et al*, 'Aldrin and dieldrin in maternal serum, cord serum and breast milk in human samples from Delhi, India', *International Journal of Analytical Chemistry*, 1991: Vol. 44, pp.253-256.
27. 'Concern over pesticide residues', *The Hindu*, 11/3/91.
28. Summarised results in a review by Kalra and Chawla, 1985, *Traces*, Oct-Dec 1987.
29. Letter to the *Financial Express*, 2/3/91, Mathew, N.M. of Voluntary Health Association of India.
30. Voluntary Health Association of India, quoted in the *Economic Times*, India, 7/5/91.
31. *Business & Political Observer*, 8/4/91.
32. *Times of India*, 30/1/91.

13. Country Report: Malaysia*

Malaysia is a major exporter of agricultural produce and has, over the last 20 years, adopted a successful policy of diversification to decrease dependence on a small number of crops. Always significant, the plantation agricultural sector has been seen as the key to economic growth, and agrochemicals have been used to boost production levels.

In 1989, the annual pesticide bill amounted to $300 million, 80% of which was for herbicides. Demand has increased annually over the previous five years by about 6%, and flourished after the 1988 improvement in commodity prices. In spite of some concerns about the impact on health, particularly of plantation workers, the government believes that 'it cannot be denied that the use of pesticides has benefited agriculture.'[1] Some 8,000 agricultural labourers are estimated to work as pesticide applicators in the plantation sector, and the majority of spray work is carried out by women. Plantation workers are generally from the Tamil minority.

Health and safety

Many in Malaysia are greatly concerned about the impact of pesticides on estate workers, rural communities, and in food residues. The National Union of Plantation Workers believes that 'Hundreds have lost their lives and limbs because of wrong handling of pesticides, besides having permanent scars and loss of finger nails.'[2] With an average wage of around $10 per day, conditions on plantations are poor. The union would like to see tighter regulation, with workers trained in the use of sprayers and then licensed by the Ministry of Agriculture.

In spite of the concern, and attempts by consumer and environment organisations and some sections of industry to promote pesticide education and training, blatant and careless abuses are still common. One brand of rat poison which resembled candy was distributed to rice farmers by a pesticide company in Seberang Perak for testing in their rice fields. One child was admitted to the Teluk Intan District Hospital, having mistaken the poison

---

* The material for this case study was provided by Pesticides Action Network (PAN) Asia and the Pacific. Much of it is based on a survey carried out by PAN and Tenaganita, now published as *Victims Without Voice* (1992), together with press reports from Malaysian papers.

for candy. The poison was distributed in white plastic packets, with inadequate labels and warnings, and the name could not be identified.[3]

Extent of poisoning and death

Consumer groups argue that most poisonings are not identified, particularly chronic pesticide poisoning. The figures available are confused by the high levels of pesticide-related suicides in Malaysia, but the reported cases of accidental poisonings and deaths are still high (see Table 13.1), and are a cause for concern with the authorities. In Negri Sembilan State, the government is considering methods of enforcing stricter control on the use of weedkillers in estates in view of the substantial numbers of paraquat poisonings each year.[4]

Paraquat is a major concern, and consumer groups believe that death due to paraquat poisoning is increasing. Many believe that banning or severely restricting its availability would improve the situation in Malaysia. The environmental group, Sahabat Alam Malaysia (SAM), has called for a six-year ban: Mr Varatha Rajoo, commenting on four deaths in one week in 1990 from paraquat noted that, 'We understand that it is one of the cheapest pesticides available in the market, but the government must not forget that it is also the most deadly.'[5] SAM carried out a survey of paraquat use on 30 estates, which it sent to the Pesticides Board, the Labour and Agriculture Ministries, and the Prime Minister's Department. However, although the government indicated that it would investigate, it has not yet done so.

Table 13.1 Reported cases of accidental pesticide poisonings in two Malaysian states.

Cameron Highlands[6]		
1989:	9	accidents; one death. Six of children under 10.
Negri Sembilan[7,8]		
1989 (Jan-Oct):	43	deaths (one child under 12), of which 40 were accidental consumption of paraquat.
1988:	29	cases of accidental poisoning, primarily paraquat: a number were fatal.
1987	18	accidental cases, primarily paraquat.

Source: As referenced in table.

The majority of accidents are assumed to occur on plantations, but this is not always the case. In 1989, an 11-year-old schoolboy, S. Sivakumar, from Bahau, Seremban, died and his 10-year-old cousin, B. Gopi, was reported seriously ill in hospital. Traces of paraquat were found in the urine of the two boys and health authorities in Bahau conducted throat swabs and urine samples on 30 other schoolchildren in Bahau. There was no cause to admit other students, but it is not known how the two boys were poisoned.[9]

Chronic health effect

These statistics do not reflect the chronic health impact. In 1991 two local groups conducted a random survey of 50 women pesticide sprayers from six estates in the State of Selangor. The interviews revealed the pervasive health hazards related to pesticides.[10]

Sprayers interviewed showed a high level awareness of the hazards of pesticides. All believed that pesticides could be dangerous to human beings when exposed to high levels, or exposed over a long period. All were aware of the dangers of swallowing or breathing pesticides. Many said that if they breathed in pesticides in their concentrated form, the fumes are so strong that it causes nausea and burning sensations in their respiratory tract.

Almost 20% of those interviewed were not aware that pesticides could be absorbed through the skin and a number said that neither the plantation management nor the health authorities had informed them of this possibility. Yet skin contact is common, even with concentrated active ingredients. Workers mix pesticides with their hands, and treat regular ill-effects, such as nose-bleeds, headaches and nausea, as part of the job (see Chapter 3).[11]

The survey asked about a number of pesticides commonly sprayed on the estates: paraquat, 2,4-D, carbaryl, dimethoate and lindane, and found many symptoms associated with working with these pesticides. The symptoms are not fatal but cause intense discomfort to pesticide applicators, whose jobs will involve spraying 6-10 hours a day for up to 10 months of the year. Symptoms can be differentiated, depending on the active ingredient. The symptoms identified with three pesticides are summarised in Table 13.2. The women also made comments on particular pesticides.

Paraquat: Paraquat is very widely used on Malaysian plantations to clear weeds. Its notoriety as a suicide agent has distracted attention from the range of physical discomforts it inflicts on sprayers. Table 13.2 indicates that all the workers interviewed are troubled by skin rashes, most of them often. This rash is so common that, in general, workers only go to the estate clinic to see the hospital assistant when it is really bad. One woman said:

> I have skin rash. I go to see the doctor in the estate hospital. He gives me some cream. I apply the cream until I run out of it. My skin rash is still there. I must save money to go to the private clinic now. —Minah.

When contacted in a more concentrated form, workers pointed out that paraquat leaves the skin of the hands dry and fissured, sometimes resulting in loss of fingernails. In addition prolonged contact with paraquat often causes skin blistering and ulceration.

2,4-D: The chlorophenoxy herbicide 2,4-D is often promoted as unproblematic, compared with the widely-banned chlorophenoxy herbicide 2,4,5-T. However, almost all sprayers interviewed suffered some problems when using 2,4-D and said that prolonged inhalation sometimes causes dizziness.

Table 13.2 **Incidence of symptoms and complaints of sprayers working with three pesticides commonly applied on six Malaysian plantations—paraquat, lindane and dimethoate.**

Symptoms of illness/complaint	Paraquat (bipyridyl) (sample 50)			Lindane (OC) (sample 36)			Dimethoate (OP) (sample 35)		
			Total			Total			Total
	A	B	%	A	B	%	A	B	%
Skin rash	5	45	100%	18	18	100%			
Discoloured, irregular nails	10	20	60%						
Nose bleeds	1	1	4%						
Vomiting	7	4	22%	7	3	30%			
Nausea				22	7	80%	-	35	100%
Stomach pain				22	7	80%			
General muscle ache	4	5	18%						
Muscular weakness				29	7	100%			
Tight feeling chest							7	7	40%
Difficulty breathing									
Sore/ red/watering eyes	9	20	58%				35	-	100%
Blurred/darkened vision							14	7	60%
Cough	4	5	18%						
Difficulty breathing				11	7	50%			
Dizziness				18	10	80%	20	7	80%
Headache							35	-	100%
Tiredness							-	35	100%
Unusual sweating							14	7	60%

A = Number suffering from stated symptoms occasionally
B = Number suffering from stated symptoms often
Source: Supplied by PAN Asia and the Pacific, based on interviews for Victims Without Voice, 1992.

Carbaryl: The respondents identified a number of symptoms associated with spraying carbaryl, most commonly: headache, tiredness, stomach pains and dizziness. Two reported occasional blurred and darkened vision. Some workers testified that on days when they mix Sevin (carbaryl) and inhale concentrated fumes, they have difficulty breathing and an unusual amount of sweating occurs. This passes if they rest.

General symptoms

The treatment for irritation by, and exposure to, many pesticides is to bathe and shampoo with soap and water to remove chemicals from skin and hair.

Eye contact demands flushing with copious amounts of clean water for 10-15 minutes. However there are no washing facilities in the field where pesticides are sprayed, and it is impossible to wash. This is a normal situation in Third World countries. Occasionally, if skin contact is high, they will get water from the nearby monsoon drains (only in the rainy season, at other times these drains are dry). The drains are also contaminated by spray drift and run off.

Symptoms which are associated with mild or moderate exposure to organophosphates were widely reported. These include: dizziness, headache and nausea—experienced by 95% of the workers often or occasionally; and anxiety and restlessness, prominent in 90% of the workers interviewed. These symptoms are invariably treated as flu by the medical officer from the nearby hospital.[12] The interviewer concludes that:

> Repeated exposure to organophosphates at significant dosage, although in amounts not sufficient to cause acute poisoning, may be the cause of persistent headache, tiredness and tearing among the workers interviewed..

The majority of sprayers seek medical attention when needed from hospitals, which are free, but are resigned to receiving scant treatment and believe they must go to private clinics to receive proper attention.

Paraquat—suicide issue

Paraquat is highly toxic, and has no known antidote. It is freely available in Malaysia, and is responsible for a large number of suicides. From 1986 to March 1990, a total of 1,156 people committed suicide by drinking pesticides, primarily paraquat. The highest numbers are from the main plantation areas, in particular Selangor (323); followed by Negri Sembilan (171); Pahang (151); and Johor (14). The main reasons are family problems, depression, debt, failure in love, examination failure. But the easy availability of pesticides is undoubtedly a contributing factor, and these figures prompt calls for measures to control the availability of pesticides.[13]

In some instances the line between suicide and accident is blurred, and the easy availability of paraquat leads to unnecessary death. In Tanah Rata, three girls who were threatened with bodily harm by a villager drank paraquat in school. One of the girls, Vanaja Gopal, had died and, at the time the incident was reported, the other two were in a critical condition. All three lived on a nearby estate and one had brought the bottle from home.[14]

Environmental impact

There are few studies of the environmental impact of pesticides in Malaysia. In one study, local scientists confirmed rice farmers' belief that fish and other life forms in paddy fields have been adversely affected by pesticides, creating a sudden and obvious drop in fish and amphibians.[15] The scientists expressed concern that nearby rivers and lakes are also affected. A similar study carried out by Universiti Malay in Tanjong Karang area of Selangor, two years previously, made the same observations.[16]

Legal

Pesticides are regulated under the Pesticides Act 1974. In 1991 the Pesticides Board issued a draft of Pesticides (Advertising Regulations), designed to further tighten up the manner of advertising pesticides, and ensure that advertising complies with the FAO Code. Under the new regulations all advertisements must be approved by the board, unless they do not make claims to efficacy and safety.

In 1991, 19 people were charged with violating the Pesticides Act. Common offences were adulteration of pesticides by shopkeepers and manufacturers and production of pesticides below specifications. The arrests resulted from 2,500 raids and inspections on shops over the year, and resulted in products worth more than $3,000 being impounded.[17] This is an indication of the extent of the problem of adulteration. Most Third World countries do not monitor or enforce quality control, and Malaysia cannot pick up all cases of adulteration and repacking.

Education, training and labelling

Training at the state level is poor. The National Union of Plantation Workers would like to see the Ministry of Agriculture be responsible for the training and licensing of sprayers.

ICI Malaysia launched a product stewardship programme five years ago. Dr. Susannah Jacobs, medical adviser with the company has made regular visits to estates since initiating the programme, and the company believes that proper handling of pesticides has improved among workers, medical staff and management personnel.[18] ICI employs one stewardship officer, who meets smallholders in land settlement schemes and smallholdings for group discussions on safety. The company also holds contests on 'Safe Storage of Pesticides', 'Read the Label' and children's drawing competitions to increase awareness. More recently ICI has sponsored a puppet show depicting one day in the life of a spray operator, carrying the safety messages.

Fundamentally, ICI, like all pesticide corporations, believes that it 'cannot be held accountable for abuse of their products by farmers who may not read product labels or fail to understand them'.[19] Unfortunately, promotion of 'safe' use has a similar impact to promotion of pesticides. Like all advertising, it is consciousness of a product name which prompts a sale. Nor does ICI have the capacity to educate the majority of the farmers in the country. Without government backing, plantation owners have little incentive to reduce pesticide use, as it is not their health, but that of their workers, which is affected.

Labelling

At a meeting hosted by the Malaysian Agricultural Chemicals Association, S.H. Tan of the Department of Agriculture's Pesticide Control Branch asked for improved labelling practices in the country. He said there was a lack of commitment by certain companies to ensure that product labels were accurate.

Food residues

Little information is available on pesticide residues. In September 1991 an incident occurred with pesticide residues in a dark green-leaf vegetable for local consumption, *sayur manis* (also known as *pucuk manis*). Klang health authorities found residues of methamidophos more than 500 times the permitted level. Eleven people were hospitalised, although there may have been more casualties, some with milder forms of food poisoning, depending on how the vegetable was cooked. (A soup would impart milder effects than stir fry). Methamidophos is normally sprayed on potatoes, edible fat and edible oil, peaches, citrus fruits, water melon, brinjal, cucumber, capsicum, tomato and leafy vegetables. The authorities suspect this incident originated on the big farms in Subang or Sungai Buloh as the small or backyard farmers would not use so much pesticides.[20]

An anomaly of Malaysian law was the fact that use of pesticides registered under the Pesticide Act 1974 could contravene the Food Act of 1983, which regulates pesticide residues in food. The maximum residue levels established under the Food Act are based on Codex maximum residue levels (MRLs). Codex MRLs tend to be agreed several years after a product's commercialisation, and new products have no Malaysian MRL, making any food residues illegal.[21]

Alternatives to pesticides

There is recognition in some quarters of the need for new ways to control pests, weeds and diseases. The Agriculture Minister, Datuk Seri Sanusi, called for a reduction in the 'alarming' increase in the use of pesticides at the opening of an International Conference on Biological Control in Tropical Agriculture. In 1991, Law Hieng Ding, the Science, Technology and Environment Minister, called for a review of the rising trend of chemical pesticide usage and pointed to successes in Malaysia using biological controls, for example against oil palm bagworms and rhinoceros beetles in coconut trees and rearing sheep in rubber plantations to reduce the need for weed-killing chemicals.[22]

A further success has been the use of owls to control rats in Selangor paddy fields where pesticides have failed.[23] This biological method will be used extensively following the successful pilot project by the State Agriculture Department three years ago. The cost of the project is around $250,000, mainly the cost of building owl coops in strategic spots in paddy fields. Each coop costs about $250, but lasts up to 20 years. The coops must be built to attract owls, who would normally seek shelter in tall buildings and roofs. Owls are more economical that pesticides, with one pair consuming 3000 rats a year. It is worth noting that, in spite of the success of this scheme, one pesticide corporation uses the programme to promote its product in competition: Rhône Poulenc advertises its pesticide, Draw Bait, saying that it will, 'together with the owl exterminate rats.' The ad implies that the only way to get rid of rats 100% is to use pesticides to supplement the owls. If this were the case, the owls would leave the area and the programme would be undermined.

Malaysian Agricultural Research and Development Institute (Mardi) runs a project to promote integrated pest management to vegetable farmers in the highland areas. It has been running for two years and, according to Mardi senior research officer Dr. Syed A. Rahman, it has proved successful.[24] Mardi hopes to introduce the scheme to lowland farmers shortly. Malaysia grows more than 50 types of vegetables, tropical and temperate species, cultivated on 14,000 ha, of which 2,000 are in highland areas. Dr. Syed pointed out that, 'The use of chemical pesticides has decreased tremendously, especially among Cameron Highlands farmers. From 1989 to 1990 there has been a decrease of more than 50%.' The Department of Agriculture has been monitoring pesticide residue levels and found drastic reductions.

Conclusion

Health and environmental organisations in Malaysia have campaigned for many years for tighter regulations on pesticides use, but the country has widespread problems of pesticide misuse because of difficulties enforcing the law and lack of political will. Surveys, such as that referred to in this case study, indicate that pesticide-related chronic ill-health is prevalent among agricultural labourers. Because of the importance of plantations to the Malaysian economy, the necessary education and training or investment in more sustainable agricultural production techniques, would involve a major political commitment from the government. There is a growing body of work and experiments on non-chemical alternatives which would reduce the present scale of pesticide use in the country if it were systematically adopted.

References:
1. Parliamentary Secretary to the Agriculture Ministry, Encik Mohamed Shariff Haji Omarm, quoted in the *New Straits Times*, 14/8/91.
2. Krishnan, N., research officer at the National Union of Plantation Workers, quoted in the *New Straits Times*, 1/12/90.
3. 'Poison—candy in the hands of farmers', *Business Times*, 5/12/89.
4. *New Straits Times*, 22/2/89.
5. 'Call to ban paraquat: time for action on suicide potion— SAM', *Malay Mail*, January 1990.

6. *New Straits Times*, 21/4/91.
7. Mohamed, Dr. Taha Arif, director of the State Health and Medical Services in Seremban, quoted in *New Straits Times*, 14/1/90.
8. *New Straits Times*, 22/2/89.
9. *New Sunday Times*, 19/2/89.
10. Arumagum, V., *Victims Without Voice: a survey of women pesticides sprayers*, Tenaganita and Pesticides Action Network Asia and the Pacific, Malaysia, 1992.
11. Material collected for *Victims Without Voice, op. cit.*, 1992.
12. *Ibid.*
13. '1,156 suicides from drinking pesticides', *New Straits Times*,. 4/6/90.
14. *The Star*, 18/1/90.
15. 'Insects threaten agri-lifeforms', reported in *New Straits Times*, 18/5/91.
16. Rani Abdullah, Dr. Abdul, pesticide chemist, quoted in *The Star* and *New Straits Times*, 28/8/91.
17. '19 charged with violation of Pesticides Act', *Nation*, 2/9/91.
18. 'Educating planters on safe use of pesticides', *The Star*, 6/9/91.
19. 'Companies not to blame for pesticide abuse', quoting Iain Brown, general manager and director of ICI Agrochemicals (Malaysia) Sdn. Bhd., *Malay Mail*, 11/12/90.
20. 'Greens horror: more than 500 times permitted pesticides in sayur manis', *Malay Mail*, 11/9/91.
21. *Agrow*, No. 161, 12/6/92, p. 20.
22. 'Law: need to review the use of chemical pesticides', two-day seminar on Pest Management and the Environment in the Year 2000, reported in *New Straits Times*, 8/5/91.
23. 'Owls pass rat test', *Malay Mail*, 26/11/90.
24. *Straits (Business) Times*, 9/5/91.

14. Conclusion

There has been considerable international policy directed to reducing the health and environmental hazards of pesticides over the last 10 years particularly, though not exclusively, through the FAO Code and its PIC provisions. These have focused on assisting developing countries to build a capacity to manage chemicals, tighter controls and education and training. This book has primarily looked at the assumption that better management of chemicals in international trade will reduce and eliminate the hazards of pesticide use in developing countries. The evidence presented in this report suggests that pesticide problems have not been substantially reduced in Third World countries, and in some cases may have increased with growing pesticide use. The focus on pesticide safety needs to be balanced with a focus on safer, non-chemical alternatives for sustainable agriculture and rural development.

The country reports published here bring new information, but unfortunately not new issues. There is a continuing cause for grave concern on the health and the environmental impact of pesticides, in spite of undoubted effort. The conditions guiding the training and handling of pesticides in industrialised countries are not uniform standard practice in those countries and cannot be achieved in the majority of countries in Asia, Latin America and Africa, where literacy may be a problem, and where basic washing facilities are often lacking and medical facilities are distant. It may conceivably be possible for certain large-scale agricultural schemes to provide this level of training. However, indications show this is not a priority. Even among some of the richer developing nations, such as Malaysia and Brazil, expectations of good occupational health and safety support for the plantation workforce is remote.

Campaigns and trade controls have reduced the availability and application of a number of older, environmentally persistent organochlorine pesticides, although some remain in common use. But problems persist. Their replacement by organophosphate and carbamate pesticides has adversely affected the health of pesticide applicators and others exposed in Third World countries. Few of the pesticides responsible have yet been included in the PIC process. Until these are incorporated, PIC will not be addressing the substantial health problems in Third World countries.

There is almost no monitoring of the health impact of pesticides, although some non-governmental organisations have conducted surveys. Other information comes from hospitals and poison centres, but this tends to be distorted by suicide incidents, and does not provide a guide to occupational poisoning. Where surveys of occupational poisoning exist, such as in Brazil, Costa Rica and Guatemala, the incidence of poisoning is high.

There are a negligible number of scientific studies on the environmental impact of pesticides in Third World countries, but country reports indicate environmental concerns. In particular in rural areas where pesticides are regularly used, there are problems guaranteeing clean water, maintaining fish supplies, and preservation of flora and fauna for a balanced ecology. Insect resistance and resurgence is a great problem.

Training aimed at improving health and safety awareness is essential, but cannot by itself address the fundamental issue of poverty, which intensifies the problems of pesticide use, and means many small farmers cannot read labels, afford protective clothing, or risk experimenting with other methods of agricultural production. Agricultural labourers are rarely in a position to dictate the terms of their employment. It is questionable whether those who can afford protective clothing could wear it in tropical conditions, and technical or engineering controls for safety are rarely available. The issue is not only one of safety but also one of economy: where insect resistance and resurgence has been created through pesticide use, farmers have suffered economic loss, and governments have lost revenue.

Impact of PIC
While it is too early to assess the impact PIC might have, most countries have welcomed the procedures. In many Third World countries, the United Nations is their strongest source of information, and the PIC process can only strengthen this. It is hoped that related developments, such as making a data base available, will transfer substantial information, and also strengthen the existing information exchange function of the International Register of Potentially Toxic Chemicals.

Although the initial list is small, it offers the potential to include any pesticide banned or severely restricted for health or environmental reasons, or which is hazardous to health or the environment under conditions of use in developing countries. However, there is concern that some governments might only participate superficially, by receiving information, but not acting on this to prevent hazardous imports. Until non-hazardous alternatives to pesticides causing health or environmental concerns are available, the ability to act on the information may also be limited, as alternatives could be more hazardous, or non-existent.

At present European countries export only a small proportion of the pesticides on the PIC list. This is partly because the first pesticides on the list are old, are not widely used (or used at all) in Europe, and are out of patent. Several are now manufactured in India, Taiwan or South Korea.

Taiwan in particular exports many of the more hazardous pesticides and is not participating in PIC. Unless all producing countries are required to participate in the PIC process, the availability of these hazardous pesticides cannot be reduced. Technology transfer to Third World countries is desirable, but this needs to take place in a manner which does not pose threats to Third World communities, and should not consist of technologies and products rejected by industrialised countries.

The initial criticisms of PIC are the time it has taken to get underway and the limited number of pesticides—many of which are in diminishing use—which have so far qualified for inclusion in the process. While delays are understandable in the initial phases, it is now time for governments to use the opportunity PIC presents. If the PIC list remains small and restricted only to pesticides already in limited use, then the scheme will fail to meet its intentions. PIC offers a partial but important basis for preventing unwanted imports of hazardous products. It offers a clear structure for action; and a process which non-governmental organisations, community groups and others can relate to when they seek to eliminate hazardous pesticides and promote safer alternatives.

Addressing the issues

Agricultural production needs to incorporate the precautionary principle and to adopt and develop methods that are not only productive in the long term, but also pose minimal hazards to people and the environment.

In the meantime, relevant pesticide-testing data needs to be carried out for Third World countries and resources put into monitoring impacts of pesticides used. Pesticide registration schemes are being implemented in many more countries, but a recent workshop in Sweden on the role of science in pesticide management pointed out that, with the possible exception of India, no Third World countries had the necessary independent scientific bodies able to carry out risk assessment in pesticide management. In particular, there is often a lack of liaison between health, environment and agriculture ministries, and most countries are desperately short of toxicologists. Legislation relating to pesticide distribution and use is essential. However a number of countries in this study have comprehensive legislation which is ignored in practice. The political will and resources for enforcement are lacking.

Two recent international conventions have taken a broader stance on pesticides in their region. Under the Barcelona Convention, 17 Mediterranean countries pledged, in 1991, to phase out organophosphates hazardous to health and the environment by 2005. In 1991, 12 African countries seeking to ban the import of hazardous substances which have been banned, cancelled or refused registration, or voluntarily withdrawn in the country of manufacture for human health or environmental reasons, drew up the Bamako Convention on the Ban of the Import into Africa and the Control of Transboundary Movement and Management of Hazardous Wastes within Africa. In the United States, environmental organisations have lobbied for 'circle of poison' legislation, to ban the export of pesticides banned or not registered for use in the US.

These conventions and circle of poison legislation underline the urgency of a need for positive alternative agricultural strategies, based on sustainable alternatives. The resources available for conventional, chemical-based agriculture are far greater than those for alternatives. In addition, the pesticide industry supports institutions which influence agricultural production, such as universities and agricultural colleges. In a number of the countries reported in this book, directors of agrochemical corporations are government advisers or politicians.

Regulations and information exchange are unlikely to reduce the majority of health and environmental problems in Third World countries. These are caused by poverty and lack of resources to use pesticides safely. Education and training initiatives are welcomed, but resources must be committed to providing substantial support for a range of policies aiming to reduce pesticide use, drawing on the experience of integrated pest management, the agro-ecology, low external inputs for sustainable agriculture, organic farming and sound land husbandry. Without this, countries will not be in a position to ban the import of pesticides on the PIC list, as their agricultural production will be dependent on their use.

The lack of a body with responsibility for monitoring or enforcement of the FAO Code and related practice means that these tasks are left to voluntary efforts. The information here points to further recommendations for reducing pesticide problems.

Recommendations

Prior Informed Consent Provisions

❑ Implementation of the PIC procedures should not be constrained by lack of resources. Financial, technical, educational and regulatory support should be forthcoming from industrialised countries to assist implementation of PIC procedures in developing countries.

❑ Governments should be required to make available to non-governmental organisations and the public generally the information they receive through the PIC procedure.

❑ The PIC procedures should be strengthened, to ensure that all pesticides causing health and environmental concern are included in the process.

❑ The information-sharing on pesticides which are not included in the PIC process should be supported and extended.

❑ Measures taken to limit trade in hazardous pesticides and to promote sustainable agriculture, must not be regarded as a restriction to free trade and thus blocked by potential agreements under the General Agreement on Tariffs and Trade.

Strengthening implementation

❏ The FAO Code and its PIC provisions remain voluntary. Governments should adopt the FAO Code and Prior Informed Consent as national legislation. The European Community has adopted a Regulation to ensure compliance with PIC in member states. Consideration should be given to encouraging legally binding processes, with resources for monitoring and enforcement.

❏ Exporting countries should introduce government licensing schemes to prevent exports of unwanted pesticides on the PIC list.

❏ Third World countries should require testing data showing suitability of pesticides relevant to conditions of use in the agro-ecological zone, and under the social and economic conditions of use.

❏ Governments should introduce import bans for PIC pesticides and any others they consider too harmful for use in their countries.

❏ Exporting countries should ban the production and export of pesticides prohibited for use in their countries for health or environmental reasons.

Health and environmental impact

❏ There should be a programme of research into the costs and benefits of pesticide use, taking account of the indirect health and environmental costs.

❏ The precautionary principle should be accepted for agricultural production, and agricultural systems should be adopted which prevent the need for chemical inputs, as in organic farming and LEISA.

❏ The use of internationally acceptable standards of health and safety in the manufacture of hazardous chemicals should be introduced into all manufacturing and formulation plants.

❏ If pesticides are to be used in an area where new land is being put to agricultural use, a full ecological study of prevailing fauna and flora and studies on the existing ecological relations should be carried out.

Reducing risks

❏ The World Health Organisation has developed 'use categories' for pesticides, in recognition of the need to restrict certain pesticides to trained licensed, professional operators, commercial applicators and permitted users. Use categories for pesticides are helpful and should be promoted to reduce access to hazardous pesticides.

❏ Education and training programmes to reduce the risks of pesticides are welcome, but cannot address low levels of literacy, inaffordable protective clothing, lack of washing facilities and distant medical facilities. As training is primarily aimed at those who in turn train others, it should only be run in the context of safe, available alternatives.

❏ Pesticide use should not be advocated if conditions for safe use do not exist. This implies the need for more monitoring of the health of pesticide applicators and the environmental impact. In particular it is apparent from this report that although the pesticide impact on health is widely identified, the pesticides causing problems cannot all be identified.

❑ The practice of aerial spraying should be eliminated as a standard agricultural practice.

Transport, storage and disposal

❑ FAO guidelines on transport, storage and disposal should be implemented.

❑ Pesticide disposal needs to be more closely regulated, and industry should develop more technical and engineering controls with a view to safe disposal of containers, and operate a return-to-sender policy for collecting used containers.

❑ The 'polluter pays principle' should be applied to manufacturers of pesticides which damage the environment, and not only to individual farmers.

Freedom of information

❑ Pesticide manufacturers need to ensure that information is available, including technical data, hazards, restrictions on use, requirements for safe use, antidotes, and references to independent research.

❑ There needs to be more transparency in pesticide trade, in particular full data on pesticide exports, including bulk shipments of the active ingredient, should be available.

Alternatives

❑ Resources should be directed to providing information on promoting and implementing safe alternatives, and in particular non-chemical alternatives which promote sustainable agricultural production.

❑ The joint FAO/Netherlands government conference on Sustainable Agriculture and Rural Development recommended that inventories and studies of 'diverse forms of agriculture systems, including low external input sustainable agriculture and organic agriculture farming systems' should be undertaken to 'determine the scope of their agronomic, environmental and socio-economic viability in different farming and population density conditions, as well as evaluating their environmental and social performance.' This should be adopted by governments as part of a programme for developing more sustainable agricultural systems.

Annex 1

Product Stewardship

A survey of the 13 largest agrochemical corporations based in Europe and the United States sought to establish the approach industry has taken to comply with the provisions of the International FAO Code of Conduct on the Distribution and Use of Pesticides (the Code). The questionnaire was open-ended, as set out below, and the summary sets out the companies' views of their responsibilities and policies, and does not attempt to provide an analysis of the effectiveness of these policies.

*** *** ***

Questionnaire to Agrochemical Corporations

1. Policy:
a. What is the company's stewardship policy? Please attach any documentation setting this out.
b. What are the lines of communication within the company to ensure the policy is implemented? Who within the company is ultimately responsible for ensuring the policy is correctly implemented, and what measures would be taken if it was found that the policy was not working as envisaged?
c. What is the budget allocation to operate the stewardship policy?

2. Labelling:
Does the company use the GIFAP pictograms and the appropriate local language on all products marketed in Third World countries?

3. Advertising:
The PAN/Pesticides Trust recent publication, *The FAO Code: Missing Ingredients*, showed that in spite of major improvements in advertising practices, there are still many instances where pesticide advertisements are contrary to the FAO Code of Conduct. What is your advertising policy? And what measures does your corporation take when subsidiaries place advertisements contrary to the Code?

4. Training:
a. Does your company co-operate with aid and development agencies (World Bank, FAO, USAID, ODA), to ensure that a stewardship element is included in agricultural projects or rural training? In what ways? If possible, please let us have examples of this.
b. Does your company undertake work with agricultural colleges/extension workers?

5. Technical information:

In what ways is technical information and background research on products made available in Third World countries using your products?

6. Distribution:

a. What measures are taken to ensure safety during transportation?

b. How are distributors in Third World countries vetted to ensure they are qualified to sell and provide advice on the agrochemicals they stock?

c. What guidelines does your corporation provide on where and how pesticides can be sold? For example are there caveats on selling through food/grocery shops? Are instructions against repacking pesticides issued to distributors?

d. Do you recommend that dealers:

Sell protective clothing?

Display posters showing sprayers wearing full protective clothing?

Sell safety equipment?

Stock a good supply of free booklets on safe use?

Display the GIFAP pictograms?

e. What educational/training material is made available for dealers (videos, posters, workshops, courses)?

7. Safe use at farm level:

a. How does your company ensure that information is widely available about the dangers of repackaging pesticides, reusing containers, and care and disposal instructions? Please give details.

b. Please comment on other measures taken (in addition to the above) to ensure that pesticides are used safely at farm level.

8. Registration:

Please comment on the company's policy on registration of pesticides in their local markets? How would the company like to see registration of products applied?

NB: We are happy to receive policy documents, and articles written about the stewardship policy, as answers to any of the questions above.

Please reply by: 30 June 1991.

Summary of company responses

Product stewardship has become the means for companies to translate into policies the recommendations contained in the Code. While voluntary, the Code covers corporate obligations to: adequately and effectively test all pesticides (article 4.1); reduce the availability of hazardous formulations and containers (article 5.2); meet regulatory and technical requirements (article 6.2); carry out evaluations on products and make this information available (article 8.1); ensure packaging, storage and disposal of pesticides conform to FAO guidelines (article 10.3); and comply with advertising guidelines (article 11.1).

Companies believe health and environmental obligations can be met through product stewardship, as expressed by Cyanamid: 'We believe that safety and environmental responsibility are fully compatible with the efficient, productive and profitable use of today's agricultural products. Tomorrow's agriculture, and the products farmers will need, require a responsible balance between environmental considerations and the development and application of new technology.'

All the major companies have adopted some form of product stewardship that puts into effect these obligations, although no company was prepared to indicate its budget for product stewardship. The industry association, GIFAP, plays a lead role in developing guidelines to help implement the Code, and many of these agrochemical corporations have a significant input into the work of GIFAP, both in implementing the Code, and in developing educational and training materials to improve safe pesticide use.

Many of the corporations mentioned their belief that agrochemicals are essential to provide food for an increasing world population, and to the estimated 30% annual crop losses due to pests and disease prevented by pesticides. ICI believes there will be increasing use by smallholders on food crops such as vegetables, rice, beans, maize and fruit which would be partly retained for domestic use and partly sold for cash.

Occupational health and safety is a key issue in Third World countries, where conditions make it difficult to ensure that pesticides can be used safely. It is hard for stewardship programmes to reach field level, and in particular to address the problems faced by agricultural labourers. As Bayer said, 'We believe a lot of material is readily available, yet the problem often is their distribution to every single ultimate pesticide user.'

Companies say considerable resources have been committed to labelling, education and training material. Training initiatives are undertaken both by companies directly, and through GIFAP. In October 1991, GIFAP launched three pilot Safe Use Projects, in Thailand, Guatemala and Kenya. These three-year projects aim to promote training; improve standards in manufacturing; promote pesticide control laws; introduce into rural schools an awareness of the need for proper handling of agricultural chemicals; and demonstrate that pesticides can be handled safely.

The survey does not include major Japanese companies, which at present rank below the 13 major companies on the basis of turnover, but whose position is particularly strong in Japan and certain Asian markets. The Safe Use Project, launched by GIFAP in 1991 (see point 7), is also supported by the Japanese Society of Agricultural Chemical Industry. The 13 companies which participated in the survey are:

BASF	German	Hoechst	German
Bayer	German	ICI	British
Ciba-Geigy	Swiss	Monsanto	US
Cyanamid	US	Rhône Poulenc	French
DowElanco	US	Sandoz	Swiss
Du Pont	US	Schering	German
		Shell	British/Netherlands

Table 1 provides an overview of responses, however the information was provided in many different formats, and the more detailed responses are set out below.

1. Policy

1.1 GIFAP and the Code

GIFAP co-ordinates much work on the Code, and has developed a range of guidelines to help its members implement the Code. These include position papers on freedom of information, hazardous substance export, product stewardship, and compliance with the advertising guidelines of the Code. Some companies work primarily through GIFAP. **Rhône Poulenc** said the Code is the 'principles of which our company adheres through GIFAP'. Other companies have contributed to GIFAP's thinking, and support and develop its work on the Code.

A number of working groups have been set up by GIFAP on a regional basis and on aspects of the Code. The current composition is as follows, though it should be noted that participation of all major companies is sought by rotation every couple of years.

Africa/Middle East: Bayer, Ciba-Geigy, Cyanamid, DowElanco, FMC, Hoechst, ICI, Monsanto, Rhône Poulenc, Sandoz, Schering, Shell.
Asia: BASF, Bayer, Ciba-Geigy, Cyanamid, DowElanco, FMC, ICI, Monsanto, Nihon Noyaku, Rhône Poulenc, Schering, Shell, Sumitomo
Latin America: BASF, Bayer, Ciba-Geigy, DowElanco, Du Pont, Hoechst, ICI, Monsanto, Rhône Poulenc, Rohm & Haas.

1.2 Overview of company policies

All 13 agrochemical corporations officially endorse and promote the Code. Several of the companies (**ICI, Shell, Du Pont**) point out that they were actively involved in its development. Product stewardship develops pledges under the Code into company policy. As **Hoechst** pointed out, 'we understand product stewardship to mean the translation into action of the recommendations contained in the Code.'

While some companies were not specific about the extent of their stewardship, others indicated far-reaching intentions. **BASF** said that 'responsibility for products extends beyond the warehouse', while **Cyanamid** said it will 'develop and market only products that can be manufactured and used in a safe and environmentally sound manner to help produce a reliable, plentiful supply of low-cost food and fibre.'

Bayer, Ciba-Geigy, Cyanamid, ICI, Monsanto and **Sandoz** noted that they relate product stewardship to clean production, as well as to marketing, education and training. **ICI** pledges to take foremost account of safety and health and to manage activities to benefit society, including acceptability to communities, reducing adverse effects on the environment to a 'practicable minimum': 'Product stewardship embraces both a philosophy and a set of policies and activities which aim to ensure that ICI Agrochemicals develops, manufactures, promotes, distributes and markets its products in a socially and environmentally responsible way.'

In January 1990, **Monsanto** made a pledge which promises to reduce all toxic and hazardous releases and emissions working towards an ultimate goal of zero effect; to ensure no Monsanto operation poses an undue risk to employees and communities; to work to achieve sustainable agriculture through new technology and practices; to ensure groundwater safety; to keep plants open to communities and involve the community in plant operations; to manage all corporate real estate, including plant sites, to benefit nature; and to search world-wide for technology to reduce and eliminate waste from its operations, with the top priority being not making it in the first place.

Ciba-Geigy employees receive a Vision statement covering their responsibility for 'Economy, Society and Environment'. The company expends considerable energy ensuring that this message is understood throughout the company, and that equal weight is placed on the three responsibilities of the vision. It sees that funds for quality generate tangible returns, and company policy is to ensure long-term gains are not sacrificed for short term profits. **DowElanco** sees its primary responsibility as the promotion of health, safety and the protection of the environment, and 'to a strong desire to help our customers and suppliers in aspiring to these same goals.' **Du Pont** has a policy 'to conduct our business in a way that assures our products can be made, used, handled, and disposed of safely and in an environmentally sound manner.'

Most companies implied that they would apply standards even-handedly in all countries where they operate. **ICI** specifically mentioned that it 'applies similar standards of product stewardship in all the countries in which it operates, taking due account of the different constraints imposed by the legal and regulatory requirements in individual countries.'

Companies also pointed out their willingness to investigate infringements of the Code. **Schering** said it would 'investigate all infringements and take the necessary actions to ensure compliance with these basic rules.' **Sandoz** said there 'remain only few significant incidents which we obviously correct as soon as we detect them.' All companies expected their subsidiaries to follow the Code.

1.3 Budget allocation for product stewardship

No company revealed its specific budget allocation for product stewardship, several pointing out that this information is confidential (**Cyanamid, Monsanto, Shell**). **Shell** also pointed out that the overall budget for stewardship is considerable if the central and local expenditures are added together. Others indicated that the management is part of general management in crop protection, and a separate budget cannot be established (**BASF, Bayer, Ciba-Geigy, Dow, Du Pont, Sandoz**). **Ciba-Geigy** noted that 25% of its R&D budget is for product enhancement, concentrating on reducing toxicity, improving biodegradability, making IPM compatible, seeking safer packaging or safer application techniques, such as water soluble bags.

1.4 Implementation of company policies

Companies have implemented their policies in a number of different ways. Some have set up separate departments with responsibility for product stewardship, removing it from marketing pressures, others rest authority with the chief executive officer, or a high-ranking manager.

Separate department established

BASF set up a separate 'Product Safety' department in 1987 to deal with registration, environmental chemistry, communication and product stewardship. Responsibility for product stewardship is shared by agro-representatives world-wide.

Ciba-Geigy. The 'qualified and experienced' personnel responsible for ensuring implementation and monitoring of the Code have a budget which is independent of management, and thus not subsidiary to financial considerations. An extensive programme of visits and education operates to ensure implementation.

ICI established a separate Stewardship and Safety Department in October 1991, which reports to the R&D Director. It manages the product stewardship programme through its infrastructure of national sales companies and distributors. It has a network of product stewards who ensure the public receives a 'fair, accurate account of the safety, health and environmental issues relating to agrochemical products'. The stewards implement ICI agrochemical stewardship policies; make recommendations to management on priorities for improving local company stewardship; participate in reviews of standards on product use and the design and implementation of education and training programmes to ensure safe and effective product use. The company is developing systems to monitor the

Code and identify infringements. ICI advice is sought by other major agrochemical companies to establish their product stewardship programmes.

Hoechst combined its organisational groups to form the Product Development—Product Safety section in 1989 in response to increasingly stringent safety requirements. Product safety managers are in regular contact with specialist departments, sales offices and government bodies in Germany and abroad. This, with the company's guiding principles, are seen as the most important factors for putting product stewardship into practice.

Rhône Poulenc created a Department of Ethics and Environment, which reports directly to the corporation's general management. It has no commercial responsibility, and is responsible for introducing product stewardship on a world scale. The company created product stewardship specialists in more than 20 countries, and is expanding this resource in other countries, particularly by running awareness programmes on aspects of product stewardship at the local management level. Each national subsidiary has initiated a policy of product stewardship tailored to the specifics of its markets and clients, and to regulatory requirements. The company backed up product stewardship in 1989, with a world-wide assistance network of toxicologists, technicians and engineers on call 24 hours a day.

Shell set up a department with responsibility for product stewardship in 1985 and made it a key part of the Crop Protection business strategy. It issued guidelines to all subsidiaries and associated companies in 1987. Stewardship focal points were established in all its operating companies to introduce the strategies and to initiate plans of action. The corporate lines of communication on product stewardship are between Shell International product managers and the operating company crop protection managers. For policy matters and general principles and practice, the communication is between the product stewardship department and the operating company focal points. The crop protection manager is responsible for implementation within Shell.

Board-level responsibility

Cyanamid gives key responsibility for environmental stewardship to the president of American Cyanamid. Each division is ultimately responsible for ensuring that the policy is correctly implemented. The lines of communication to ensure that this policy is implemented extend from the Chairman of the Board and Chief Executive Officer to the President of the Company, the Division Presidents, their Directors and Managers, and each and every employee.

DowElanco stewardship is monitored by a Health, Safety and Environmental Council, with two standing committees and two subcommittees, which include representatives from sales, research and development, scientific and regulatory departments. Geographical liaison operates through administrative personnel in North America, regulatory personnel in Europe, Latin America and the Pacific. Subsidiaries and distributors are monitored for compliance with the Product Stewardship Policy.

Du Pont extends the responsibility and communication to ensure implementation of stewardship policy from the chief executive officer to individual business leaders.

ICI board has overall responsibility for environmental policy, with one executive director nominated to maintain an overview of safety, health and environment matters across the group. The principal executive officers are responsible for provision of environmental standards and reporting procedures internationally. In subsidiaries, the chief executive officer and/or his board are responsible for environmental policy, consistent with local laws and company standards and procedures. On health and safety issues, the main board has overall responsibility, and division chairmen and departmental heads are responsible for implementing and monitoring. It is the duty of all employees to exercise personal responsibility and to co-operate in preventing harm to the environment. ICI encourages subsidiary companies to establish and implement policies in accordance with its stated product stewardship policies.

Monsanto rests responsibility for implementation with the executive vice-president for Environmental Safety, Health and Manufacturing. Within Monsanto Agricultural Company, responsibility for stewardship rests with the vice-president, Environmental and Public Affairs. The director of Registration and Regulatory Affairs is the contact point for matters concerning the Code. Implementation is through two vice-presidents and a director of registration and regulatory affairs. It also relies on its well publicised pledge as a stand by which it can be monitored and judged by employees, stockholders and the public. In 1989, the Agro sector created the Ethics and Environment (E&E) Management in charge of Product Stewardship and Regulatory Affairs. The E&E director reports directly to the Agrochemical general manager. This reporting system and control of registration team give E&E strong authority. It may make decisions on purely ethical concepts in complete independence from business constraints.

General management function

Bayer set up an internal Code working group in 1986 to ensure the implementation of the various product stewardship areas addressed in the Code. This working group draws on personnel from the various line functions: it is assisted by the head of the product safety, advertisement, production safety department and others. Everyone in these departments has stewardship functions and implementation lies in the hands of the respective departments, while the Code working group co-ordinates, sets goals and communicates to subsidiaries.

Sandoz policy is based on responsible management. **Sandoz** had developed specific product stewardship functions which make contact with the appropriate line functions to take corrective measures if and where necessary.

Schering rests responsibility for meeting the requirements of the Code with company headquarters, through heads of relevant functions, such as development, production, sales, marketing, with one person in Germany responsible for co-ordinating all issues. In subsidiaries, responsibility to implement and monitor the Code lies with top management, the divisional manager, or heads of Schering delegations

1.5 Measures taken if policy not working

Not all companies elaborated these measures. **Ciba-Geigy** has established a series of internal audits and 'adequate' corrective actions for ongoing implementation. **Cyanamid** stated it would determine in what ways it was not working then take corrective action to resolve the specific error. **DowElanco** said it would take remedial action as necessary to correct valid complaints. **Shell** stated that if or when deficiencies arise these would be notified to the crop protection manager for remedial action.

2. Labelling

There is little variation between practices followed by the companies, whose policies are to:
(a) Comply with national laws and regulations;
(b) Follow the Code;
(c) Label with required information on product activity, use, and precautionary measures;
(d) Use main local languages, or comply with local regulations regarding language;
(e) Check for compliance with the Code;
(f) Encourage the use of pictograms, and use these in countries which allow them. The Code says industry should use labels that 'include appropriate symbols and pictograms whenever possible'.

Cyanamid requires that product labels must be reviewed and approved by legal, medical and technical disciplines before it can be used on a product. **DowElanco** actively promotes the concept of uniform classification of risk and safety phrases in developing countries. **ICI** developed a guide for label-writers, based on four principles: clarity, completeness, conformity, consistency. **Rhône Poulenc** states it has reviewed all labels existing in developing countries, and has also carried out work on safer packaging. **Shell** produced the 'Shell Agriculture Guidelines for Pesticide Labelling' and distributed these to all its companies. Some governments use these to help establish local labelling legislation. **Bayer** has 'Recommendations for pictogram use on Bayer product labels' which are regularly updated and sent to all subsidiaries.

Table 1. Summary of corporate product stewardship

Stewardship Check List	BASF	Bayer	Ciba Geigy	Cyanamid	Dow	Dupont	Hoechst	ICI	Monsanto	Rhone Poulenc	Sandoz	Schering	Shell
POLICY													
Does company policy include Code	Y	Y	Y	Y	Y	Y	Y	Y	Y	Y	Y	Y	Y
Is there a structure to implement	Y	Y	Y	Y	Y	Y	Y	Y	Y	Y	Y	Y	Y
Is implementation a separate structure	Y	N	N	N	Y	N	Y	Y	Y	Y	N	N	Y
Is ultimate responsibility with board	-	Y	Y	Y	Y	Y	-	Y	Y	Y	-	-	Y
Is implementation monitored	-	Y	Y	Y	Y		-	Y	Y		Y	-	-
Is budget separate(S) or part of normal management functions(M)	M	S	M	S	M	M			M		M		S
Is there a structure for remedial action if policies not working		Y	Y	Y	Y		Y				Y		Y
Does policy cover production as well as distribution		Y	Y	Y				Y	Y		Y		
LABELLING													
Labels comply with FAO Guidelines on good practice	Y	Y	Y	Y	Y	Y	Y	Y	Y	Y	Y	Y	Y
Pictograms used on labels where permitted	Y	Y	Y	Y	Y	Y	Y	Y	-	Y	Y	Y	Y
ADVERTISING													
Does company follow Code or equivalent	Y	Y	Y	Y	Y	Y	Y	Y	Y	Y	-	Y	Y
Does company produce material on safe use	Y	Y	Y	Y	Y	Y	-	Y	-	-	Y		
TRAINING													
Does the company work with aid and development agencies on training		Y	Y	Y	Y			Y	Y				Y
Does the company undertake its own and/or GIFAP training in safe use	Y	Y	Y	Y		Y		Y	Y		Y	Y	Y
Does the company work with agricultural colleges/extension workers	Y	Y	Y	Y	Y	Y		Y	Y		Y	Y	Y
Does the company initiate other safe use education for the public		Y	Y	Y				Y					
TECHNICAL INFORMATION													
Is technical information the same in industrialised and developing countries		Y	Y	Y	Y	Y		Y	Y			Y	Y
Is additional technical information targeted at developing countries			Y	Y				Y					Y

Stewardship Check List	BASF	Bayer	Ciba Geigy	Cyanamid	Dow	Dupont	Hoechst	ICI	Monsanto	Rhone Poulenc	Sandoz	Schering	Shell
DISTRIBUTION													
Comply with strict guidelines, eg GIFAP on transport	Y	Y	Y	Y	Y	Y		Y	Y		Y		Y
Vet Third World Distributors for suitability			Y	Y	Y				Y		Y		Y
Is repacking prohibited (* see 6.1)		Y	Y	Y	Y	Y		N*	Y		Y		
Are distributors deselected if they sell foodstuffs		Y	Y			Y					Y		
Is it recommended that dealers sell protective clothing	Y	Y	Y	Y		Y		Y	Y	Y	Y		Y
Is it recommended that dealers sell safety equipment		Y	Y					Y	Y		Y		
Are dealers supplied with good stock of safety booklets	Y		Y	Y		Y		Y	Y				Y
SAFETY AT FARM LEVEL													
Rely mainly on label instructions													
Carry out own safety demonstrations at farm level		Y	Y	Y		Y			Y		Y	Y	Y
Participate in GIFAP programmes		Y	Y	Y					Y	Y	Y		Y
Involved in safe campaigns for users		Y	Y			Y			Y			Y	Y
REGISTRATION													
Only sell to Third World pesticides registered in US, EC, or OECD country	Y	Y	Y	Y							Y	Y	Y
Only sell if products actually registered in country of purchase		Y	Y	Y					Y		Y		
Complies with local regulatory requirements		Y	Y		Y	Y	Y				Y		

Y=Yes; N=No; Blank indicates company did not respond to this point.

Pictograms

Shell chaired the GIFAP/FAO working group on pictograms. These are now used in some 65 countries, unless their use is not permitted by regulatory authorities (mainly the European Community). Several other companies, such as **ICI, Bayer, Du Pont,** have been involved in the GIFAP working group to improve and establish use of pictograms.

3. Advertising

All companies endorse the Code on advertising for themselves and subsidiaries. GIFAP has developed a checklist of the advertising guidelines in the Code. Hoechst has developed its own checklist. Several mentioned their readiness to correct problems drawn to their attention, for example:

'Corrective actions are made if pertinent.'—**Ciba-Geigy**

'There have been a few occasions in which we have recalled advertising placed by subsidiaries which the company believed was not consistent with Code.'—**Cyanamid**

'We would instruct any subsidiary found to be in violation of these to immediately bring their advertising into compliance.'—**Du Pont**

'Will investigate any complaints about product advertisements that may not meet the intent of the FAO Code and will take corrective action where appropriate.'—**Dow**

'If we detect an advertisement which is not up to FAO Code standards we request an immediate correction.' —**Sandoz**

'If an infraction is observed or notified, we inform local crop protection manager and request remedial action.'—**Shell**

Cyanamid pointed out that PAN/Pesticides Trust and GIFAP have differing interpretations of some aspects of the Code. Thus not all advertising cited in the Missing Ingredients report was withdrawn.

ICI publishes detailed guidance on the Code, with examples of general expressions which are not permitted, such as: 'safer, non-poisonous, harmless, non-toxic, low toxicity, high degree of safety, wide safety margin, safe to the environment, harmless to wildlife etc, environmentally acceptable, wide safety margin in the environment.' This list is more comprehensive than that in the Code.

Monsanto was the only company which objected to PAN monitoring of advertising. It pointed out that it complies with requirements of the Code, and does not agree with PAN allegations that some of its advertisements were in violation: it said these allegations were vague or without foundation. Monsanto questioned whether the publication of these types of allegations by PAN without verifying their authenticity could in itself be a violation of Article 5.4 of the Code (which asks public-sector groups to 'try to distinguish between major differences in levels of risk among pesticides and uses' in order to 'avoid unjustified confusion and alarm among the public').

4. Training / working with aid agencies

We asked companies for information both about general training work in which they are involved, and whether they worked with development agencies on agricultural schemes.

GIFAP launched a 'Safe Use Project' in 1991, which is supported by all the major world-wide agrochemical companies, and the Japanese association of agrochemical manufacturers, the Society of Agricultural Chemical Industry. This is elaborated under point 7.

In 1988, GIFAP produced a training video and two new training manuals, one for training extension staff to give courses in safe pesticide use to small farmers; one to guide the training of retailers to give better advice to farmer customers on using and applying pesticides more safely and effectively. GIFAP has developed the courses with the Agricultural Education and Training Unit of the Wolverhampton Polytechnic (UK).

As part of their product stewardship programmes, companies are increasingly involved in education and training in safe use of their products. The approach is in general 'training the trainers', and companies aim their materials primarily at dealers, retailers and extension officers. No companies indicated the number of countries where education and training was directed, compared to the number where their products are sold. As there is some variation depending on the size and orientation of the company, their comments are summarised below:

BASF provides 'optimal information' on the use of agrochemicals with an emphasis on end user and intermediate levels in every country, and on training in proper handling. 'Training programs of each separate company are paralleled by intensive educational and training programs dealing primarily with the safe use of pesticides.' These train primarily extension officers and dealers, i.e. people who can pass along their expertise on to end users.

Bayer has its own technical service which works with farmers 'in the field', using posters, brochures and films on the safe use. It holds farmers' meetings on safe use and application technology to which it invites dealers. The technical service also operates in some Third World countries, and Bayer has tried a number of approaches: in one country it distributed the film on safe use to retailers to try to reach more farmers, in others, specially equipped 'film cars' visit villages to show it. The film has been translated into many local languages. Bayer did not indicate the Third World countries where this has taken place.

Ciba-Geigy directs training on correct and safe use of pesticides at farmers, distributors, dealers, representatives of authorities, development agencies and extension services. Courses are held in the application station in Switzerland, or under realistic conditions in many countries including Third World. GIFAP and/or Ciba-Geigy training material is disseminated. Discussions are presently underway on strengthening awareness, for example, more communication of good agricultural practice, precautionary measures and better hygiene. Ciba-Geigy has invited representatives of Third World agricultural colleges to Swiss training centres for courses on safe use.

Cyanamid conducts its own training programmes in product stewardship, and participates in programmes of USAID, GIFAP and local government agencies. It works closely with agricultural colleges and experimental stations and sponsors students with scholarships and assistantships. The current level of stewardship co-operation with aid agencies is on an 'as-needed' basis: the only agricultural products subject to such projects are malathion and temephos (ABATE). When these uses were being developed in the 1950s and 1960s, Cyanamid provided technical assistance to ensure their safe, effective use.

Dow supplies appropriate information to extension officers, and runs extensive programmes to support research by agricultural colleges in the countries in which it operates. Dow states it is committed to, and actively co-operates with, international aid and development agencies, such as FAO, USAID and the World Bank to promote the safe use of crop protection products. It particularly supports 'train the trainer' programmes.

Du Pont develops and distributes information on the safe use and handling of products through marketing channels and information sources, including aid and development agencies. Du Pont is involved in global industry training activities for safe use developed under GIFAP. Du Pont trains dealers and distributors to conduct their own information and demonstration activities. The company often supports these activities and provides or collaborates on information materials on safe-use and proper handling. For example, in a pilot programme in Costa Rica, GIFAP has developed, in co-operation with the government, safe use training to rural elementary school children as a regular part of their curriculum. This pilot programme and its implementation has been particularly supported by Du Pont, while being sponsored by major companies.

ICI believes that effective crop protection will continue to depend on the intelligent use of agrochemical technology for the remainder of this century and the beginning of the next, and thus emphasises the need for safe use, Integrated Pest Management and other strategies. ICI indicates that it has carried out a wide range of education and training for over 20 years as part of normal market development. In addition to its own material and programmes, ICI participates in the GIFAP initiatives on safe use, and promotes their material.

ICI policy recognises the importance of 'farmer education and training as a professional company activity alongside the development, marketing and sale of products' and has established a Farmer and Education and Training Section (FEATS), based in the UK. The work of this section includes monitoring the impact of programmes; impact of past initiatives; tailoring for 'target populations'. It is intended to reach smallholders and farm labourers. ICI recognises that there are limitations on the resources for delivering to field level, and states that it is open to suggestions for further improvements. Much of the training work is also aimed at retailers, extension workers, rural paramedics and schools, all of whom have direct contact with users.

FEATS has carried out knowledge, attitude and practice surveys in Malaysia, Central America, Brazil, Indonesia, Paraguay, Thailand, Pakistan,

Colombia, and has plans to extend the surveys. Conclusions were: 'There is little doubt that the integration of mass education techniques with practical training methods in properly managed programmes, tailored to fit local circumstances and targeted at local needs, is the best strategy for improvement, even for the individual company. However, success requires active collaboration between private and public sectors. Both sides need to recognise their shared interests and work towards common goals.' ICI emphasised the need for locally developed programmes; mass education techniques and campaigns to create awareness and change attitudes; prioritising training the trainers; educational videos are used only occasionally.

The most important components to ensure safe use are labels, on-pack leaflets, improved label design and pictograms, all of which 'travel' with the product pack. Also useful are wall posters, mass media, videos and other educational aids. In Malaysia, the company has developed a cartoon booklet ('Adventures of the Grow Safely Team') aimed at increasing awareness in children.

ICI has carried out studies on the potential effectiveness of posters: a survey in Malaysia showed that posters displayed in retail shops achieve only two hours per annum exposure, where those in the dealer shops where smallholders sell rubber would achieve 30 hours per annum exposure. This points to the need for co-operation with public sector organisations so posters reach right into rural areas and are not left with agro-chemical retailers.

Monsanto co-operates with AID/ROCAP in Central America on safe use of pesticides educational programmes through participation in the Latin American Working Group of GIFAP, and actively supported education programmes through local industry associations in Southeast Asia and Latin America. It also undertakes work with agricultural colleges/extension workers. Monsanto pointed out that pesticides are being excluded from most development agency funding on agricultural projects.

Rhône Poulenc has initiated a new regional direction for Africa recently.

Sandoz encourages country managers to participate in training programmes, mostly arranged by local associations. Occasionally a representative from Sandoz works with agricultural colleges/extension workers. The company's major contacts with aid and development agencies is through GIFAP, but it says it would like to increase its co-operation.

Schering believes that education and training are the best vehicles to encourage people to use any product in its correct and safe way.

Shell has co-operated on many occasions with aid and development agencies, both independently and via GIFAP. In the early eighties the company originated the 'train the trainer' courses, which were subsequently developed by the International Agricultural Training Programme (a UK charity) and GIFAP. Shell run a comprehensive course on the safe and effective application of crop protection products, but did not indicate in which countries and how widely this course is run. The company undertakes work with agricultural colleges and extension workers.

5. Technical information

Groups working with small farmers in the Third World and agricultural workers, including their unions, have frequently indicated they have difficulty finding out detailed information about products used. All companies are required to provide full technical information and registration dossiers on each product, but most do not make available additional technical information in Third World countries, or seek to make technical information more accessible under conditions prevailing in Third World countries. Posters and pictograms are, as indicated above, widely used in countries with high illiteracy. Other approaches adopted by companies are:

Bayer's technical service works with local colleges and extension workers, and exchanges information and co-operates with the German aid authorities when requested.

Ciba-Geigy carries out practical demonstrations. Technical information is made country-specific, within an overall framework provided from Switzerland. This is monitored by the company to ensure technical information 'is not sacrificed for sales'.

Cyanamid has a field presence through agronomists, who furnish up-to-date technical information to distributors, growers and researchers through literature, training meetings and field demonstrations. Technical Information Reports and Technical Bulletins, above and beyond the registration dossiers, are distributed to researchers and users, giving extensive information on background research with products. These are routinely translated into Spanish, and into other languages by local subsidiaries.

Dow supplies safety data sheets available on all products to distributors. Many are in several languages. The company encourages its scientists to publish research in scientific journals, and to present work at national and international scientific conferences, ensuring access by the scientific community. However this is not necessarily accessible in Third World countries.

ICI produces a wide range of technical information bulletins for individual products. In some areas, this has been collated into advisory handbooks, e.g. the Tropical Africa Product Handbook, which gives details on products to use on 19 crops for major pests—by crop and pest—and summarises key information: timing and number of applications; restrictions on use; application; dosage rates; safety precautions.

Monsanto will supply detailed technical follow-up briefings on request. The company works with local universities or agricultural extension officials to generate local efficacy data and use recommendations for the farmers in individual countries.

Shell provides technical information in its regulatory review documents, and widely distributes its detailed Shell Agriculture Safety Guide.

6. Distribution

6.1 In transport

Companies emphasised their compliance with the Code, and the GIFAP guidelines, as well as company-specific directives which emphasise, for instance, separation of agrochemical products from food and feed, avoidance of non-professional repacking. GIFAP has produced a Checklist for Production, Formulation and Packaging which is widely followed by its members. Other points made were:

Cyanamid pointed out that Material Safety Data Sheets accompany products in transport. All transportation companies are made fully aware of the properties and potential hazards of products. Safety brochures and emergency telephone numbers are provided.

Du Pont requires its dealers to adhere to the FAO Code and handle its products according to label instructions.

ICI uses 'Transport Emergency' (TREM) cards with all shipments and complies with all road, rail, air and sea regulations.

Sandoz attaches specific safety/emergency data to each shipment. Affiliates are advised to increase their efforts in training truck drivers. Local Associations make general instruction leaflets and some have produced a video for training purposes.

Shell carries out haulier audits where practical. TREM cards are produced in a wide range of languages. Incidents are monitored for lessons and remedial action. Stickers and posters are made available, warning against transporting pesticides with foodstuffs.

6.2 Third World distributors

A number of companies vet distributors in Third World countries. GIFAP publishes a 'Checklist of Industry's Responsibilities for Marketing, Distribution and Sales of Pesticides'. The checklist provides the following guidance:

- standard 1-2 is generally acceptable but might be further improved by attention to specific aspects;
- standard 2+ (but not up to 3) is marginally acceptable but remedial action may be required on specific aspects;
- standard 2.5+ is less than acceptable and remedial action is essential if the company is to continue with the distributor;
- standard 4 (and just below) indicate a high-risk location where immediate withdrawal of company business is recommended until a significant improvement in standards is achieved.

Some additional comments include:

Ciba-Geigy believes that pesticide dealers should be licensed and monitored.

Cyanamid explicitly states that it sells highly toxic products only to distributors meeting its safety standards. In selecting distributors in the Third World (as elsewhere) 'We ensure they are fully qualified to sell agricultural chemicals and to provide correct advice to end user.' Hands-on training courses and workshops are all used where appropriate for training dealers, distributors and their staffs. The company's Corporate Safety Loss Prevention Auditors periodically pay visits to distributors to ensure that safety measures are being followed. The majority of distributors in the Third World are subsidiaries of other large, research-based multinational chemical companies.

ICI uses both GIFAP's and its own safety check list.

Monsanto pointed out that US anti-trust laws limit its ability to select, refuse or control the operations of dealerships.

Sandoz selects distributors, which are informed and trained. Some may be involved during the final development phase.

Shell uses a distributor audit checklist, which is completed by company sales staff when they visit distributors.

6.3 Safe selling/repackaging

Most companies allow only authorised repackaging, and follow FAO Code recommendations where applicable.

Bayer pointed out that the industry tries to avoid dealers which repack products, and have sought to minimise this by developing package sizes to suit respective markets.

Cyanamid seeks to ensure its products are sold safely and according to label directions through field reps. It prohibits repackaging of finished toxic and hazardous products into smaller packages by anyone other than approved formulators, and allows repackaging of less toxic products in approved containers meeting Cyanamid specifications, under proper supervision, with approved labels.

ICI allows repackaging only through approved repacking units which have been checked for safety. The company does all in its power to prohibit illegal repacking.

Monsanto pointed out that the Code encourages governments to prohibit repackaging, but does not prohibit repackaging per se, nor does it require dissemination of information about the dangers. It asks industry to provide an appropriate range of pack sizes to avoid the need. Monsanto complies with this.

Sandoz distributors are not to repack unless they have the necessary facilities and equipment and written agreement with appropriate instructions.

6.4 Protective clothing/equipment

Generally, companies recognise the difficulties of wearing protective clothing in tropical climates, and support FAO and GIFAP initiatives. New GIFAP guidelines aim to make protective clothing locally accessible, at reasonable price, to all farmers, field-workers, professional applicators and other users, particularly in hot and humid climates. While all emphasise use of protective clothing and equipment in promotional and educational material, this does not mean such protection is affordable, wearable or accessible. There was some indication that companies are trying to make sure protective clothing is more widely available, for example that it is issued free through their distributors. However, it should be noted that technical and engineering controls are preferable to sole dependence on protective clothing. A number of companies indicated efforts in this direction.

BASF co-operates with national crop protection associations and distributors to make gear available to users, but recognises it needs to improve protective clothing.

Bayer is putting together a 'Bayer safety kit' which will be sent to subsidiaries. Some subsidiaries sell or give away protective items.

Ciba-Geigy supports the idea that dealers should distribute pesticides and adequate application material, protective clothing and information necessary for correct and safe use.

Cyanamid ensures the use of, and in some cases provides, protective clothing, safety equipment and pictograms when selling highly toxic products. Dealers and distributors are encouraged and given incentives to sell and/or provide protective clothing and safety equipment. Company reps work to ensure a sufficient supply of safety gear and literature are available where its toxic products are used. Cyanamid also works closely with equipment manufacturers to adapt and modify application equipment to minimise potential operator exposure in the field.

Du Pont encourages dealers to have available protective clothing in relation to label requirements.

ICI has developed the electrodyne sprayer for use in tropical climates. Its spray action is safer, and eliminates the need for protective gloves during spraying. This was the main specific technical or engineering solution to safer spraying in the tropics mentioned by companies. ICI pointed out that recent research has shown that the barrier properties of normal cotton farm clothing are adequate for the safe application of most pesticides used in the tropics. Its own surveys have shown that most smallholders wear adequate clothing and exercise sufficient personal hygiene when applying products, without resort to special sets of protective clothing. ICI uses the GIFAP safety clothing to illustrate good practice in its training work for distributors and extension workers.

Rhône Poulenc pointed out that the international companies have decided to use a certain percentage of their normal promotional budgets in developing countries for putting at the disposal of users 'protective clothing' designed by a group of experts of GIFAP. The company has developed, with a specialised subsidiary, Horstine Farmery in UK, specific machinery to apply granules in soils without any contact to the user, and ensure proper safe application, however it did not indicate the relevance of this to Third World countries. Rhône Poulenc has made efforts to introduce safer technical controls, which include steady-flow containers to eliminate splashing, solid handles instead of hollow, water dissolvable bags that can be dropped directly into the applicator tank; bags with pouring spouts for filling application equipment without coming into contact with the product. Given the difficulty of preventing the reuse of empty packaging in the Third World, Rhône Poulenc has modified internal coatings of packaging systems to prevent absorption of product residue.

Shell has developed 'Gardman' protective clothing packs.

6.5 Training dealers

GIFAP has a retailer training programme, which is supported by a number of the international companies. A reorganisation of GIFAP is in progress to create a special structure whose responsibility will be specifically to 'take care of developing countries'. Most companies recognise that dealers and distributors need safety information, and they are an easy target to reach. Several noted their work with dealers, for example **ICI**. **Du Pont** pointed out that it trains dealers and distributors to conduct their own information and demonstration activities. Like other companies, it supports these activities and provides or collaborates on information materials on safe use and proper handling.

7. Safe use at farm level

In general, companies emphasise an approach of 'training the trainer', combined with clear labelling, safe-use posters, videos, cartoons, and so on, as set out under No. 4 above. GIFAP runs an Education and Training programme which is generally supported by all companies.

In addition, GIFAP launched a 'Safe Use Project' in 1991 in Guatemala, Kenya and Thailand (see box) to increase safety awareness at farm level in these three countries, and to increase understanding of methods to improve safety. These are intended to serve as pilot projects, and GIFAP hopes to reach further developing countries where pesticide use is significant by the end of the decade. The Code is accepted as the common standard which should be applied everywhere. The project is a recognition that improved safety and environmental responsibility is essential. GIFAP note in their 'Safe Use Project' leaflet that 'crop protectants are not being handled safely and efficiently in many countries. That situation must change to protect the health and safety of those who handle and use these products, to protect our environment, and to ensure the continued availability of these crop protection tools.'

Companies made the following comments on safe use:

Bayer has developed policy guidelines for environmental protection and safety, which must be applied from production of the product through to use at farm level. Its technical service trains at farm level and also invites dealers to farmers' meetings.

Ciba-Geigy believes safe use at farm level is best achieved through labels and packaging leaflets, and through dealers and farmers participating in instruction meetings. It has developed a brochure 'Safety Depends on You', which includes extensive information on pesticide problems and safe practices. It pays for advertisements on safe use. In addition to supporting GIFAP safe-use projects, Ciba-Geigy runs projects in Mali, Mozambique, Nigeria, Indonesia, Pakistan, Philippines, Colombia and Dominican Republic; and has conducted special studies in Zimbabwe, India and Mexico.

Cyanamid says it refuses to sell highly toxic products in markets where safety cannot be assured. Company agronomists provide technical service where pesticides are sold. Regular grower/farmer meetings are held to instruct on safe use and the dangers of repackaging and misuse of products. The importance of strict adherence to label instructions is always stressed. Safety manuals and audio-visual materials are provided to emphasise proper use, handling and disposal of pesticides. Cyanamid product labels and other literature provide full instructions for the safe disposal of containers. The company says it provides or makes available cholinesterase testing kits to banana growers to monitor worker blood levels when terbufos (Counter) insecticide-nematicide is used.

DowElanco provides a range of package sizes to suit the needs of small-scale farmers to avoid the risk that resellers will repackage products into unlabelled or inappropriate containers.

Du Pont sales reps conduct meetings with groups of farmers. Field tours and seminars provide the opportunity for demonstrations. The company did not indicate that these were specifically geared to Third World countries.

ICI has produced an Instructors Manual for training farmers and advisors in safe and effective pesticide use. Some examples of the training and education material aimed at safe use at farm level are a safety campaign conducted in Thailand using a poster, leaflets, video and stickers; in Malaysia a puppet show illustrates safe mixing, spraying and storing; in Brazil a smiling scarecrow is promoted to emphasise pesticide safety. These are part of product stewardship programmes which rely heavily on using a country's traditions or cultural connotations.

Rhône Poulenc states it reviews its range of products regularly to take appropriate action if it considers that a proper product stewardship programme cannot be managed in certain countries, especially in developing countries as far as WHO class 1a and 1b products are concerned. The

Three pilot 'safe-use projects' of GIFAP

These three projects were launched in November 1991.

Guatemala: The Safe-Use Project in Guatemala aims to train 200,000 farmers in the proper and safe handling, use and disposal of crop protection chemicals over a three-year period. This will be done in co-operation with the Guatemala Ministry of Agriculture and with Agrequima, the country's National Agricultural Chemicals Association. Similar training will be provided for technicians in the Social Security and Health Ministries, agricultural chemicals sales staff, distributors and dealers. Efforts will be made with the Ministry of Education to introduce safe and environmentally responsible use of crop protection products as a subject taught in rural schools.

Other elements of the Project include promotion and adoption of new, and/or enforcement of existing, pesticide control laws, supporting two new toxicology information centres, ensuring availability of antidotes for accidental pesticide poisonings, and developing, supplying and encouraging use of protective clothing.

Kenya: The Safe-Use Project in Kenya has a goal of training 400,000 farmers over a three-year period. To achieve that, a multiplying number of trainers will be instructed in how to educate farmers in the safe handling and use of pesticides. The project intends to expand the number of trainers from 60 to more than 1,000. These training efforts will be undertaken in co-operation with the Pesticide Chemicals Association of Kenya, the Pest Control Products Board, the Ministries of Agriculture, Health, Education and Environment, and interested non-governmental organisations.

The Kenya project will also focus on safe and environmentally responsible containers and waste disposal, and improving distributor and dealer handling of agricultural chemicals.

Thailand: As in the pilot countries in Latin America and Africa, the focus in Thailand will be on education and training. The Project, which will be developed in collaboration with the Thai Pesticide Association, the Department of Agriculture, the Department of Agricultural Extension and non-government organisations, will stress developing safe-use trainers within industry and government and educating dealers in safe and environmentally responsible handling and storage of pesticides.

The Project will provide support for a new and extensive farmer training effort being undertaken by Thailand's Department of Agricultural Extension. The training effort aimed at dealers will include an accreditation programme. The Thailand Safe-Use Project will also include a programme to provide safe pesticide-use education to young people in rural schools, supply pesticide antidotes to medical facilities to deal with accidental poisonings and promote the use of protective clothing.

company has special guidance for its most sensitive products to establish very precise recommendations for local units in terms of storage, transport and use and organises special training sessions.

Shell pointed out that it widely distributes local language literature. Farmer days and workshops are held. Special initiatives include: blood cholinesterase monitoring at farmer meetings in Thailand; village training using cotton flip charts in the Philippines; a mobile video van in Pakistan; a booklet for farmers' children, warning about pesticide hazards in the Philippines.

8. Registration

Companies comply with national regulations, however registration schemes do not exist in all Third World countries and the agrochemical industry supports implementation of registration schemes in all countries. **Dow** pointed out that countries lacking the necessary infrastructure to review and interpret complex scientific reports should be able to rely on evaluations and approvals by major developed countries in granting registrations of similar or identical products for local uses. **Du Pont**, like other companies, said it strongly encourages responsible registration and regulation of pesticides through competent regulatory authorities, and works through local and international trade and United Nations organisations to foster and develop regulatory competency. **Monsanto** said it: 'supports the efforts of the EPA Office of International Activities to provide training to regulators in developing countries on how to make decisions which meet their specific needs on regulation of pesticides.'

Companies are also lobbying for harmonisation of registration standards for pesticides throughout the world, although **Sandoz** suggested regional harmonisation. Companies believe that international harmonisation of national registration schemes would benefit both regulators and industry. In particular it would 'facilitate wider distribution of approved products' (**Dow**). **Bayer** pointed out that harmonisation could avoid double testing and associated bureaucratic work, 'which could save time and manpower for more practical work in the field.' However, if this is the case, some double testing should perhaps be built into harmonisation procedures.

8.1 When no registration scheme exists

Most companies will only sell their products to that country if the pesticide is approved in at least one authority of a country with high registration standards, for example the USA, UK or Japan (**BASF, Bayer, Schering**), or if that country is a member of the Organisation of Economic Co-operation and Development (OECD) (**Ciba-Geigy**). **Cyanamid's** policy on registration is that all products must be registered for the specific use in each market before they can be sold. **Monsanto** requires registration of the pesticide in the actual user country.

8.2 Pesticides which are not registered in country of production

In general, companies do sell a product which is not registered where it is produced unless it is registered in another country with high registration standards. (This can occur when a crop is not grown in the producing country.) **Cyanamid** qualified this by pointing out that 'registration approval may not have been granted in the US, EC or other OECD country at the time of a first sale to a Third World country, only because the review of the data had not been completed. An initial registration submission would have been made, and Cyanamid would intend to pursue that registration to final approval.'

9. PIC

The PIC provisions are at a preliminary phase. GIFAP has developed 'A Guide to its Working' to help companies meet their obligations. Member companies indicated they would follow procedures if one of their products is identified for inclusion in the PIC process. **Cyanamid** has been actively involved in implementation, with the Manager of International Registrations participating as GIFAP representative in relevant working groups during development and implementation, and has thus informed and helped educate all its relevant company personnel on the topic.

Contacts for enquiries:
BASF: Contact GIFAP, BASF local representative, or marketing department in the Plant Protection Division, Landwirtschaftliche Versuchsstation, Postfach 220, 6703 Limburgerhof, Germany
Bayer: Dr. Frohling and A. Dollacker, Bayer AG, Pflanzenschutzzentrum Monheim, Alfred-Nobel Strassse 50, Postanschrift 5090 Leverkusen, Bayerwerk, Germany
Ciba-Geigy: I. Spiess-Hilf and Dr. R. Immler, Ciba-Geigy AG, CH-4002 Basel, Switzerland
Cyanamid: Dr. Richard J. Nielsson, American Cyanamid Company, Agricultural Research Division, PO Box 400, Princeton, NJ 03543-0400, USA
ICI: Mr. M.J. Whitaker, Safety and Stewardship Department, ICI Agrochemicals, Fernhurst, Haslemere, Surrey GU27 3JE. UK
Sandoz Agro: The manager of the affiliate in the country.
Schering: Dr. Susan J. Crisp-Jungklaus, PF-Strategy and Corporate Affairs, Schering AG, Gerichtstrasse 27, 1000 Berlin 65, Germany

Specific contacts were not given for DowElanco, Du Pont, Monsanto or Rhône Poulenc. These could be reached through their main agent in the country, or through the head office.

Annex 2

Producers of PIC Pesticides Still Available

Active ingredient	Common trade names	Producers	Details of use
aldrin	Al-Tox	All India Medical Corp (AIMCO)— India *(?) Shell—discontinued	Insecticide.
chlordane	Chlordane Chloro-Tox Niran (granular) Velsicol	Velsicol—US Northwest Industries—US Sandoz—US	Persistent broad spectrum contact insecticide for termites, wireworms, ants, soil insects and insects on vegetable and field crops.
chlordimeform	Bermat Fundal Galecron	Agro-Quimicas— Guatemala Quimica Estrella— Argentina Sintesu—Brazil	Ovicide/larvicide for the control of bollworm and tobacco budworm.
cyhexatin	Rospinex 25WP	Oxon Italia—Italy	Wide range of phytophagous mites.
dieldrin	Dieldrin	Shell—discontinued	Widely used for termite, tsetse fly and locusts.
dinoseb		Drexel—US Hoechst—Germany AH Marks & Co—UK Uniroyal—US	Herbicide.
DDT	DDT Hildit	EniChem Synthesis—Italy Hindustan Insecticides —India PT Montrose Pesticido— Indonesia	Now mainly used on public health programmes. Until recently India sold for use on fruit, vegetables, cotton and livestock. Some timber and industrial use.
EDB	Bromofume Celmide Nephis Soilbrom	Excel Industries —India United Phosphorus —India	Fumigant.

heptachlor	Heptachlor Hep-Tox	Velsicol Chemical Corp—US	Insecticide applied to corn, sugar-cane, rice, wheat, barley, cotton, sorghum and termites.
hexachloro-benzene	Anti-Carie Hexachloro-benzol	Compania Quimica	Fungicide.
paraquat**	Sold under many trade names and formulations including: Gramoxone Dexuron Gramocil Gramonol	ICI is the producer and key supplier. Production plants in UK, US, Japan, Brazil and India. Formulation facility in Malaysia.	Herbicide, widely used for weed control, and in tropical areas used on tree-crop plantations (cocoa, coffee, palm oil, rubber etc) for weed control.
parathion OP insecticide	Folidol E605 Ethyl Parathion Parathion (various) Seis-Tres 6-3	Bayer—Germany Cheminova—Denmark	Field crops, vegetables, fruit, etc.
parathion ethyl OP insecticide	Folidol Thiomex EM	Bayer—Germany Cheminova—Denmark	Insecticide and acaricide.
parathion methyl (some formulations) OP insecticide	Methyl Parathion Folidol-M Metacide Penncap-M Paratox	Bayer—Germany Cheminova—Denmark	Contact and stomach insecticide with some fumigant action. Lower mammalian toxicity than parathion. Recommended for cotton boll weevil control.
thallium sulphate	Thallium Sulphate Tharattin	Ameco—Belgium Marman—US Hentschke & Sawatzki—Germany	Molluscicide.
toxaphene / camphechlor		Production in Nicaragua	

* (?) Possible producer. ** Not yet confirmed in the PIC process.

Source: Decision Guidance Documents for Prior Informed Consent.

Annex 3

Producers of Potential PIC Pesticides

Active ingredient	Some common trade names	Basic Producers
aldicarb	Temik	Rhône Poulenc (formerly a Union Carbide pesticide)—France Equitable Trading—Taiwan Forward International—Taiwan
amitrole	Aminotriazole Ustinex	Bayer —Germany Makhetshim-Agan—Israel Rhône Poulenc—France
arsenic compounds	Arsenic Acid	Atochem—US (supplier)
captafol, fungicide	Captafol	AIMCO—India(*?)
carbofuran acaricide, insecticide, nematicide	Carbodan Carbofuran Furadan	FMC—US AIMCO—India (*?) Makhteshim-Agan (*?)—Israel
chlorobenzilate acaricide	Benzilan Chlorobenzilate	Makhteshim-Agan—Istrael
chloropicrin Soil fumigant/grain store	Added to methyl bromide mixtures as warning	Great Lakes Corp—US International Minerals and Chemical Corp—US Niklor Chemical Co—US
demeton-s -methyl	Metasystox	Biesterfeld—Germany Bayer—Germany (discontinued) Mobay—US (discontinued)
dichlorvos	Cypona DDVP Detmolin Devikol Duravos Nogos Nuvan Nuvanex Phosvit Unifos Unitox Vapona and others	AIMCO—India Bayer—Germany Ciba-Geigy—Switzerland Defensa Industria—Brazil Denka—Netherlands Hightex—Spain Jin Hung Fine—Korea Kenogard—Sweden Makhteshim-Agan—Israel Montecina—Spain Nippon Soda Co—Japan Quimica Estrella—Argentina Quimica Lucava—Mexico
dicofol	Dicofol Hilfol Kelthane Mitigan	Hindustan Insecticides—India Makhtesim-Agan—Israel Rohm & Haas—US and others
endosulfan	Thiodan	Hoechst—Germany

gamma-HCH and lindane	BHC Gamma-Col Gammalin Gammexane Lindane	Hindustan Insecticides—India ICI—UK (discontinued) Rhône Poulenc—France
methamidophos	Gilmore Methamidophos Monitor MTD-600 MTD Technical Nitofol	Agro-Quimicas—Guatemala Bayer—Germany Chevron Chemical Co—US Jin Hung Fine—Korea Quimica Estrella—Argentina Taiwan Tainan Giant—Taiwan
methomyl	Methomyl Lannate Methomex Pillarmate	Diachem—Italy Du Pont—US Gilmore—US Makhteshim-Agan—Israel Pillar—Taiwan Pyosa—Mexico Rhône Poulenc—France Sorex—UK Sundat—Singapore
methyl bromide	Methyl Bromide Haltox	Ameco—Belgium Degesch/Detia—Germany Great Lakes—US Marman—US
methoxychlor	DMTD Higalmetox Gustafson Marlate Methoxcide Prentox	Cequisa—Spain Drexel—US Gustafson—US Hightex—Spain Hopkins—US Kincaid Enterprises—US Prentiss Drug and Chemical—US
monocrotophos	Aimocron Azodrin Hilcron Monocron Monodrin Nuvacron Pillardrin	Ciba-Geigy—Switzerland Drexel—US Jin Hung Fine Chemicals—Korea KenoGard AB—Sweden Makhteshim-Agan—Israel National Organic Industries—India Quimica Estrella—Argentina Shell—UK/Netherlands Taiwan Tainan Giant—Taiwan
pentachloro-phenol Fungicide, herbicide, insecticide (termiticide), molluscicide	Block Penta Chem-Tol Dowicide Dirotox Fungifen Pentacon and others	Canada National Product Co—China Pola Quimia—Mexico Preservation Products—Mexico Rhône Poulenc—France Vulcan Materials—US

phosphamidon Insecticide, acaricide	Dimecron Phosphamidon Phosron Pillarcron	Bharat Pulverising Mills—India Ciba-Geigy—Switzerland Hui Kwang—Taiwan Pillar—Taiwan United Phosphorus—India
phosphin generators Fumigant, insecticide	Arrex (phosphine) Phostoxin	AIMCO—India Degesh—US and South Africa Excel Industries—India Inventa Corp—India Pestcon Systems—China
sodium fluoride Insecticide	Florocid	Olin Chemical Co—US Osmose Chemical Co—US
strychnine Molluscicide	Strychnine Nitrate	Nova-Chem Inc—US Marmon—US

*? Possible producer of potential PIC pesticide.

Sources: Decision Guidance Documents for the PIC procedure. *International Pesticide Directory*, 11th edition, October, 1991. Additional German information supplied by PAN Germany, through Biologische Bundesanstalt: Hundertelfte Bekanntmachung Uber die Zulassung von Pflanzenschutzmitteln Vom. 18, Mai 1991 and Vom. 17, Marz 1991

PAN Regional Offices

Africa, Anglophone: Environment Liaison Centre International, PO Box 72461, Nairobi, Kenya. Tel. 254 256 2015. Fax. 254 256 2175

Africa, Francophone: Environnement et Developpement du Tiers Monde (ENDA), BP 3370, Dakar, Senegal. Tel. 221 22 5565. Fax 221 22 2695.

Asia and the Pacific: PAN Regional Centre for Asia and the Pacific, PO Box 1170, 10850 Penang, Malaysia. Tel. 604 870271. Fax 604 877 445.

Europe: (Temporary) PAN Europe, 23 Beehive Place, London SW9 7QR. Tel. 44 71 274 8895. Fax. 44 71 274 9084.

Latin America: RAPALMIRA, Calle 37, #29-35, Palmira, Colombia.

North America: PAN North America Regional Center, 965 Mission Street #514, San Francisco, CA 94103, USA. Tel. 1-415 541 9140. Fax 1-415 541 9253.

Abbreviations

a.i.	Active ingredient (of a pesticide)
Agenda 21	The action plan for the 21st century agreed at UNCED
ANDEF	Associatiaco Nacional de Defensivos Agricolas— National Association of Pesticides Companies in Brazil
Earth Summit	United Nations Conference on Environment and Development
EC	European Community
EPA	Environmental Protection Agency, USA
FAO Code	The FAO International Code of Conduct on the Distribution and Use of Pesticides
FAO	The Food and Agriculture Organisation of the United Nations
GATT	General Agreement on Tariffs and Trade
GIFAP	Groupement International des Associations Nationales de Fabricants de Produits Agrochemiques (International Group of National Associations of Pesticide Manufacturers)
IARC	International Agency for Research on Cancer
IPCS	International Programme on Chemical Safety of the WHO
IPM	Integrated Pest Management
IRPTC	The International Register of Potentially Toxic Chemicals
LEISA	Low External Inputs for Sustainable Agriculture
MRL	Maximum residue level
NGO	Non-governmental organisation
OC	Organochlorine pesticide
OECD	Organisation of Economic Cooperation and Development
OP	Organophosphorus pesticide
PAN	Pesticides Action Network
PIC	Prior Informed Consent Provisions of the FAO Code
ppb	parts per billion
R&D	Research and development
SARD	Sustainable Agriculture for Rural Development, a policy adopted by the FAO
UNCED	United Nations Conference on Environment and Development, also known as the Earth Summit
UNEP	United Nations Environment Programme
UNIDO	United Nations Industrial Development Organisation
USAID	US Agency for International Development
WHO	World Health Organisation

Glossary

Acaricide pesticide which kills spiders, mites and tics.

Active ingredient (a.i.) the chemical part of the pesticide which kills pests.

Agro-ecology farming techniques which are compatible with the ecology of an area—similar to LEISA. This term is increasingly used, and comes particularly from practices developed over the last 10 years in Latin America.

Agrochemical same as pesticide, i.e. a chemical used in agriculture, generally applied to the companies producing pesticides (agrochemical company).

Anticholinesterase substance that inhibits action of cholinesterase, especially in people sensitive to anticholinesterase compounds (about 15% of the population).

Biological control regulation of plant and animal pests through encouraging or actively introducing their natural predators.

Biotechnology genetic manipulation of living matter to produce new plants, animals, material etc. Can be controversial in that many companies are manipulating plants for resistance to pesticides, rather than resistance to insects or diseases.

Botanical pesticides plants with pesticidal properties.

Carbamates insecticides made from an ester of carbamic acid, which have anti-cholinesterase properties.

Cholinesterase an enzyme found in blood plasma that breaks down acetylcholine; this helps regulate the activity of nerve impulses and is necessary for proper nerve functioning.

Circle of poison (legislation) used to describe the process where hazardous pesticides which are banned as a residue in one country are exported from that country, and then return as residues in food imported from the countries where the products have been applied to crops.

Codex alimentarius the WHO and FAO body which sets standards for pesticide residues in food.

Consolidated generics/generics pesticides which do not carry a trade name and which are therefore often cheaper, but which also may be marketed without full label advice and warnings.

Dirty dozen (pesticides) a list of pesticides which have been targeted in a campaign seeking to severely restrict or eliminate their use because of their health or environmental hazards. This list grew to more than a dozen, to include: aldicarb, camphechlor (toxaphene), chlordane, chlordimeform, DBCP, DDT, the 'drins'—aldrin, dieldrin, endrin—EDB,

HCH/BHC (mixed isomers) and lindane, heptachlor, paraquat, parathion ethyl and parathion methyl, pentachlorophenol and 2,4,5-T.

Feddan a land measurement used in Arabic countries, equal to 0.42 hectares.

Formulated products the active ingredient mixed with any other chemicals—dilutants, adjuvants, wetting agents, etc.—necessary to make the final product.

Green revolution the development of high-yielding varieties (HYV) of staple food crops, particularly rice and wheat, which are dependent on high inputs of fertilizers. These varieties come from a narrow genetic base and depend on pesticides to control pests and diseases. Although the green revolution increased crop yields, it has been criticised for its tendency to exacerbate inequality as essential inputs can only be afforded by richer farmers.

Integrated pest management (IPM) system of pest control which uses an integrated mixture of control measures, including pesticides, time of planting, biological control, use of crop rotations, new crop varieties, etc. On any given plot, the use of IPM techniques would almost certainly reduce pesticide use.

Intermediates (pesticide manufacturing) a stage in the chemical process of making pesticide active ingredients.

LD50 dose required to kill 50% of test animals.

Low External Inputs for Sustainable Agriculture (LEISA) advocates using locally available inputs and, while not rejecting pesticide use in all cases, emphasises the need for sustainability and aims to minimise chemical pesticide applications. It has been defined as agriculture which is 'economically feasible, ecologically sound, culturally adapted and socially just'.

Maximum Residue Level (MRL) maximum permitted concentration of a pesticide residue in or on a food crop.

Molluscicides pesticide which kills slugs and snails.

Nematicides pesticide which kills nematode worms.

Non-chemical pest control methods of controlling pests and diseases without using chemical pesticides, involving approaches such as IPM, LEISA or organic farming.

Organic farming farming system which does not use artificial pesticides at all.

Organochlorine (OC) pesticide pesticides containing chlorine atoms with insecticidal properties, sometimes called chlorinated hydrocarbons. These are among the most environmentally-persistent groups of pesticide. DDT is an example.

Organophosphate (OP) pesticide pesticides containing ester of phosphoric acid, acting mainly on the anticholinesterase enzyme. These began to replace organochlorines in the 1960s and 1970s have given rise to persistent health complaints in the Third World. Malathion is an example.

Pesticide the general term used to describe all insecticides, herbicides, fungicides as well as miscellaneous chemicals.

Pesticide treadmill syndrome the process where crops become dependent on pesticides to control pests and diseases, having lost their properties of resistance, and through the destruction of natural enemies which allows a small number of pesticide-resistant pest species to dominate, thus requiring further pesticide applications.

Phenoxy herbicides herbicides containing phenoxyacetic acid, hydroxyl and acid substitutes, e.g. 2,4,5-T.

Plant-growth regulators chemicals developed to regulate plant growth.

Polluter pays principle the principle that the polluter should carry out and bear the expenses of safeguarding the environment. In practice, the principle accepts that the cost of any measures would be reflected in the cost of the polluting goods or services (see Chapter 1).

Precautionary principle says that if further environmental degradation and health impacts are to be minimised precaution must be the overriding principle guiding action. Adoption of the precautionary principle implies a shift in approach from proof of environmental harm, to proof of environmental safety.

Pyrethroid pesticides developed from the naturally-occurring plant with insecticidal properties, pyrethrum, now mostly produced synthetically.

Resurgence (of pests) the process whereby insect pests become resistant to pesticides and therefore increase their numbers.

Rodenticide pesticide which kills rodents (usually rat poisons).

Sustainable agriculture a very broad term for agriculture which does not deplete the resources necessary for future production: to some this does not imply a reduction in pesticide use, but NGOs use the term to include IPM, LEISA or organic methods of production.

Synthesise the chemical process involved in making the pesticide active ingredient.

Teratogenic induces birth defects.

Thrips a small insect pest, particularly of cereal crops.

Index